TEACHING KIDS TO SING

TEACHING KIDS TO SING

Kenneth H. Phillips

SCHIRMER BOOKS
A Division of Macmillan, Inc.
New York

MAXWELL MACMILLAN CANADA
Toronto

MAXWELL MACMILLAN INTERNATIONAL
New York   Oxford   Singapore   Sydney

Schirmer Books
A Division of Macmillan, Inc.
866 Third Avenue, New York, N.Y. 10022

Maxwell Macmillan Canada, Inc.
1200 Eglinton Avenue East, Suite 200
Don Mills, Ontario M3C 3N1

Macmillan, Inc., is part of the Maxwell Communication Group of Companies.

Library of Congress Catalog Card Number: 91–26288

Printed in the United States of America

printing number
1 2 3 4 5 6 7 8 9 10

Library of Congress Cataloging-in-Publication Data

Phillips, Kenneth H. (Kenneth Harold)
    Teaching kids to sing / Kenneth H. Phillips.
        p.   cm.
    Includes bibliographical references and index.
    ISBN 0-02-871795-3
    1. Singing—Methods—Juvenile.   2. School music—Instruction and
study.   I. Title.
MT935.P53   1992
783.7′ 142′ 07—dc20   91–26288
                                                                    CIP
                                                                    MN

The paper used in this publication meets the minimum requirements of American
National Standard for Information Sciences—Permanence of Paper for Printed Library
Materials. ANSI Z39.48–1984. ∞™

This book is dedicated to the memory of Lowell Mason (1792–1872), "the father of singing among the children," who demonstrated that all children could be taught to sing.

CONTENTS ⟋⟋⟋

PREFACE

This is a vocal-technique method for children and adolescents, grades 1–12. It consists of ninety sequential techniques grouped by five major areas: respiration, phonation, resonant tone production, diction, and expression. The purpose of this method is to lead young people through a developmental program of psychomotor skills that will result in confident and expressive singing.

Vocal technique is foundational to the singing program. Technique that is faulty hinders proper tone production and limits the singing response. Proper technique leads to enjoyable music making.

This book is limited to a presentation of vocal technique; it does not address to any depth two other important areas of the singing program—music reading and song repertoire. Both of these areas are covered well in other sources. Music literacy programs—notably those developed by Kodály, Orff, Dalcroze, and Gordon—are available, and the instructor is encouraged to commit to some procedure for teaching music reading and to use it consistently in the singing program. Songbooks are readily available, and today's music series again are recognizing the importance of good song literature for young people. *Teaching Kids to Sing* specifically addresses the area about which the least has been written in music education—singing technique for young people.

Part II of this book employs, admittedly, a cookbook approach to vocal education. The author's experience has been that most music teachers feel incompetent when it comes to development of singing skills and want a method that tells them where to begin and what to do each step of the way. This method does just that. However, for those who feel confident in the teaching of singing, exercises and vocalises can be chosen selectively to supplement those already being used. The sequence of techniques also may be useful to such teachers for checking any gaps in their own curriculum. Therefore, the method may be used as a "method" in sequential order or as an "approach" at the instructor's discretion.

Vocal physiology is an important part of this text. Teachers of singing need to know something about the physical structure and action of the instrument they teach. The "motor" part of psychomotor learning demands a high degree of physical coordination of muscles, cartilages, vocal folds, and other parts of the singing anatomy. Without an understanding of these basic parts, the teacher of singing is hampered in diagnosing physical problems that result from poor alignment of the singing mechanism and correcting faulty singing techniques. Clearly, vocal physiology is an important part of vocal pedagogy.

Part I is intended to provide the teacher with the knowledge base necessary for understanding the sequence and various parts of the method in Part II. It is valuable information and should not be ignored in order to get to the how-to section of the book. The why and what of Part I prepare the instructor to understand more fully the how of psychomotor learning in Part II.

This is a research-based text. It is a synthesis of knowledge gleaned from the writings of leading authors in the field of child and adolescent voice and from the findings of many research investigations as they relate to child and adolescent singing. Research in the area of the young singing voice has yielded considerable knowledge upon which to build a pedagogy for young singers. However, much remains to be learned, and the many research citations in this text may lead others to consider singing as a field of research activity.

The study and discussion questions that appear at the end of each chapter are given for directed-reading purposes. In a class setting with sufficient time, the instructor may review each question. This will allow for further clarification and discussion. If time is limited, it may be possible to cover only Part II (the actual exercises) in depth, with a brief interval provided for clarification of specific questions. The use of the study and discussion questions, in the latter case especially, will ensure that the chapter content is covered. The use of these and other questions or activities is at the discretion of the individual instructor.

Music pitches are given throughout the text using the octave designations shown in Example P.1.

Throughout the text, symbols for phonetic sounds are used that are those of the International Phonetic Alphabet (IPA). If the reader is unfamiliar with these symbols, a listing can be found in Chapter 10.

The research, knowledge, and techniques presented in this book have evolved over many years of experience in working to improve the singing of children and adolescents. It is the author's desire that this

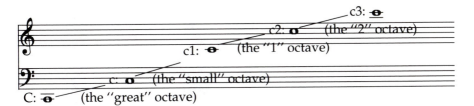

EXAMPLE P.1. Octave designations.

method will be helpful to those who have dedicated their lives to the betterment of young persons through music and that more people will develop the skills needed for experiencing the joy of singing. Let's get back to basics—let's teach everyone to sing!

ACKNOWLEDGMENTS

The author wishes to express his gratitude to the many children and adolescents who over the years have served as the inspiration for this book and who have served as the guinea pigs for the many exercises in vocal technique presented herein. Appreciation also is extended to the teachers who have used the method in pilot form and who have provided valuable feedback.

Many authors have been cited in this text as sources of research and knowledge concerning child and adolescent singing. Their findings and insights have made significant contributions to the content of this book, and the author is indebted to those writers who have helped develop a greater understanding of the psychomotor process involved in singing.

The beautiful illustrations in this book are the work of Donald Alvarado, former associate professor at the School of Medicine at Louisiana State University. The author is grateful for his expertise and contribution to this text.

Lastly, to his loving wife, Donna, the author extends his love and appreciation for her years of devotion and caring. Her steadfast belief in this work has helped bring it to fruition.

TEACHING KIDS TO SING

Part
I

THE YOUNG SINGER

Singing is a learned behavior.
—Helen Kemp

1

VOCAL PEDAGOGY FOR YOUNG SINGERS 〰

Singing is a basic form of human expression. It is an end in itself and a means to many ends. Unfortunately, there are people who never learn to sing accurately or with any measure of confidence. Those who are unable to "carry a tune" rarely experience the joy and fulfillment that singing brings to life. Worse yet, such persons think of themselves as ungifted or unmusical. How sad the adult who equates the inability to sing with a lack of musical ability in general. A lack of support for the arts may find its roots in this misconception!

Music teachers have long agreed that children can, and should, learn to sing. It is the process that remains open to question: whether it is appropriate to train young voices, and if so, which approach is most beneficial. The philosophy that serves as the basis for this book on vocal technique for young singers is as follows: developmental instruction in vocal technique is appropriate and necessary for all students (grades 1–12) and is fundamental to developing musical literacy and artistic vocal expression.

PHILOSOPHICAL AND HISTORICAL PERSPECTIVES

The prevailing attitude among some contemporary music educators is that the training of the child voice should be delayed until the vocal folds have completely adjusted to the physical changes related to puberty. Their reason for delaying is the fear that vocalises and vocal techniques may damage a young voice. There is no empirical evidence for such a belief. In fact, medical experts such as Robert Sataloff and Joseph Spiegel (1989) believe that it is possible and proper to train young voices to sing. They caution against vocal abuse and recommend an approach based on gradual development of vocal musculature and control. It is really a matter of endurance; one should not expect youthful voices to endure long periods of practice or vocal exercises. A balance of song and singing instruction is most important. In a carefully monitored program of voice development, child and adolescent voices will thrive and avoid abuse.

The Song Approach

The song approach—which in recent years has been the one most widely used to teach young people to sing—places primary emphasis on expression, with secondary emphasis on technique. The student learns to sing by singing songs. This is not to say that vocal technique cannot be taught using this approach; rather, it is the song that serves as the vehicle rather than specific exercises or vocalises.

Elementary methods texts emphasize the song approach almost exclusively. It is uncommon to find in such sources any directives to the actual training of the child voice. The song-approach literature often neglects such technical areas as vocal quality, registers, dynamic level, duration, and range. The mastery of singing technique is not presented as a developmental skill.

Most music students receive voice training in college or university voice studios that use the song approach rather than the older, bel canto technique. The bel canto school of training emphasizes the mastery of singing technique before song repertoire is studied. Today, vocal students begin to acquire almost immediately a repertoire of song literature, using it as a vehicle by which to learn to sing. However, the acquisition of repertoire often assumes more importance than the development of technique. Thus, a vocal student may spend a great deal of time learning songs, but never really understand the fundamentals of voice production. Likewise, vocal pedagogy courses are directed most often to the adult singer and provide little help for understanding the child and adolescent voice.

A survey of public school music teachers' ratings of their undergraduate training in music education found that training for teaching a beginning vocalist was among the lowest-rated areas of preparation (Colemann, 1980). Apparently, college vocal training does not sufficiently prepare teachers to face the problems they encounter in teaching children to sing. Also, some schools do not require instrumental majors to study voice, yet many of these students take jobs that require vocal teaching. Similarly, vocal pedagogy for children and adolescents is not a topic covered to much depth in methods classes. Given this lack of training and given that almost all methods texts present only the song approach, is it any wonder that beginning teachers often feel so ill equipped to handle the child and adolescent voice? This, of all areas, should be emphasized in the preparation of teachers of vocal music.

The song approach does fulfill an important goal of music education: it involves children in singing. The problem arises when this approach emphasizes the teaching of songs to the neglect of the singing voice. It is important for students to learn a large repertoire of varied songs, but they also must be taught good singing habits, which can adapt to the needs of different songs. If the teacher is not familiar with child and adolescent vocal production, and does not understand the tone quality and voice placement one should expect from these voices, it is doubtful that the skill of singing will be taught. The inherent danger in the exclusive use of a song approach with children and adolescents is that while it may appear that singing is being taught, what is being learned is song repertoire.

The song approach may result in the unconfident singer being neglected. By the upper elementary grades, discipline problems and refusals of boys to sing are the rule in music classes. James Mursell, a noted mid-twentieth-century American music educator, believed that the two most common reasons children abandon singing are the lack of vocal development and the peer pressure that ensues when children compare their singing to that of others. What is often mistaken as a belligerence toward singing among some students may in reality be a state of embarrassment brought on by a lack of confidence in the singing voice. The song approach encourages children to sing with voices that often are unequal to the task, and by the fourth or fifth grade, the resulting embarrassment and loss of confidence may produce a negative attitude toward singing.

The song approach has another inherent danger. Children who flourish under this approach may do so even as they develop poor vocal habits. In addition, the song approach may give the teacher a false sense of security by masking problems of technique. While a child's singing may sound good in general, his technique may be faulty. This may lead to future vocal problems, though no immediate problems may be apparent. With poor-sounding children's voices, one can assume that good vocal production is lacking.

The Roots of Systematic Vocal Instruction

The song approach is a rather recent pedagogical development. Voice training for children in the United States has a history dating from the early "singing school" movement of the eighteenth century. In the nineteenth century, vocal instruction was advocated by America's first public school music teacher, Lowell Mason, but continues today mostly in the training of boy choirs and professional children's choirs. How did vocal instruction, appropriate for all children in Mason's time, fall from favor in the school music curriculum?

The beginning of the child-singing movement in the United States is credited to Mason, who is considered the "father of singing" among American schoolchildren (see Figure 1–1). Mason was responsible for the first formal inclusion of music in the Boston public schools in 1838. He put together one of the first music methods, the *Manual of the Boston Academy of Music for Instruction in the Elements of Vocal Music on the System of Pestalozzi*, first published in 1834. Its purpose was to cultivate music literacy and proper vocal production among children.

FIGURE 1–1. Lowell Mason (1792–1872). (Special collections in music, The University of Maryland, College Park. Used by permission.)

Singing among public school children was not fostered in America until Mason demonstrated that it was possible. After working for a year without compensation with the children of the Hawes School in Boston, Mason gave a public concert that convinced the Boston School Board that all children could learn to sing. In the *Manual*, Mason states that singing instruction should begin when a child commences to read and continue throughout the child's education.

Late-Nineteenth- and Early-Twentieth-Century Writers

The name of Francis E. Howard is not as well known as that of Lowell Mason, but at the end of the nineteenth century, Howard was one of American education's most influential authorities on the child voice. His publication *The Child-Voice in Singing* (1895) became one of the most extensively used texts on child vocal instruction. Howard believed that every music teacher should have a physiological understanding of child vocal production and that if good singing habits were taught, students' singing would improve. Two of Howard's main theses were that children should sing only at a soft dynamic level and that children should sing only in the thin, or head, register. While these principles are today questionable (soft singing requires greater skill, and exclusive use of head voice results in a weak middle register), his influence on child vocal pedagogy remained strong until the 1930s.

E. H. Curtis was another late-nineteenth-century American authority on the child voice. She wrote, along with H. R. Palmer, a series of training manuals and readers for use with children, which became known as the Palmer-Curtis series. These manuals covered the areas of voice culture, ear training, sight-singing, and children who could not sing. Concerning voice culture, Curtis, in *Children's Voices* (1895), recommended specific exercises and vocalises for vocal development, noting that perhaps half the time of all early music classes be devoted to vocal instruction.

Emil Behnke and Lennox Browne, in *The Child Voice* (1885), were established vocal authorities in the late nineteenth century and were advocates of the English tradition of choirboy training. The authors recommended that vocal instruction commence between six and ten years of age, with much emphasis given to the development of proper breathing. They warned against children developing the habit of "collarbone" breathing, recommending instead the development of "midriff" and "rib" breathing. Behnke and Browne believed in the same training procedures for girls and boys prior to puberty.

John J. Dawson, an early-twentieth-century educator, was a music teacher in the public schools and taught at the Pratt Institute in Brooklyn, New York. In his book *The Voice of the Boy* (1902), Dawson challenged the traditional view that the "voice break" was a necessary phenomenon of the adolescent male. He believed the voice break resulted from the practice of keeping boys singing in the pure upper voice (according to the English model) without permitting the lower voice to develop. Dawson recommended that boys be allowed to develop the lower register as they approached puberty, thus permitting the voice to descend gradually without acquiring the traditional break. He also recommended that the voices of boys and girls be trained in the same manner up to about the age of twelve. Of this training, Dawson noted that "disordered muscular conditions" were among the greatest causes for poor singing among children. Shallow, upper-chest breathing he gave as one of the main reasons for inadequate singing, and he noted that instruction in deeper breathing almost always resulted in improved vocal production.

A number of authors in the early 1900s advocated training of American children's voices according to the traditional English boy-choir model, stating that such training was applicable for all children. Proper breath management was one area that was often stressed, and Jerome Bates, in *Voice Culture for Children* (1907), prescribed a well-ordered method of breathing exercises rarely found in any other publication. Bates advocated the practice of breathing exercises both at school and at home.

Frank R. Rix was a strong advocate of child vocal training in the public schools. He believed that children should be taught to sing upon entrance to school and that suitable vocalises be used on a daily basis. Breathing exercises utilized natural activities such as smelling, blowing, yawning, laughing, sighing, and stretching. Rix stated that all singing classes should begin with a brief routine of breathing exercises and vocalises. His books *A Manual of School Music in Elementary Grades for Supervisors and Class Teachers* (1909) and *Voice Training for School Children* (1910) were written for public school music teachers.

Thaddeus P. Giddings, a prominent music educator in the early 1900s, was a firm believer in early vocal training for children (see Figure 1–2). In *Grade School Music Teaching* (1919), Giddings declared that proper breathing was the basis for good singing and should be taught from kindergarten on. To those who questioned the advisability of early vocal training, Giddings stated, "The singing a child does in school, when the work is properly carried on, requires but a tithe of the number of pounds of pressure a child puts on his vocal chords [*sic*] in yelling or crying" (p. 19).

School music classes in the early twentieth century placed much emphasis on learning to read music, in addition to learning to sing well. Lowell Mason advocated the use of the seven-syllable, seven-note movable-do system, and it became the basic approach in the urban centers of the

FIGURE 1–2. Thaddeus P. Giddings teaching breath support. From a 1939 issue of *Minneapolis Journal*. (Special collections in music, The University of Maryland, College Park. Used by permission.)

northern United States. Following Mason's lead, numerous people published primers devoted to teaching music literacy. Thus, the thrust of teaching in the elementary music class consisted of developing vocal confidence through a dual program of vocal technique instruction and sight-reading.

A Change in Philosophies

By the 1930s, much progress was being made in preserving the child voice, and many teachers believed that vocal instruction was appropriate at the elementary level. At the same time, there was a noticeable change in attitude from an exercise approach to a song approach to vocal pedagogy. Karl Gehrkens, in his influential book *Music in the Grade School* (1934), was among the first to advocate a move from formal instruction and vocalises to this new song approach. Believing that vocal training could be fostered through the aesthetic experience, he suggested that the old idea of using exercises for training the voice, which involved a considerable amount of class time, should be replaced by a modern approach designed to teach the child through the singing of beautiful songs. The lack of information on child vocal pedagogy in methods texts from Gehrkens's publication to the present demonstrates that this song approach became very popular among public school music teachers.

The change in child vocal instruction philosophy in the 1930s is better understood in light of the state of music teaching at that time. Early music education, like education in general, was drill-oriented. Sight-singing manuals were used extensively in the classroom, and vocal instruction was a regular part of the routine of music teaching. Pestalozzianism, with its stress on the instructional side of teaching, was prevalent, and music teachers emphasized the rudiments of music. As reforms in education were instituted, more creative expression was expected from students. Music educators became concerned about aesthetics and the need for children to experience more "real" music—more songs with beauty and charm. Thus, the pendulum swung from a drill-oriented approach to a more creative one in which music instruction centered around song for art's sake. Unfortunately, child vocal instruction ceased to be an important part of formal music teaching; children learned to sing by singing songs.

The song approach worked as long as teachers were able to employ old methods in a new setting. New teachers, however, received little knowledge of child vocal pedagogy or sight-singing methodology. The song approach then became nothing more than that—an approach to teaching songs. This change of attitude may be seen in the early writings of James Mursell and Mabelle Glenn (1938), who cautioned against drilling on vocal habits. Two decades later, however, Mursell (1956) was warning against omitting specific training of the voice. The results of the song approach were beginning to be heard in America's classrooms.

Advocates of Vocal Technique Instruction

A number of music educators in the 1930s continued to advocate vocal instruction. Claude E. Johnson (1935) and Hollis Dann, author of the Hollis Dann Song Series (1936), both stressed vocal training for children, believing that children more easily and more quickly acquired good habits than did adults and that all children should be taught the essentials of deep breathing via specific breathing exercises. Prominent choral directors of the period such as William J. Finn (1944) and T. Tertius Noble (1943) continued to advocate child vocal training in the boy-choir tradition. Both men emphasized breathing as the basis of good vocal tone.

William E. Ross, voice teacher for many years at Indiana University, wrote *Sing High, Sing Low* in 1948 as a guide for teachers of public school music. Ross's approach to children's singing involved specific training exercises and was a reaction to the song approach, which was then growing in popularity. His method regarded singing as both an art and a science. Ross stated, "There is no doubt that the actual singing of songs should be the artistic side of singing. However, when a singer is unable to meet the demands that the literature for his particular voice calls for, then he must call on science for the development of a physical skill that will meet those demands" (p. 3).

Other prominent authors of the day, notably P. W. Dykema and H. M. Cundiff (1955), also recognized the importance of voice instruction for children. These authors recommended one minute devoted to the right kind of breathing exercises at the beginning of the music period. They emphasized exercises in the form of games, such as smelling a flower, mooing like a cow, or buzzing like a bee. They believed, however, that the best way to teach breathing for singing was through the sentiment of the words and proper phrasing. This was an approach that seemed to embrace both formal exercises and the song approach.

The Demise of Instruction in Vocal Technique

Elementary music classes at mid-twentieth century became mainly singing classes. As in the philosophy of James Mursell, music became a way of socializing and producing healthier, happier children. While Mursell did return to advocating vocal instruction and music reading, the broader implications of musical involvement overshadowed the systematic teaching of musical skills. Rote teaching became the fastest route to the desired goal—a pleasurable experience with music.

The a cappella choir movement, based upon the model of F. Melius Christiansen, was advancing in the nation's high schools at a fast pace at the very time the song approach was becoming common at the elementary level. In numerous high schools, a cappella choir programs began to rival their instrumental counterparts (Kegerreis, 1970). The emphasis of the a cappella choir was on performance, and the limited repertoire produced a polished perfection heretofore unknown among high school singers. While choral music was given a new prestige by this movement, it also thrived via the song approach. Little attention was given to music-reading skills, and music was taught largely by rote. Vocal technique may have suffered as the "straight tone" became the means of achieving choral blend.

America was shocked in 1957 to find that a false sense of security had developed in its educational system. *Sputnik* and other advances in Soviet space technology resulted in the Woods Hole Conference of 1959 and the Yale Seminar of 1963. These meetings led to calls for the complete restructuring of American education, including the music curriculum.

During this same period, Zoltán Kodály inspired a method of vocal music literacy that became successful in the elementary grades of Hungary. It aroused an interest in American music educators who were struggling to find ways in which to make music more viable in this new age of accountability. In Germany, Carl Orff pioneered his own approach to music education, and the Swiss educator, Émile Jaques-Dalcroze, was becoming known for a music curriculum involving the relationship of movement to music learning. All of these particular approaches or methods found a way into the American music curriculum at a time when music teachers were desperately seeking a new direction for music education.

The renewed interest in music literacy, as found in the curricula of Kodály, Orff, Dalcroze, and others, was just that—a renewed interest in developing music-reading skills. There was little to be found in any of these curricula that would develop confidence in the singing voice through any type of voice instruction. Kodály stressed beautiful singing, but the method presupposed the ability to sing beautifully; there was nothing in the original Kodály method concerning vocal technique. Trying to teach music reading before the skill of singing is like the proverbial cart before the horse. Singing technique and music-reading skills must develop together.

While voice instruction was a central part of music pedagogy from the time of Lowell Mason up to, and including, the 1930s, it was not a major part of the new music curricula that began to appear in the 1960s. Use of the singing voice seemed to be something that was caught but not taught. The song approach was considered the best form of vocal instruction, and some music educators even warned against specific vocal pedagogy for children. The tradition of child vocal training in the United States, which was rooted in boy choirs, children's choirs, and early public school music programs, was lost to a generation of vocal music educators and children in the second half of the twentieth century.

Contemporary Advocates

Not all music educators abandoned child vocal instruction in this new age of music literacy. Frederick J. Swanson, in a work that grew out of thirty years of working with boys, *The Male Voice Ages Eight to Eighteen* (1977), became a leader in junior high music and became known for his work with the Moline (Illinois) Boys Choir. Swanson believed in group vocal training for children as young as eight, but called for instructional techniques that were appropriate for adolescents and children. His techniques for working with boys' changing voices are discussed in Chapter 4.

The contemporary children's choir movement among church groups continues to stress the importance of vocal training for children. M. W. Sample, in *Leading Children's Choirs* (1966), relates the appropriateness of instruction for children's voices from the viewpoint of the American Academy of Teachers of Singing, which states that the principles of good singing are the same for all age groups and that the muscular action needed to produce a good sound is identical from youth to maturity (p. 76). Ruth Krehbiel Jacobs, founder of the Choristers Guild in 1949, wrote *The Successful Children's Choir* (1948), which recommends a thorough knowledge of child vocal pedagogy for teachers as the basis for the proper training of children's voices. Jacobs considers both posture and breathing as fundamental techniques for children to learn. Helen Kemp, internationally known as a specialist in the training of young voices, summarizes her approach to child voice instruction in the statement "Singing is a learned behavior" (1985, p. 68). By this, Kemp stresses that singing is something that children can learn to do when given the proper help. Connie Fortunato emphasizes in *Children's Music Ministry* (1981) that singing involves psychomotor learning, or sequenced instruction in the mental and physical coordination activities of respiration, phonation, resonation, and articulation. Shirley McRae, specialist in Orff Schulwerk and children's choirs, relates the following perspective in *Directing the Children's Choir* (1991): "By middle elementary years, children may be taught the physiological aspects of singing and basic concepts about posture, breathing, and diction. . . . Good habits at this stage not only produce more-musical performances but also protect the child against vocal damage" (pp. 131–132).

Harvey Smith, director of the Phoenix Boys Choir, is a strong advocate of a developmental program of voice skills for children. Basing his work on that of voice teacher Laura Browning Henderson (1979), Smith has produced a set of videotapes that detail his training instruction with the boys of his choir. Particularly important in his approach is the establishment of proper posture and breathing. Smith associates the physical coordination needed for singing to that needed for sports activities, which appeals to young people, especially boys.

A number of influential publications have appeared in recent years advocating vocal instruction for elementary school children. The authors include such vocal specialists as Jean Ashworth Bartle (1988), Betty Bertaux (1989), Mary Goetze (1988), Doreen Rao (1987a), and Linda Swears (1985). Doreen Rao, founder and past chairman of the Children's Choir Committee of the American Choral Directors Association, summarizes the contemporary philosophy of child vocal instruction when she states:

> The first task of the teacher is to teach the students to think of the singing voice as an "instrument." This approach will encourage a more "objective" response to singing. Because the voice is regularly used for self-expression it is closely associated with personal feelings. There is a need to objectify the idea of singing so as to alleviate the student's self-consciousness. Treating the voice as an "instrument" like other instruments will accomplish this objective [1987b, p. 7].

The author's own methodology and research (Phillips, 1983; cf. Aaron, 1990) has demonstrated the applicability of vocal coordination instruction on the improved singing of elementary students. Most vocal pedagogues hold that correct breathing is the basis of correct singing. "Chest heaving" begins early in a child's life and is a detriment to good vocal production. Research has shown that attention to posture alone will not correct the breathing habits of children who are chest heavers. Regular breathing exercises can be incorporated into the child's vocal program with positive benefits for singing.

Vocal development at the secondary level will continue the program that has been started in the elementary school. When such a foundation is lacking, the secondary teacher must consider implementing such a program. While many fine high school choral organizations exist, far too many adolescents use faulty vocal production to achieve the desires of their directors. It is surprising to note the number of high school singers who, when asked about basic vocal instruction in their school choral programs, appear totally ignorant of the fundamentals of singing. Every secondary vocal-music teacher has the obligation to be voice teacher as well as choral director. For most students, the only voice instruction they receive will be from their chorus director.

M. Lynne Gackle (1987) examined the effects of selected vocal techniques and vocalises on the improvement of tone production in the junior high school female voice. Her results showed that those students who received vocal training improved in breath management skills and sang with more security of pitch.

Another advocate of vocal instruction for adolescents is Sally Herman (*Building a Pyramid of Musicianship*, 1988a), whose career has focused on teaching junior high vocal music. Her approach to vocal instruction is based upon the development of vocal confidence through specific training of the adolescent voice.

The December 1988 issue of the *Music Educators Journal* is a special-emphasis issue on choral music education. Articles by Mary Goetze, Sally Herman, Donald Neuen, and Kenneth Phillips are recommended for further reading on current philosophies regarding child and adolescent voice instruction. All four authors agree that singing is a learned behavior and present ideas to foster better singing through a skills-related sequence of vocal techniques.

A PSYCHOMOTOR APPROACH

The idea that singing is a psychomotor skill is certainly not a new one, but its serious implications have been overlooked far too long in regard to children's singing. The process of singing is complex, requiring many psychomotor coordinations. The piano teacher does not expect the coordination needed to play the piano to appear naturally, nor does the band instructor; they spend hours teaching children eye-hand coordination and fine muscle motor control. However, many teachers of child and adolescent singers seem to expect that coordination of the singing voice will happen automatically! These teachers have not been equipped with the knowledge necessary to teach singing correctly. They continue to admonish children to "sing out" because they do not know anything else to do—and "singing out" usually means "belting."

The Five Components of Vocal Technique

Most vocal authorities recognize proper breathing as the basis for good singing technique, yet learning to breathe correctly is often a slow and methodical task for children. If nothing else is done in the way of child vocal training, children should, and can, be taught to breathe properly!

A second area of vocal technique in which children can be instructed is that of phonation. Speech activities are a vital link to the development of the singing voice. The study of elocution used to receive more emphasis than it does in today's schools, but the advent of the amplified sound system has eliminated the need for voice projection. Children need to be encouraged to develop their speaking voices as a natural part of voice training, in terms of timbre, dynamics, pitch, and registration (see Chapters 3 and 4).

The study of breathing and phonation leads to the third area of vocal instruction, resonant tone production. Children and adolescents can be taught simple, enjoyable vocalises that will not hurt their voices. The word to remember in this case is *endurance,* as children's voices cannot be expected to endure long practice sessions or demanding vocal exercises. This is analogous to organized sports activities, in which children play only for short periods: children are not forbidden to play ball because their muscles and bones are still developing, but are allowed to endure less so that they do not become fatigued and hurt themselves. Thus, in singing, no more than five or six minutes of a typical thirty-minute music class should be given to vocal training at the elementary level. At the high school level, approximately 10 percent of the choral rehearsal time is adequate for vocal instruction. A competent vocal instructor will not permit students to strain their voices, because he or she will be aware of endurance limits for child and adolescent singers.

Regarding the possible damage to a child's larynx by early vocal training, it should be noted that the larynx is far more likely to suffer damage from loud play on the playground and misuse in speaking than in the music classroom. Why not teach a child from an early age the proper way to use and protect the voice—on the playground, while speaking and singing? Surprisingly, those who object to child vocal training often feel that it is safe for children to sing without any instruction. A child will learn to sing properly or improperly; better that children be taught correctly how to use the voice, rather than that the "learning" happen by chance!

A teacher should be familiar with the sound of properly produced vocal tone before trying to teach students to sing. The distinguished children's choir director Helen Kemp (1965) has noted that by the time children are seven years old, they often will have developed one of two types of singing voice: the whispery, breathy, puny voice, or the loud, boisterous, neck-swelling sound. The quality produced by the exclusive use of chest voice in singing, so often cultivated in America's classrooms, not only results in a harsh vocal quality but also is harmful physiologically to the voice (see Chapter 5).

The fourth area in which students need vocal instruction is that of diction. This area is a constant source of trouble for adult singers and needs to be emphasized when students are beginning their vocal study. Diction study that emphasizes uniform vowels and rapid, exaggerated consonant articulation will help both word intelligibility and beauty of vocal sound.

The fifth area of emphasis for child vocal instruction is that of expressiveness, which leads to meaningful interpretation. By expressiveness is meant the study of phrasing, increasing vocal range, dynamic and tempo variation, agility, and meaning and mood. Appropriate exercises and vocalises can be employed to help students develop in all of these areas.

Pitch ranges of songs in the early basal series often required that children sing to f^2 of the treble staff. Today, pitch ranges generally have been lowered, to the chagrin of those who believe that all children can be taught to sing in their upper voices. Could it be that early song series included upper-range songs because children in those days were taught how to produce their upper voices properly? The evidence from publications of those times suggests this to be the case. The lowering of song ranges is indicative of poor instruction in vocal technique!

Who and When?

When should child vocal training begin? Adult modeling of techniques can begin for the child during infancy and be continued throughout early childhood. However, formal instruction may begin at about age eight, preferably in a group setting. At age eight the lungs develop fully and the child is able to generate the interthoracic pressure needed to sustain the upper voice. In the present method, students begin in the first grade to develop the proper breathing motion without overt attention to management skills. Learning to breathe naturally is important before one begins to support the voice.

Vocal instruction should be for all children, and not reserved only for those in choral groups. Special emphasis should be given to those who are not developing vocally. Research involving inaccurate singers suggests that by the intermediate years poor pitch matching may be a result not of poor pitch discrimination but of the inability to coordinate the vocal mechanism. A study of seventy-two mono-tones found that many inaccurate singers could be helped through early vocal coordination training over a gradually extended pitch range (Joyner, 1969). The topic of the inaccurate singer is discussed in detail in Chapter 2.

The Select Choir

One of the dangers of the elementary school choral program, if not handled correctly, is that it may tend to foster the idea of musical "elitism" at an age when just the opposite should be occurring. In their desire to produce superior musical results, music teachers often leave children out of choral organizations who do not measure up to audition expectations. Or worse yet, children who do not sing accurately in the classroom and who are told to be "listeners" or not to sing at all never have the courage to audition for the chorus! Being chosen or not chosen for the elementary chorus may very well carry with it the label of "singer" or "nonsinger."

Select choirs have their place, but not if they are the only opportunity for children to experience the joy of choral singing. Select choirs are permissible when *all* children have the basic opportunity to experience the joy of group singing in a choral situation. Having a group of highly motivated students perform in a select organization can provide a special opportunity for those children who really love music. It should not be, however, at the expense of those students who show no early inclination for the musical art. All children should have equal opportunity to grow musically.

One way to provide for equality is through the establishment of a training choir. Those students who do not match pitch accurately may be given extra help in a training organization, while still feeling a part of a choir. This makes an excellent feeder system and provides for the needs of all children.

Do not overlook the needs of handicapped children in the choral program. While mainstreaming is an important concept in today's education, some students may need more specialized programs. Patricia Coates (1988) offers helpful ways to create a successful choir for handicapped students.

Research on Singing

There is growing interest among researchers and music educators in the topic of the child and adolescent voice. This is evident in the number of research studies that are cited in this text. Included in this growing quantity of research are a number of articles that summarize or review the literature on child vocal research. Many useful articles are included in a special bibliography at the conclusion of this chapter.

The Case of Justin

Justin was a fifth-grade student when a program of vocal development was begun in his music class. Justin disliked singing, sank down low in his seat, and participated very little. One day he expressed his dislike of singing to the instructor, who then asked the boy if he could yet drive a car. "No!" was Justin's response. "I'm not old enough!" To which the instructor responded, "Will you learn to drive when you are old enough?" "Of course," was Justin's reply. "How do you know you will?" asked the instructor. "Because anyone can learn to drive, and my dad will teach me," replied Justin. "And that's how it is with singing," replied the instructor. "You learn! Everyone can. It's just like driving a car!" "Oh," replied Justin with a new look of understanding. He had thought that singing was some type of "gift" and he wasn't gifted! Justin's attitude changed, and he learned to enjoy singing.

Why is singing so threatening to students? Because singing is a very complex skill. A writing teacher would not tell students to take out a piece of paper and write with no previous instruction in writing. But in music, we just expect students to open their mouths and sing! Those that can do; those that can't learn very quickly not to be heard. When one sings, one shares the inner self. That in itself can be intimidating, especially if one lacks confidence in the delivery system!

Lowell Mason demonstrated in 1838 that all children were capable of singing. What was true then is true today: singing is a learned behavior. Let's get back to basics—let's teach everyone to sing!

STUDY AND DISCUSSION QUESTIONS

1. State the two contemporary philosophies regarding the appropriateness of vocal instruction for children and adolescents. Which view does the author recommend and with what precautions?
2. Describe the song approach. What are its advantages and disadvantages as a pedagogy for vocal instruction?
3. Why was Lowell Mason important in early music education, and what was his philosophy for teaching children to sing?
4. What was the common theme concerning child vocal instruction among late-nineteenth- and early-twentieth-century writers? Were any of the ideas expressed by these authors unique for the time? Explain.
5. In what ways did the English tradition of choirboy training influence the singing instruction of American children in the early 1900s?
6. Why did the shift in philosophy away from child vocal instruction occur in American education? When did this happen, and what was the result of this change? Was it successful? Explain.
7. Describe the prevailing philosophy of American vocal-music education at mid-twentieth century both at the elementary and secondary levels. Who were the prominent proponents of these philosophies?
8. Why did American music educators turn to European curricula after 1957? What were the results of adopting these European approaches and methods to instruction in the United States?
9. Summarize the views of prominent late-twentieth-century authors on child vocal instruction.
10. Why is a program of vocal instruction important at both the elementary and secondary school levels? What are the five areas of study to be included in such a program and why is each important?
11. How much time should be spent on vocal instruction in both the elementary vocal-music class and the high school chorus? Of what precaution must the vocal teacher be aware regarding the time element and the use of exercises and vocalises?
12. What has brought about the lowering of song ranges in today's music series? Is this justified? Explain.
13. What is the recommended age to begin child-voice instruction? Why? What are the dangers in delaying such instruction?
14. Discuss the advantages and disadvantages of the select chorus at the elementary school level.
15. Why is singing a threatening experience to many students? What strategies can you suggest for encouraging confident singing by all children?

References

AARON, J. C. (1990). *The effects of vocal coordination instruction on the pitch accuracy, range, pitch discrimination and tonal memory of inaccurate singers* (Doctoral dissertation, The University of Iowa).

BARTLE, J. A. (1988). *Lifeline for children's choir directors.* Toronto: Gordon V. Thompson Music.

BATES, J. (1907). *Voice culture for children.* London: Gray & Novello.

BEHNKE, E., & BROWNE, L. (1885). *The child's voice.* Boston: Oliver Ditson.

BERTAUX, B. (1989). Teaching children of all ages to use the singing voice, and how to work with out-of-tune singers. In D. L. Walters and C. C. Taggert (Eds.), *Readings in music learning theory* (pp. 92–104). Chicago: G.I.A. Publications.

COATES, P. (1988). Enabling the disabled choral singer. *Music Educators Journal, 73*(5), 46–48.

COLEMAN, H. (1980). Perceptions of music teacher competencies through a survey of public school music teachers in selected school districts: A positive response to accountability for higher education (Doctoral dissertation, Memphis State University, 1979). *Dissertation Abstracts International, 40,* 3861A.

CURTIS, E. H. (1985). *Children's voices.* New York: John Church.

DANN, H. (1936). *Hollis Dann song series: Conductor's book.* Boston: American Book Co.

DAWSON, J. J. (1902). *The voice of the boy.* New York: E. L. Kellog.

DYKEMA, P. W., & CUNDIFF, H. M. (1955). *School music handbook.* Evanston, IL: Summy-Birchard.

FINN, W. J. (1944). *Child voice training in ten letters.* Chicago: H. T. FitzSimons.

FORTUNATO, C. (1981). *Children's music ministry.* Elgin, IL: David C. Cook.

GACKLE, M. L. (1987). The effect of selected vocal techniques for breath management, resonation, and vowel unification on tone production in the junior high school female voice (Doctoral dissertation, University of Miami, 1987). *Dissertation Abstracts International, 48*(04), 862A.

GEHRKENS, K. (1934). *Music in the grade school.* Boston: C. C. Birchard.

GIDDINGS, T. P. (1919). *Grade school music teaching.* New York: C. H. Congdon.

GOETZE, M. (1988). Wanted: Children to sing and learn. *Music Educators Journal, 75*(7), 28–32.

HENDERSON, L. B. (1979). *How to train singers.* West Nyack, NY: Parker.

HERMAN, S. (1988a). *Building a pyramid of musicianship.* San Diego: Curtis Music Co.

HERMAN, S. (1988b). Unlocking the potential of junior high choirs. *Music Educators Journal, 75*(4), 33–36, 41.

HOWARD, F. E. (1923). *The child-voice in singing* (rev. ed.). New York: H. W. Gray. (Original work published 1895.)

JACOBS, R. K., (1981). *The successful children's choir* (rev. ed.). Chicago: H. T. FitzSimons. (Original work published 1948.)

JOHNSON, C. E. (1935). *The training of boys' voices.* Boston: Oliver Ditson.

JOYNER, D. R. (1969). The monotone problem. *Journal of Research in Music Education, 17*(1), 115–124.

KEGERREIS, R. I. (1970). History of the high school a cappella choir. *Journal of Research in Music Education, 28*(4), 319–329.

KEMP, H. (1965). Vocal methods. In N. P. Tufts (Ed.), *The children's choir,* vol. 2 (pp. 66–86). Philadelphia: Fortress Press.

KEMP, H. (1985). Understanding and developing the child's voice. In D. Rotermund (Ed.), *Children sing his praise* (pp. 66–86). St. Louis: Concordia.

MASON, L. (1839). *Manual of the Boston Academy of Music for instruction in the elements of vocal music on the system of Pestalozzi* (5th ed.). Boston: J. H. Wilkins & R. B. Carter.

MCRAE, S. W. (1991). *Directing the children's choir.* New York: Schirmer Books.

MURSELL, J. L. (1956). *Music education, principles and programs.* Morristown, NJ: Silver Burdett.

MURSELL, J. L., & GLENN, M. (1938). *The psychology of school music teaching.* New York: Silver Burdett.

NEUEN, D. (1988). The sound of a great chorus. *Music Educators Journal, 75*(4), 42–45.

NOBLE, T. T. (1943). *The training of the boy chorister.* New York: G. Schirmer.

PHILLIPS, K. H. (1983). The effects of group breath control training on selected vocal measures related to the singing ability of elementary students in grades two, three, and four (Doctoral dissertation, Kent State University, 1983). *Dissertation Abstracts International, 44,* 1017A.

PHILLIPS, K. H. (1985). Teaching children to sing: Changing attitudes. *Choristers Guild Letters, 36*(9), 165–168.

PHILLIPS, K. H. (1988). Choral music comes of age. *Music Educators Journal, 75*(4), 22–27.

RAO, D. (1987a). *Choral music experience, Vol. 1: Artistry in music education.* Oceanside, NY: Boosey & Hawkes.

RAO, D. (1987b). *Choral music experience, Vol. 2: The young singing voice.* Oceanside, NY: Boosey & Hawkes.

RIX, F. R. (1909). *A manual of school music in elementary grades for supervisors and class teachers.* New York: Macmillan.

RIX, F. R. (1910). *Voice training for school children.* New York: A. S. Barnes.

ROSS, W. E. (1948). *Sing high, sing low.* Bloomington: Indiana University Press.

SAMPLE, M. (1966). *Leading children's choirs.* Nashville: Broadman.

SATALOFF, R. T., & SPIEGEL, J. R. (1989). The young voice. *The NATS Journal, 45*(3), 35–37.

SMITH, H. (n.d.). *Growing and singing: Parts I and II.* Statesville, NC: Video Teaching Aids.

SWANSON, F. J. (1977). *The male voice ages eight to eighteen.* Cedar Rapids, IA: Ingram.

SWEARS, L. (1985). *Teaching the elementary school chorus.* West Nyack, NY: Parker.

Bibliography of Child Vocal Research Reviews

APFELSTADT, H. (1988). What makes children sing well? *UPDATE: Applications of Research in Music Education, 7*(1), 27–32.

ATTERBURY, B. W. (1984). Children's singing voices: A review of selected literature. *Bulletin of the Council for Research in Music Education, 80,* 51–63.

FRANKLIN, E., & FRANKLIN, A. D. (1988). The uncertain singer. *UPDATE: Applications of Research in Music Education, 7*(1), 7–10.

GOETZE, M., COOPER, N., & BROWN, C. J. (1990). Recent research on singing in the general music classroom. *Bulletin of the Council for Research in Music Education, 104,* 16–37.

PHILLIPS, K. H. (1984). Child voice training research. *Journal of Research in Singing, 8*(1), 11–25.

PHILLIPS, K. H. (1985). Respiration for singing: Torso movement and related research. *Journal of Research in Singing, 9*(1), 1–10.

ROSBOROUGH, K., TRONCOSO, L., & PIPER, R. (1972). *Teaching the young child to sing: A literature review with annotated bibliography.* Alamitos, CA: Southwest Regional Laboratory for Educational Research and Development.

RUTKOWSKI, J. (1988). The problem singer: What does research suggest? Part I: The nature of the problem. *General Music Today, 2*(3), 19–23, 32.

RUTKOWSKI, J. (1989). The problem singer: What does research suggest? Part II: Song materials and remediation strategies. *General Music Today, 2*(4), 24–29.

WELCH, G. F. (1979). Poor-pitch singing: A review of the literature. *Psychology of Music, 7*(1), 50–58.

2

THE PSYCHOMOTOR PROCESS ♾

The vocal instrument is a wonderfully complex mechanism. Its psychoacoustical and physiological properties combine to produce an incredible result—singing. For some people, the ability to sing seems to come naturally; the complex coordination of muscles, cartilages, tissue, breath, perception, and memory, among other things, align without much conscious effort. For others, singing remains forever elusive; some breakdown occurs in the machinery that hinders vocal coordination. This chapter discusses those various aspects of pitch perception, tonal memory, and vocal coordination that are involved in the psychomotor process of singing. The causes of inaccurate singing are discussed in relation to these parameters of pitch production.

The area of learning involving skills development has become known as the psychomotor domain. This mode of learning is skills oriented—that is, motor activity that directly proceeds from mental activity. Music making relys heavily upon psychomotor learning. Both psychological and motor responses combine to result in some type of performance.

The psychomotor process for teaching, in its simplest form, may be conceptualized in four steps: (1) the teacher provides a model or stimulus, (2) the student perceives and decodes the model, (3) the student imitates the model, and (4) the student analyzes feedback regarding their effort. Each of these steps is important to the skills-learning sequence,

23

and each step is discussed in this chapter as it relates to vocal production.

Elizabeth Simpson (1966) has developed a more complete taxonomy of psychomotor behavior, one that has had rather wide acceptance for its applicability to the learning of musical skills. There are seven levels to this taxonomy, representing a hierarchy, with upper-level behaviors requiring the skills contained in the lower levels. The main levels, from lowest to highest, are as follows:

1.0   Perception: the process of becoming aware of objects, qualities, or relations by use of the sense organs

2.0   Set: preparatory adjustment or readiness for a particular kind of action or experience

3.0   Guided response: overt behavior action under the guidance of an instructor

4.0   Mechanism: the learned response becoming habitual

5.0   Complex overt response: smooth and efficient performance of a complex motor act

6.0   Adaptation: ability to change a performance to make it more suitable

7.0   Origination: ability to develop new skills

While a number of the main areas in Simpson's taxonomy have subsets, those for set 2.0 are especially important when considering the psychomotor process. These subsets are as follows:

2.1   Mental set: readiness to perform a motor act (cognitive awareness)

2.2   Physical set: having made the anatomical adjustments necessary for a motor act

2.3   Emotional set: readiness in terms of favorable attitude

While 2.1 Mental set and 2.2 Physical set are commonly acknowledged parts of the psychomotor process, 2.3 Emotional set is also important. Without the proper attitude, the psychomotor process breaks down. Students who do not like to sing resist instruction and are observed to drone along without interest. American boys, especially, seem to think that singing is less a masculine activity than a female one (Castelli, 1986) and withdraw early from active participation. Teachers must work to overcome this macho attitude, using male role models, whenever possible, to note the contributions of male singing to musical culture.

Ramona Clark (1989), a middle school teacher in Iowa, reports success in changing students' negative attitudes toward singing through a letter-writing project to major athletic teams. Students sought to determine if professional athletes participate in music; they found that many do! Bulletin boards and scrapbooks were made from the many pictures and responses received from the players. Enrollment in Clark's middle school choral program went from 38 students to more than 250, for which she gives partial credit to the "Musical Athletes" project. Stressing the physical and athletic nature of the psychomotor process is an effective means of increasing interest in singing.

Vocal pitch production is dependent upon both psychological and physiological factors. The ability to hear and decode pitch (pitch perception) and to remember pitch (tonal memory) are the psychological requirements. The physiological action involves the closing and tensing of the vocal folds and the pressure of the breath. If these parameters are not coordinated properly, accurate pitch production is hampered.

PITCH PERCEPTION

Poor pitch perception can have psychological or physical origins. Fortunately, the majority of the student population does not have a physical hearing problem. Those students who do have a hearing loss can be helped through the use of sophisticated hearing devices. Hearing problems must be referred to medical specialists, and most schools offer routine hearing checks to uncover such problems.

The psychological problems of poor pitch perception may stem from a number of factors. Among these are attention to pitch, proper feedback, and mode of teaching.

Attention to Pitch

Inattention, or lack of focus, is especially problematic among younger children. This lack of attention to pitch may be simply a result of where the child is seated within the classroom. Children who sit at the edge of the class and who sing inaccurately may be helped by moving them to the center of the group. A change in physical placement seems to provide the type of focus that these children need for better pitch concentration.

Distractions within the environment also may contribute to focusing problems. Every attempt should be made to create a classroom environment that is free of distracting elements, such as students coming and going and interruptions from outside of the classroom. Some teachers report success in gaining a student's attention to pitch by placing the student's face between the teacher's hands and singing directly into the face of the child. Not only does this focus the student's attention, but the child can feel the teacher's voice and interact with it.

Proper Feedback

Lack of proper feedback is a reason not only for inattention but for the inability to decode pitch. Aural, visual, and kinesthetic forms of feedback all have been found to aid pitch perception and production.

Aural feedback is most important to the perceiving and decoding of pitch. In order for people to make the appropriate adjustment to the vocal mechanism, they must have auditory information. The importance of children monitoring their own vocal production in relation to the sound source has been noted by Mary Goetze, who states, "Inattention to one's singing voice may result in a singing response which is similar to singing without auditory feedback" (1985, p. 15). Child voice research specialist Graham Welch has found that "knowledge of results" is an important aspect of self-monitoring. Welch states, "Children who sing out of tune can become pitch accurate if the learning condition contains both qualitative information about pitch error and sufficient practice for this information to be applied" (1985, p. 246).

Children who experience singing only as a sensory experience without auditory feedback may not link the kinesthetic production of pitch to its psychological parameter. Research has found that primary school children are more likely to sing in tune individually than in a group (Goetze, 1985). Perhaps an aural masking effect takes place in group singing that interferes with aural perception. Thus, young children who are unable to hear their own voices are forced to sing only by kinesthetic association, which by itself is not sufficient to produce accurate singing results. Goetze notes that by the third grade, pitch accuracy no longer seems to be affected by group singing; older children who sing inaccurately will do so in either situation—individually or in a group.

Likewise, children who develop only an aural mode of discrimination may actually hear or perceive pitch correctly, but be unable to reproduce it accurately. The importance of kinesthetic learning (the physical feeling of sound sensation or production) to "audiation" (inner hearing) is related by Betty Bertaux:

> In effect, a singer who is low in vocal-kinesthetic aptitude and inattentive to his own voice, and who is consequently unable to exercise precise control over his vocal mechanism, may fail to associate kinesthetic sensation with the music that is audiated. Such a singer may develop habits of kinesthetic disassociation when singing, causing singing to become a sensory experience exclusive of the auditory dimension. Conversely one may perceive music as an auditory experience exclusive of singing. If an individual who is low in vocal-kinesthetic aptitude but high in tonal aptitude never learns to make the aural/kinesthetic connection, singing may actually interrupt and interfere with his aural perception, and he may never develop accurate audiation. He certainly will not learn to sing [1989, pp. 93–94].

Visual feedback has been found to be another aid to pitch perception. Pictures of high and low objects, or "pitch targets," placed on a chalkboard will help some students in the psychological process of voice direction. Moving students' hands in the direction of high and low also will help some children to connect to the pitch.

The use of microcomputers for providing visual feedback on pitch accuracy to inaccurate singers has been explored in a study by Welch, Howard, and Rush (1989). An author-designed software program, SINGAD, enabled students to have a real-time visual feedback of vocalized pitch (displayed as a line moving across the screen) in relation to pitch targets displayed on the computer monitor. Results of the study showed that use of the computer program produced significant improvement in pitch accuracy and that "verbal feedback on its own appears to be less powerful in promoting learning than real-time, meaningful visual feedback" (p. 156).

While the use of microcomputers for improving singing accuracy may have the potential for helping with inaccurate singers, a certain amount of caution must be expressed. Students using such a program without the help of a teacher may develop the wrong kinesthetic associations in a determination to produce the correct pitch, for instance straining at the laryngeal level. While the use of microcomputers in the music class has obvious advantages, care must be taken to monitor for both psychological and motor responses in the psychomotor process.

Teaching Mode

Teaching mode is a third parameter that affects pitch perception. A teaching mode that merely drums notes by rote does not actively engage students in the learning process. The manner in which musical examples are presented has a direct effect upon how students listen. When teachers are enthusiastic, students are apt to be more focused. Students can be involved directly in the learning process of a song by structuring a sequence of activities in which they make judgments and decisions about the music being studied, such as whether the students are able to find the same musical motive repeated in another part of the composition. Music learning should be a student-centered process.

The degree to which teaching and learning modes affect pitch perception is a question that has begun to interest researchers in music education (Apfelstadt, 1986a, 1986b; Persellin, 1988). There are three general learning modalities—visual, auditory, and kinesthetic—and individuals usually learn better in one of these modes (primary modality). A visual learner will respond better to books, visual aids, and other visual forms than an auditory learner, who prefers aural stimuli, or the kinesthetic learner, who learns best through the senses.

The teaching modality preference of teachers does influence teaching direction, that is, those who are visual learners teach with an emphasis toward visual instruction. Many students, however, are not good visual learners and therefore respond better to auditory or kinesthetic approaches. What this means to music teachers is important: a mixed modality of teaching-learning styles is best for classroom instruction if students are to be reached. When students are learning a song, visual activities may include learning to read notation and using word sheets, while auditory learning may use modeling and echo singing. The kinesthetic component will involve movement and adding actions to songs. For students whose primary mode of learning is not auditory, pitch perception and production may be aided by both visual and kinesthetic activities.

Another important area of teaching modality is that of vocal modeling. Research has shown that children are more likely to perceive pitch accurately if the model they hear is an accurate representation of what they are to produce and presented in their own singing range (Clegg, 1986; Petzold, 1966).

Voice quality, as part of the vocal model, also affects accuracy of pitch perception and production. The female vocal model (when produced correctly) is superior for this purpose (Clegg, 1966; Hermanson, 1971; Petzold, 1966; Sims, Moore, and Kuhn, 1982; Small and McCachern, 1983), as is the child voice (Green, 1987).

The male voice singing an octave below seems especially troublesome for children who are inexperienced singers. Males must cultivate a lighter, head-voice production suitable for child vocal modeling. At least three research studies report that children find pitch level at a higher rate of accuracy when the male model sings in the falsetto voice, as opposed to the fuller, natural male quality (Kramer, 1985; Montgomery, 1988; Wolf, 1984). It is recommended that males who teach singing to children develop the ability to sing an octave higher than normal (male alto) so as not to confuse pitch perception, especially among younger, inexperienced children. As children become more confident singers, male falsetto modeling becomes less necessary.

TONAL MEMORY

A second psychological factor involved in accurate pitch production is tonal memory. A student must be able to remember what is heard. Research in tonal memory seems to suggest that a certain amount of inaccurate singing may be the result of poor tonal memory (Aaron, 1990). A number of investigators have found that students who are deficient in tonal memory also are deficient in pitch perception.

Tonal memory seems to be affected by age and the amount of material to be remembered at one time. Memory span generally increases with age: "Children's songs are short, and their listening experiences are also. At least, our pedagogical folklore implies an agreement of the timespan of remembered music works increases with age" (Cady, 1981, p. 84). It also is known that tonal memory decreases as the length of patterns increases, and that both perception and melodic contour appear to affect tonal memory (Long, 1977, p. 281).

Music psychologist Edwin Gordon (1981) has coined the term *audiate* to denote the process of inner hearing required for tonal memory. Gordon stresses that in learning music, children do not memorize individual notes any more than people memorize individual words to derive meaning from speech. According to Gordon, children learn to audiate in relation to musical syntax, or musical patterns. (For in-depth information on this topic, see Choksy, 1988, and Gordon, 1989.)

Activities for improving tonal memory may include vocal games such as the echo singing of tonal patterns. An important element in this type of instruction involves singing inside before outside—that is, singing part of a song inside (on a cue from the teacher) and then outside for the remainder of the song. Also, students should practice thinking the beginning pitch of a song before singing it and should be encouraged to begin a song without the first pitch being given. Veteran teachers know that students do this easily.

Establishing the concept of "same-different" is another important factor in developing tonal memory. Young children often do not recognize subtle changes in tonal patterns. Playing or singing paired phrases for student evaluation of sameness or difference should be incorporated early into the music curriculum.

Another factor in developing tonal memory is that children need much repetition in the learning process. Children should not be expected to master a song from hearing it sung as a whole. Songs are best taught whole-part-whole, allowing for multiple repetitions of individual phrases before the whole is mastered.

VOCAL COORDINATION

Singing is a psychomotor skill. Not only must sound be perceived psychologically, but it must also be produced vocally. The motor process involves coordination of the vocal folds (located within the larynx), breath, resonators (primarily the pharynx and mouth), and articulators (tongue, teeth, jaw, lips).

Research on the effects of vocal coordination on pitch accuracy presents a variety of findings. Early research on inaccurate singing points to deficiencies in pitch perception and tonal memory. Later research, however, suggests that inaccurate singers may have a problem of vocal control (Welch, 1979). Other research suggests that pitch perception and vocal production are interrelated; the more singing experience, the better the pitch perception. One recent study has found no significant difference among inaccurate singers in the fourth, fifth, and sixth grades on a test of pitch perception (Aaron, 1990). However, the experimental group receiving vocal coordination training significantly improved in vocal range and pitch accuracy over the control group, which only took part in regular singing activities. Thus, it would appear that many intermediate-age children may hear, but not be able to coordinate, the vocal mechanism to produce pitch accurately.

Pitch is the product of two physical actions—movement (vibration) of the vocal folds and the flow of the pressurized air column. If there is a motor coordination problem in either of these areas, accuracy of pitch is likely to be affected.

Phonatory Adjustments

A technical discussion of the action of the vocal folds is presented in Chapter 8. It is important to note, however, that the adjustments necessary to produce a wide range of pitches are basically involuntary, requiring no overt action on the part of the singer. The pitch-adjusting muscles respond automatically to the mental perception of pitch and adjust accordingly. However, a child must experience kinesthetically and aurally a wide variety of these adjustments if confidence in accurate pitch production is to become automatic.

Singing in the upper voice requires a thinning and lengthening of the vocal folds. If the child never experiences this sensation, matching pitches in the upper range may present a problem. Children sing more naturally in the lower, chest voice mechanism, because it is the voice they experience in speaking. However, singing only in the lower voice throughout the vocal range produces a harsh quality that can be injurious to the vocal folds. Pitch-exploration exercises are prescribed in this method as a means of helping children develop the flexibility of the vocal muscles and experience a variety of sensations as an introduction to the actual singing of prescribed pitches.

Breath Coordination

The breathing process for singing is discussed in detail in Chapter 7. Basically, the air column has to provide the correct breath pressure if accurate pitch is to be produced. Too much pressure may cause sharping, and too little may cause flatting or gross pitch inaccuracy. The vocal folds vibrate as a result of the pressurized air column flowing between the folds. Learning to balance the tension of the vocal folds with the flow of the energized air column is one of the basic requirements for singing. Children tend to breathe in the upper chest, which is incorrect for singing, and compensate for this lack of breath energy by using too much pressure and tension and the vocal-fold level. Such "pressed voice" singing results in poor quality, lack of vocal freedom and accuracy, and often injury to the vocal folds.

The breathing process is "bimodal," that is, one can breathe mostly with the intercostal muscles (between the ribs), which tends to be a shallow breath, or one can employ the diaphragm, which results in a deeper, fuller breath. The first mode, chest or clavicular breathing, is used for a fast inhalation-exhalation cycle, such as needed for running or other strenuous physical activities. This type of breathing is difficult to manage and is not recommended by vocal authorities for singing. The second mode, abdominal-diaphragmatic-costal breathing, permits greater control over the breathing process and aids pitch production through activation of an energized air column.

Young singers need to understand the bimodal nature of breathing and learn how to manage the breath consciously until the proper breathing response becomes automatic. Sometimes, merely calling attention to the fact that improper breathing is being used will bring about the correct action.

Older children often do not respond quickly to instruction in proper breathing. Ingrained habits change slowly, and upper-chest breathing is the norm for singing by the intermediate grades. The method presented in this book prescribes a sequence of large-to-fine motor control exercises that gradually change the style of breathing from thoracic or chest to diaphragmatic. Breathing exercises are the foundation of this vocal method, and much inaccurate pitch production can be helped by establishing the proper breathing mode. A number of researchers report the favorable effects of vocal coordination instruction on singing accuracy (Aaron, 1990). Such instruction should begin as early as the first grade and needs to reflect the levels of maturity and endurance exhibited at each stage of development.

INACCURATE SINGING

Many terms have been used to label students who sing off pitch: uncertain singers, monotones, out-of-tune singers, nonsingers, poor-pitch singers, droners, untuned singers, conversational singers, defective singers, backward singers, unsure singers, problem singers, tone-deaf, tune-deaf, pitch-deficient, singing-deficient, singing-disabled, singing-impaired, blue jays, submarines, and inaccurate singers (Aaron, 1990, pp. 2–3). The term *inaccurate singer* is perhaps the most accurate of all.

The frequency reported for inaccurate singing among children varies according to the criteria used to measure pitch deviation and the grade levels being measured. A. Oren Gould (1968), in one of the largest studies on children's singing, reported that 18 percent of American school children sang inaccurately, but figures vary widely. Results of the National Assessment of Educational Progress for 1971–1972 showed that 50 percent of the nine-year-olds, 45 percent of the thirteen-year-olds, 35 percent of the seventeen-year-olds, and 30 percent of the adults were unable to sing the song "America" with acceptable pitch. Whatever the numbers, inaccurate singing is a persistent problem in music education.

Two facts concerning the frequency of inaccurate singers seem certain: (1) there are more boys who sing inaccurately than girls, and (2) the number of inaccurate singers decreases with age. Both of these findings would appear to be related to age: boys mature more slowly than girls, and both genders improve in singing accuracy as they mature. Both psychological and physiological maturity affect singing accuracy.

Causes of Inaccurate Singing

A number of in-depth reviews of research on inaccurate singing have appeared in recent years (Aaron, 1990; Apfelstadt, 1988; Franklin and Franklin, 1983; Rutkowski, 1989; Welch, 1979, 1985). The results of the numerous investigations reported are often in conflict, and yet, a number of conclusions as to the causes of inaccurate singing among children and adolescents have been identified. The causes of inaccurate singing generally fall into four categories: (1) environmental, or lack of exposure to music; (2) organic, including retarded maturation, physical defects, and diseases; (3) psychological, such as poor pitch discrimination, poor pitch memory, and lack of confidence; and (4) poor vocal control, because of poor breath support, lack of kinesthetic awareness in the vocal mechanism, inability to shift into the upper register, and straining (Aaron, 1990, pp. 6–7). Most of these factors were discussed earlier in this chapter, as they relate to the correct functioning of the psychomotor process for singing. One additional influence, the environment, also needs to be discussed.

There are a number of studies that have investigated the effects of home environment on musical development and singing. One study reported a strong relationship between the singing ability of pre-kindergarten children and their home musical environments (Kirkpatrick, 1962). Excellent to good environments produced singers and partial singers with few nonsingers, but poor environments produced no singers and many partial and nonsingers. Another study found similar results for first-grade children, noting that children who were rated "musical" had frequent opportunities to hear and participate in singing in the home (Shelton, 1966). Early childhood specialists conclude:

Evidence is mounting that musical environment does have great effect upon a young child's musical development. Not only has it been shown that musical children come from homes where the family listens to, is interested in, and participates in musical activities, thereby providing much informal, incidental music "instruction" for youngsters ... but that preschool children from musically disadvantaged homes can develop neglected musical skills through planned instruction and intervention [McDonald and Simons, 1989, p. 40].

The evidence that children from disadvantaged homes can be helped musically by early intervention in school music programs is good news for music educators. Unfortunately, the most neglected area of music instruction is often at the kindergarten and prekindergarten levels. The music education profession must do more to influence stronger music programs in these early years of the child's life.

An important period of musical growth for the child is between the ages of eighteen months and three years. This is when the child is developing a repertoire of tonal patterns and tonal memory is being shaped. If, however, parents do not sing (as is all too often the case), where will children receive their musical nurturing? Some research has shown indications that nursery and church school experiences aid musical development (Simons, 1978, p. 13). With so many children being placed today in day-care and preschool centers, the challenge is before directors and teachers in those environments to help provide for the musical culture lacking in many homes. "Fortunately, vocal development is not strictly bound by time. Experience is the more important ingredient. . . . A good program of vocal instruction in the elementary school can do a great deal to insure optimum vocal development for every child" (Swears, 1985, p. 27).

Remediation for Inaccurate Singing

Remedial help for inaccurate singing is the one area of the psychomotor process included in most texts on elementary music methods. These techniques generally fall into three categories: (1) pitch perception, (2) additional drill in the singing of songs and exercises, and (3) instruction in vocal technique.

Pitch Perception Activities. The results of studies on the effects of pitch-discrimination training on singing accuracy are conflicting, probably because of the type and/or approach to the instruction involved. However, at least four studies (Jones, 1979; Shriro, 1980; Welch, 1985; Welch, Howard, and Rush, 1989) were successful in helping inaccurate singers with pitch-discrimination instruction when both aural and visual feedback were present. This suggests that teachers may have some success with inaccurate singers by using verbal feedback as well as some type of visual feedback, such as shooting an imaginary basketball toward a hoop for higher pitches or moving the student's hands in the direction of the desired pitch. As noted earlier, feedback is an important part of psychomotor learning, and a combination or aural and visual feedback seems to be more effective than aural feedback alone.

The presentation and order of the pitches to be matched for inaccurate singers seems to influence singing accuracy. Short, familiar tonal patterns in a variety of keys are better for tone matching than are individual pitches. Also, inaccurate singers may be able to match patterns before they can discriminate between high and low pitches within an octave. Such skills appear to be developing simultaneously (Jones, 1979). Finally, descending patterns are often easier to match than ascending ones.

Children often have difficulty distinguishing between their speaking and singing voices. Pitching tonal patterns high enough to avoid the chest register will help in finding the singing voice. Pitches between a^1 and c^2 are above the break and are conducive to singing in the upper voice as opposed to the chest or speaking register. A simple reminder to use the singing voice also helps younger children to remember to use the upper quality in their singing.

Singing accurately requires that students hear accurately. Students need a time for inner hearing before giving a response—that is, singing on the inside before they sing on the outside. Children also need to develop the ability to compare tonal patterns for sameness and difference. Having students cover or cup one ear with the hand also helps them to hear and attend to the pitch model.

Another suggestion concerning pitch perception and singing accuracy involves the students in analyzing their own responses and what they need to do to correct them. "In this approach, the teacher functions as a facilitator for self-discovery by setting up a vocal task, listening for the desired sound, watching for the appropriate physiological response, and suggesting alternatives. After the vocal task is performed, the teacher encourages discussion about what was felt as opposed to suggesting what *should* have been felt" (Bertaux, 1989, pp. 96–97). Discussion is central to this experience, and there is no right or wrong way to relate sensation. This is another form of feedback, but this type originates with the student.

The psychological process of pitch perception as it relates to singing accuracy can be summarized as follows: (1) provide a stimulus (tonal pattern), (2) require a time for "silent" singing, (3) request a singing response within the vocal range of the student, and (4) provide for feedback, first from the student and then from the teacher. Positive reinforcement is extremely important, and teachers must shape the response to the desired goal. Providing many opportunities for young children to sing alone, after a model, also is important.

Additional Song Experiences. The second area of remediation for inaccurate singers has been the additional singing of songs and exercises. Research in this area has produced little objective evidence to suggest that more singing, in and of itself, is an effective means of helping inaccurate singers. One study has reported a significant difference between treatments in favor of remedial vocal training using vocalises as opposed to an approach based entirely on the singing of songs (Richner, 1976). This would suggest that the use of vocal drills and vocalises may be appropriate for helping inaccurate singers. Humming is reported as the "instant voice developer" in another study (Stene, 1969), and the present method employs exercises in humming as a valuable means of warming up vocally and developing inner hearing.

Vocal Coordination. An increasing area of interest in the remediation of inaccurate singing is instruction in vocal coordination (the motor process of psychomotor learning). A growing number of research studies report the favorable results of vocal-coordination instruction on singing accuracy. A study by Viola Brody (1947) is among the earliest to investigate objectively the motor process in children's singing; she found that teaching children to breathe from the diaphragm had a positive effect on their singing accuracy. This result was later confirmed by other research (Aaron, 1990; Joyner, 1969; Phillips, 1983).

The importance of establishing the proper motor response of the singer is paramount in the present methodology. Research in this area suggests that much inaccurate singing results from failure to coordinate properly the physical process needed to establish correct pitch production. As the breath is the primary activator of the vibratory cycle of the vocal folds, its use and coordination are basic to the singing process. Lack of breath-support coordination for singing may produce either of two conditions: (1) throaty, pressed singing as a result of the laryngeal mechanism compensating for lack of breath pressure, or (2) diffused, inaccurate singing as a result of low breath pressure and lack of compensation by the laryngeal mechanism. Children who breathe improperly but learn to sing by compensating with more throat and laryngeal pressure never sing with a free or beautiful tone. Children who do not breathe properly and who do not compensate with more pressed vocal production (often a reserved or inhibited child) do not match pitch. Research suggests that while the children in this latter group may exhibit lack of pitch perception or tonal memory in the early primary years, by the time they reach the intermediate years they can hear and remember pitch but are unable to coordinate the motor process of their bodies to enable them to produce the correct tone. Learning to use the breathing muscles in pitch production is a necessary and vital part of the psychomotor process and is covered in Chapter 7 of this text.

Correct posture and breath management are the foundational elements of proper vocal coordination, but complete vocal coordination involves more than just breathing. The student must learn to apply the breath to both the speaking and singing voices. Vocal imitations, choric speaking, and chanting of texts all serve as means of establishing the various pitch levels of the voice and proper support and projection. Vocalises are another important element for the coordination of mind and motor. The method in this text uses vocalises that are appropriate to the age level of the student. Endurance must be considered when choosing music for young singers.

A program of vocal coordination also involves the areas of diction and expression. Word pronunciation depends upon the proper use of the articulators (jaws, tongue, teeth, etc.), and ease of production can be a problem when the vocal tract is under strain from a lack of psychomotor coordination. Likewise, the expressive elements of phrasing, range, dynamics, tempo, and agility are all affected when there is interference in the coordination of breath, vocal folds, resonators, and articulators. When used as an instrument, the human body requires numerous fine psychomotor responses. For some singers this coordination happens automatically, but for most people this process must be learned.

Inaccurate singers can be taught to sing accurately. While individual instruction is often best for such students, a number of researchers have had success with improving singing accuracy in a group situation. This is encouraging for music teachers, as most instruction given to students is in a classroom setting. Individual attention, however, helps quicken the process of remediation, and teachers should ask for time in their teaching schedules to work alone with students.

It is imperative to music education that all students learn to sing. Shinichi Suzuki has demonstrated that any child who has a willing attitude and the proper instruction can learn to play the violin. The same may be said for singing. Young children love to sing. It is only as they become older that they become self-conscious and learn that they do not know how to sing. Once they learn that they can be taught, their attitudes change. The importance of the psychomotor process and how its various components relate to the skill of singing need to be understood by all teachers if they are to guide their students to become confident singers. Singing is a *learned* behavior—a psychomotor skill.

STUDY AND DISCUSSION QUESTIONS

1. Define psychomotor learning. Why is it important for vocal-music teachers to understand the psychomotor process as it relates to singing?

2. What are the psychological and physiological components involved in the skill of singing?
3. How are the aural and kinesthetic modes of pitch discrimination related to the skill of accurately matching pitch vocally?
4. Why should a mixed modality of teaching styles be used in vocal-music education? Give an example of a mixed modality for the teaching of a song melody.
5. What role does proper feedback play in developing pitch accuracy? What types of feedback are appropriate?
6. Describe the components of a good vocal model as a stimulus for teaching children to sing. What special problems must the male teacher resolve when vocally modeling for young singers?
7. What techniques are appropriate for improving the tonal memory of students? Can you suggest others than those given in the text?
8. What has research shown regarding the relationship of inaccurate singing to vocal coordination?
9. How is breathing bimodal? What do children do to compensate for lack of proper breathing when singing, and what are the results?
10. What has research found regarding the most common causes of inaccurate singing, and what is known about the relative importance of each area?
11. How does home environment affect a child's singing achievement, and what are the general research findings in regard to preschool children who come from musically disadvantaged homes?
12. What two critical areas of pitch cognition are being developed between the ages of eighteen months and three years? What does this say to the music education profession?
13. Discuss the three categories of remedial techniques for inaccurate singers and the relative merits of each area.
14. When presenting exercises for pitch-matching accuracy, what are the teaching techniques that will enable the student to process and produce an accurate singing response?
15. What are the two foundational elements of proper vocal coordination, and what other areas also are involved?

References

AARON, J. C. (1990). *A study of the effects of vocal coordination instruction on the pitch accuracy, range, pitch discrimination, and tonal memory of inaccurate singers* (Doctoral dissertation, The University of Iowa).

APFELSTADT, H. (1986a). Melodic perception instruction—What is its effect upon pitch discrimination and vocal accuracy among kindergarten children? *UPDATE: The Applications of Research in Music Education, 4*(2), 6–8.

APFELSTADT, H. (1986b). Learning modality: A potential clue in the search for vocal accuracy. *UPDATE: The Applications of Research in Music Education, 4*(3), 4–6.

APFELSTADT, H. (1988). What makes children sing well? *UPDATE: The Applications of Research in Music Education, 7*(1), 27–32.

BERTAUX, B. (1989). Teaching children of all ages to use the singing voice, and how to work with out-of-tune singers. In D. L. Walters & C. C. Taggert (Eds.), *Readings in music learning theory* (pp. 92–104). Chicago: G.I.A. Publications.

BRODY, V. A. (1947). An experimental study of the emergence of the process involved in the production of sound (Doctoral dissertation, The University of Michigan). *Dissertation Abstracts, 15,* 90.000.

CADY, H. (1981). Children's processing and remembering of music: Some speculations. In R. A. Choate (Ed.), *Documentary Report of the Ann Arbor Symposium on the Applications of Psychology to the Teaching and Learning of Music* (pp. 81–87). Reston, VA: Music Educators National Conference.

CARY, D. (1949). *A study of range extension in the voices of third-grade children with singing deficiency.* Unpublished master's thesis, University of Kansas.

CASTELLI, P. A. (1986). Attitudes of music educators and public school secondary students on selected factors which influence decline in male enrollment occurring between elementary and secondary public school vocal programs (Doctoral dissertation, The University of Maryland). *Dissertation Abstracts International, 47/06,* 2069A.

CHOKSY, L. (1988). *The Kodály method* (2nd. ed.). Englewood Cliffs, NJ: Prentice Hall.

CLARK, R. (1989). Big peach headline: Would you call Too-Tall Jones a sissy? *Iowa Music Educator, 43*(1), 32–33.

CLEGG, B. (1966). *A comparative study of primary grade children's ability to match tones.* Unpublished master's thesis, Brigham Young University.

FRANKLIN, E., and FRANKLIN, A. D. (1983). The uncertain singer. *UPDATE: The Applications of Research in Music Education, 1*(3), 3–6.

GOETZE, M. (1986). Factors affecting accuracy in children's singing (Doctoral dissertation, University of Colorado at Boulder, 1985). *Dissertation Abstracts International, 46,* 2955A.

GORDON, E. E. (1981). Music learning and learning theory. In R. A. Choate (Ed.), *Documentary Report of the Ann Arbor Symposium on the Applications of Psychology to the Teaching and Learning of Music* (pp. 62–68). Reston, VA: Music Educators National Conference.

GORDON, E. E. (1989). *Learning sequences in music.* Chicago: G.I.A. Publications.

GOULD, A. O. (1968). *Developing specialized programs for singing in the elementary school* (Final Report). Washington, DC: Research in Education. (ERIC Reproduction Service No. ED025530 TE 499967)

GREEN, G. A. (1987). The effect of vocal modeling on pitch-matching accuracy of children in grades one through six (Doctoral dissertation, The Louisiana State University and Agricultural and Mechanical College). *Dissertation Abstracts International, 48,* 1410A.

HERMANSON, L. W. (1972). An investigation of the effects of timbre on simultaneous vocal pitch acuity of young children (Doctoral dissertation, Columbia University, 1971). *Dissertation Abstracts International, 32,* 3558A.

JONES, M. (1979). Using a vertical keyboard instrument with the uncertain singer. *Journal of Research in Music Education, 27*(3), 173–184.

JOYNER, D. R. (1969). The monotone problem. *Journal of Research in Music Education, 17*(1), 114–125.

KIRKPATRICK, W. C., JR. (1962). Relationships between the singing ability of prekindergarten children and their home environment (Doctoral dissertation, University of Southern California). *Dissertation Abstracts International, 23,* 886.

KRAMER, S. (1986). The effects of two different music programs on third- and fourth-grade children's ability to match pitches vocally (Doctoral dissertation, Rutgers University, 1985). *Dissertation Abstracts International, 64,* 2609A.

LONG, P. A. (1977). Relationships between pitch memory in short melodies and selected factors. *Journal of Research in Music Education, 25*(4), 272–282.

MCDONALD, D. T., & SIMONS, G. M. (1989). *Musical growth and development: Birth through six.* New York: Schirmer Books.

MONTGOMERY, T. (1988). A study of the associations between two means of vocal modeling by a male music teacher and third-grade students' vocal accuracy in singing pitch patterns (Doctoral dissertation, University of North Carolina, Greensboro). *Dissertation Abstracts International, 49/*08, 2142A.

National assessment of educational progress (1974). *The First National Assessment of Musical Performance,* Report No. 02-MU-01. Washington, DC: Government Printing Office.

PERSELLIN, D. (1988). The influences of perceived modality preferences on teaching methods used by elementary music educators. *UPDATE: The Applications of Research in Music Education, 7*(1), 11–15.

PETZOLD, R. (1966). *Auditory perception of musical sounds by children in the first six grades.* Cooperative Research Project No. 1051. Madison: University of Wisconsin.

PHILLIPS, K. H. (1983). The effects of group breath control training on selected vocal measures related to the singing ability of elementary students in grades two, three, and four (Doctoral dissertation, Kent State University). *Dissertation Abstracts International, 44,* 1017A.

RICHNER, S. S. (1976). The effect of classroom and remedial methods of music instruction on the ability of inaccurate singers in the third, fourth and fifth grades to reproduce pitches (Doctoral dissertation, University of Idaho). *Dissertation Abstracts International, 37,* 1447–A.

RUTKOWSKI, J. (1989). The problem singer: What does research suggest? *General Music Today, 2*(3), 24–29.

SHELTON, J. S. (1966). The influence of home musical environment upon musical response of first-grade children (Doctoral dissertation, George Peabody College For Teachers, 1965). *Dissertation Abstracts International, 41*, 6765–6766.

SHRIRO, M. J. (1982). Teaching vocal pitch perception and production (Doctoral dissertation, University of Pittsburgh, 1980). *Dissertation Abstracts International, 42*, 3808A.

SIMONS, G. M. (1978). *Early childhood musical development: A bibliography of research abstracts 1960–1975 with implications and recommendations for teaching and research.* Reston, VA: Music Educators National Conference.

SIMPSON, E. (1966). *The classification of educational objectives, psychomotor domain.* Washington, DC: United States Office of Education, OE5-85-104.

SIMS, W., MOORE, W., & KUHN, T. (1982). Effects of female and male vocal stimuli, tonal pattern length, and age on vocal pitch-matching abilities of young children from England and the United States [Special Issue]. *Psychology of Music,* 104–108.

SMALL, A., & McCACHERN, F. (1983). The effect of male and female vocal modeling on pitch-matching accuracy of first-grade children. *Journal of Research in Music Education, 31*(3), 227–233.

STENE, E. J. (1969). There are no monotones. *Music Educators Journal, 55*(8), 46–49, 117–121.

SWEARS, L. (1985). *Teaching the elementary school chorus.* West Nyack, NY: Parker.

WALTERS, D. L., & TAGGERT, C. C., Eds. (1989). *Readings in music learning theory.* Chicago: G.I.A. Publications.

WELCH, G. F. (1979). Poor-pitch singing: A review of the literature. *Psychology of Music, 7,* 50–58.

WELCH, G. F. (1985). A schema theory of how children learn to sing in-tune. *Psychology of Music, 13,* 3–18.

WELCH, D. F., HOWARD, D. M., & RUSH, C. (1989). Real-time visual feedback in the development of vocal pitch accuracy in singing. *Psychology of Music, 17,* 3–18.

WOLF, J. H. (1984). An investigation of natural male voice and falsetto male voice on fourth-grade children's ability to find pitch level. *Missouri Journal of Research in Music Education, 5*(2), 98–99.

3

VOCAL PARAMETERS

The voices of children and adolescents have certain definable characteristics that are important in understanding the proper sound at each level of development. Among these important vocal parameters are vocal registers, quality, range, and tessitura.

VOCAL REGISTERS

The trained adult voice is capable of producing an average vocal range of three octaves. This range is divided into areas called "registers," which may be defined as "a group of like sounds or tone qualities whose origin can be traced to a special kind of mechanical (muscular) action" (Reid, 1983, p. 296). Voice specialist Ralph Appelman states, "In the human voice, registration is a physiological and acoustical fact. Years of research . . . have contributed evidence of its existence and have verified that all voices have three registers that may be utilized in singing" (1967, p. 86).

The three registers to which Appelman refers are commonly known as the head, middle, and chest registers. While these terms are not accurate in defining the origins of these registers, the terms are generally accepted. Registers in fact result from the way the vocal folds vibrate in each mode and how the resulting sound couples with the vocal resonators. The present method uses the terms *upper adjustment, middle adjustment* and *lower adjustment* (or *registers*) to relate the vibratory and acoustical adjustments that are necessary to produce the three vocal registers (Example 3.1).

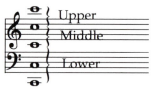

EXAMPLE 3.1.   Adult Vocal Registers.

Physiology

The theory of vocal registers was first advanced in the 1800s by the singer and voice teacher Manuel García, whose invention of the laryngoscope (hooked mirror) made possible the viewing of the vocal folds in action. García recognized three vibratory patterns of the vocal folds, which he noted as being responsible for three vocal registers: "Each of the three registers has its own extent and sonority which vary according to the sex of the individual and the nature of the organ" (1894, p. 7). García reported that only the inner edges of the vocal folds vibrate in the upper register and that the folds vibrate to the full width and length for the lower, or chest, voice. These, he said, were two different mechanical principles that overlapped in the middle vocal register.

Leo P. Reckford, a New York throat specialist who has worked with professional singers such as Jerome Hines, provides greater insight into the physiological basis of vocal registers. Reckford believes that it is not possible to mix entirely different mechanical principles. "Actually these [registers] are all produced in the same way. . . . The change from one to the other is only quantitative, with more and more, or less and less, vibration of the width of the cords" (Reckford, quoted in Hines, 1982, p. 277). He further elaborates:

> When you can finally mix it to the degree that half of the width of each vocal cord is vibrating, you have the ideal mixed tone. But it is still only a quantitative difference between the falsetto and the full tone of the head voice, and between the full tone of the head voice and the mixed voice, and from the mixed voice again only a quantitative change into the full chest voice. More and more of the width of the vocal cords is engaged for vibration. That means that it is only the quantity of vibration which changes. It is not the quality of the whole production [p. 276].

Appelman states that "professional singers more than teachers tend to believe that vocal registers do not exist" (1967, p. 86). This denial, he believes, is the result of the natural coordination found among most professionals, maturation, and vocal training. It is the goal of voice training to produce a uniformity of production that sounds like one vocal register. Nevertheless, the evidence of three vocal registers is clearly substantiated.

A singer should be able to pass from one register to the next without a noticeable break or unevenness of quality. Not only must the physical action of the vocal folds coordinate at the moment of transition between registers (sometimes called "lifts"), but the resonators also must acoustically tune to the shift in registration. The position of the larynx is primarily responsible for changes in the vocal tract, and "the position of the larynx in the phonatory tube changes much more in the trained voice than it does in an untrained voice. The greater change results from the trained singer's attempt to enlarge the pharyngeal resonators" (Appelman, 1967, p. 87).

Students should be encouraged and taught to maintain a laryngeal "at rest" position throughout the singing act. (The present method addresses this technique in Chapters 8 and 9). The untrained singer will unconsciously elevate the larynx as pitch rises, often as a result of insufficient breath pressure. This condition produces added tension at the vocal-fold level, resulting in pressed singing. The elevated larynx also reduces the size of the vocal tract ("closed throat"), thus diminishing the quality of sound, and makes transition points between vocal registers difficult. "As the larynx is lowered, it imparts to the laryngeal organs a stability they could not obtain with the vibrator at a higher point and with the phonatory tube altered in width and length" (Appelman, 1967, p. 95).

Child Vocal Registers

The presence of registers in children's voices has historically been recognized by vocal authorities. However, some early pedagogues expressed their preference for the exclusive use of upper-register singing with children (Behnke and Browne, 1885; Howard, 1895; Johnson, 1935). They warned against the use of the chest voice, noting the harshness of this register, advocating instead the English choirboy sound, with its flutelike quality.

Complete dismissal of the lower register (chest voice) is not advocated in the present method for children's singing. What is taught is a three-register (upper, middle, and lower) approach, as shown in Example 3.2. Note that the pure lower voice (full length and width of the vocal folds) is used only from middle C and lower. Middle C is the pitch where children will traditionally shift into the chest voice, if permitted. The pure upper voice (inner edges of the vocal folds) begins an octave above middle C (c^2) and extends upward. Between these two pure registers is the middle voice (c^1-c^2) which is a combination of both lower and upper registers.

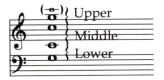

EXAMPLE 3.2.   Child Vocal Registers.

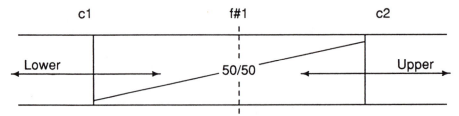

FIGURE 3–1.   Middle Adjustment (register).

The middle register, or shared adjustment, bridges the transition from pure lower to pure upper voice, and results in a 50-50 balance of the registers at approximately the pitch $f^{\#1}$ (see Figure 3–1). As described earlier by Reckford, the middle voice uses less vocal-fold width as the pitch ascends and more as it descends. The rationale behind the three-register approach is to establish a healthy pedagogy for child and adolescent vocal training. The whole voice is exercised, and when pitches are produced in the correct register, the sound is robust and pleasing.

It is commonly known that children lacking vocal instruction mostly gravitate to the chest voice for singing (Example 3.3). This is the speaking-voice register, with which they are most comfortable, and many children, never having experienced anything else, will sing exclusively in the chest voice. Because this lower register in the child's voice is quite elastic, it can be used to sing far above middle C, resulting in a harsh sound and strained technique, which is potentially damaging to the vocal folds. It can be compared to driving a car at sixty miles an hour in low gear: the transmission is not built to withstand such abuse, and neither are the vocal folds. The loud, boisterous singing of children, so commonly heard in many schools, is singing in one gear—low. Such singing, if sustained over a long period of time, can lead to permanent vocal damage. The vocal folds make far greater physical contact when singing in the lower adjustment, but such contact at high levels of tension often results in physical problems.

EXAMPLE 3.3.   All Lower Registration (incorrect) for Children's Singing.

Since chest-voice singing is so potentially damaging to young voices and produces an unmusical quality, why not eliminate its use among young singers? This is what the English choirboy model has done for centuries (Example 3.4), and the results of this pure upper-voice ap-

EXAMPLE 3.4.   English Choirboy Registration (all upper).

proach are widely admired. This author believes, however, that the English approach is not a healthy pedagogy and does not result in a sound that is equally balanced, especially in the middle voice.

English choirboys sing only one vocal part—the treble. Because they are not permitted to use even a mixture of chest and head voice, the head-voice sound is extended below pitch c^2 as low as possible. In order to keep the sound pure, the singing must be very light, and any sound below pitch e^1 becomes lifeless and does not project. Therefore, singing alto is not possible; adult males singing falsetto are used for the alto part.

The Royal School of Church Music has traditionally ignored the voice-change problem among adolescent males. Boys are kept singing totally in the upper voice as long as possible, until the voice breaks, at which time the boys stop singing for a period of adjustment. This infamous English voice break has not found much favor in American schools, where boys are encouraged to sing during the period of voice change. John Dawson (1902) was among the first American writers who openly challenged the English model, noting that a break will not occur in the voices of boys if they are permitted to develop the lower register in preparation for puberty.

The European, or Continental, approach to choir-boy singing (e.g., the Vienna Choir Boys) differs from the English model. The Continental sound introduces some chest mixture into the pure upper register, thus producing a more robust middle quality and the ability to sing an alto part. A study comparing vocal techniques used by various countries and nationalities concludes:

> Although the pure timbre of the boy chorister continues to reign, [in England] some English choirmasters are beginning to question its appropriateness to all choral situations. The Continental approach to training the unchanged adolescent male is beginning to make some inroads into the traditional English concept of what constitutes good male treble vocal quality. . . . The English choirmaster who introduces the Continental sound to his youthful charges, requires from them greater physical involvement in singing. Traditionalists find that he loses "purity" and much of the spiritual quality of the sound, although adding power and a wider range of expressiveness. Several prominent chapel and cathedral choirs are now admittedly committed to the Continental approach to the treble voice as opposed to the traditional British treble ideal [Miller, 1977, p. 150].

The method for vocal instruction in this book does not advocate a total denial of the English approach to vocal registers. The English model does produce a beautiful quality in the upper register from c^2 to c^3. This is advocated in the present method (see Example 3.2), along with a laryngeal at-rest position, to create a full-ringing sonority in the upper voice. Care must be taken that an elevated larynx not be permitted when singing in the upper register, or else the sound will be small, strained, and falsetto-like.

The author recommends the Continental approach to registration for pitches between C and c^2. When the lower register is permitted to join with the upper, the sound maintains its ring and robust quality. The joining must be accomplished from the top downward; that is, vocalises begin in the upper voice and move downward into the middle register (c^2 to c^1). This approach permits the gradual sharing necessary for a balance of vocal-fold vibration in the middle voice. Early attempts to blend these registers with vocalises from lower to upper will prove difficult; students inevitably do not shift out of the chest voice as they ascend, and can only do so once the balance is understood aurally and kinesthetically. This technique of blending registers is best learned from the top down.

The pitch $f^{\#1}$ (evenly divided between lower and upper) is the pivotal note in balancing the middle register. Pitches beginning at g^1 or higher will gradually have more and more upper quality (vibrations of the vocal folds moving to the inner edges) until the quality becomes pure upper at pitch c^2 (see Figure 3–1). Pitches beginning at f^1 or lower will gradually have more lower quality (vibrations of the vocal folds moving to the full width and length) until the quality becomes pure lower at middle C (see Figure 3–3). Young singers can be taught to listen for the changing balance of qualities in the middle register and should spend time listening to one another sing sustained pitches at different points in the middle voice. Aural evaluation will indicate if there is too much lower or upper at any point in the middle-voice scale. It is surprising how sophisticated this process can make young ears.

Developing the upper, middle, and lower registers in young singers' voices provides for exercise of the total voice and prepares the way for a healthy passage into adolescence. It also results in a fuller tone quality that is more appealing to young people. While belting in the lower adjustment must be guarded against, so must a lifeless sound, devoid of any lower quality. As the pure lower register should be used only for pitches at or below middle C, most children's singing will not be in the pure lower voice. However, all three registers (lower, middle, and upper) should be cultivated so as to produce a smooth vocal line without perceptible breaks.

Primary age children often have difficulty distinguishing between their speaking voices and their singing voices. Vocal exploration and vocalises must emphasize the upper voice so as to establish its existence and habitual use in singing. Downward vocalises and song phrases will help to blend the upper voice into the lower voice between d^1 and a^1, the best tessitura for songs in the primary grades. If the sound is kept light (but not lifeless) in this middle voice, the two registers will begin to blend automatically. Loud singing will result in all lower registration.

Adolescent Vocal Registers

Students in the adolescent years undergo a voice-change process that involves registration problems not encountered in children. The adolescent female does not face the radical voice change of the male, but she does experience a vocal adjustment. Adolescent males must learn to deal with a range that is lowered at least an octave, and realignment of the registers is a real challenge to music teachers.

The dimensions of the prepubertal female larynx are closer to adult size and weight than their male counterparts, and "thus, the prepubertal female larynx requires less growth per unit time to reach maturity" (Kahane, 1978, p. 18). However, the female larynx does increase in size, more laterally (width) than anteroposteriorly (front to back). This, along with a slight increase in vocal-fold length and thickening, results in a period of adjustment in which the voice may become breathy or sound congested. Patience and good vocal technique will help to restore the vocal coordination in a relatively short time. Junior high girls do not have to sing forever in a state of breathiness if they are taught to sing correctly!

The vocal registers of adolescent girls remain basically the same as for prepubertal children. The chest voice begins in its pure form at middle C and extends lower as the voice matures (Example 3.1). The middle voice is similar to that of the child—a sharing of lower and upper registers. The traditional treble voice break between the chest and upper registers, which occurs at approximately pitch a^1 for untrained singers, will not exist when this proper sharing of lower and upper registers is learned. The pure upper voice begins at c^2 and extends upward an octave to c^3 (Example 3.2).

There is a saying that a stone thrown at random into a group of females will likely hit a mezzo-soprano! Experienced teachers know this to be true. Females with limited ranges, who can sing neither first soprano nor second alto, are the norm. This is a registration problem. Adolescent girls seem to sing in one register—mixed or middle. As they venture to sing above pitch c^2, they fail to make the necessary adjustment of removing all of the lower vibratory pattern from the voice. This added weight of the lower voice prohibits the ease of production in the upper voice, the range of which then tends to end around f^2. This is compounded by an elevated larynx, which interferes with the lengthening and thinning of the vocal folds. All females (including altos) should be vocalised in a light manner from c^2 to c^3. This will help them to learn the feeling of moving to an inner-edge-only vibratory pattern of the vocal folds, thus eliminating all lower-voice production. The present method begins with phonation exercises that explore and strengthen the upper voice before singing is required.

The mezzo-soprano syndrome exists in part because females tend to sing below middle C in a mixed registration instead of a pure lower voice. This produces a weak and anemic type of singing in the lower register. Some voice teachers do not permit sopranos to use the chest register at all, fearing that it will harm the voice. Appelman states, "The chest voice is a necessary part of the female singer's vocal range and should be so conceived and developed" (1967, p. 93). The present author concurs. Exercising the entire vocal mechanism helps to build a total voice that is healthy and balanced.

The chest voice does present a problem in female singing when its use is permitted in its pure form above middle C. The higher this chest quality is carried, the more difficult and obvious the transition becomes and the more strident the voice sounds. Today's pop culture often presents a vocal model that is all chest voice—a model that is imitated by adolescent females. Care must be taken that this incorrect use of the voice not be allowed or encouraged among females of any age! As mentioned previously, exclusive use of the chest register above middle C is potentially damaging to the vocal folds. Increased contact of the membranes at higher rates of vibration causes friction and a wearing that may result in damage to the structure of the folds, thus limiting singing ability.

The adolescent male voice change is well documented. A study of the human prepubertal and pubertal larynx relates:

> By puberty, clear sexual dimorphism was evident in the larynx. Linear and weight measurements of the pubertal male larynx were significantly larger than in the female. Though the angle of the thyroid laminae was not significantly different in pubertal male and female cartilages, the thyroid eminence (Adam's apple) was clearly more prominent in the male. The vocal folds in both sexes reached essentially their adult length by puberty; however, the absolute length of the male vocal folds had increased by over two times that of the female. The significantly greater growth of the male vocal folds compared with female explains, in part, the structural bases for the dramatic drop in fundamental frequency in the male voice during puberty [Kahane, 1978, pp. 11, 18].

The drop in range experienced by adolescent boys presents registration problems. The adult male sings in two registers, the pure lower from approximately middle C downward two octaves and a mixed register (sometimes called the "passagio" or "head" voice) in the top third of the range, from middle C to c^2 (Example 3.5). It is possible for the adult male to sing in a pure upper voice (sometimes called the falsetto), but this voice generally is not recognized as being a legitimate voice, except for some types of choral and pop singing. It should be used, however, in developing the passagio quality.

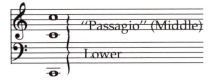

EXAMPLE 3.5. Adult Male Registers.

The boy singer who enters adolescence begins to lose the ability to sing in his pure upper register for the pitches c^2 to c^3, as his range in the lower register begins to expand downward. This does not mean that adolescent boys lose the ability to sing in the pure upper voice; the English choirboy model has demonstrated that boys can continue to sing in the upper voice throughout the voice change. The upper register of the pubertal boy must remain in use in what was his middle register (c^1 to c^2) if the new top of his range is to be successfully handled for singing. Richard Alderson states, "While the boy's voice is changing he should rely on head voice techniques for his highest notes" (1979, p. 234). The present author concurs, as does Sally Herman (1988), who states that vocalising adolescent boys in the upper register is the secret for developing the high school tenor.

The adolescent male can no longer sing in what was his middle voice in childhood (c^1 to c^2) with the same balance of upper and lower registers. The length and thickness of the growing vocal folds disturbs this coordination, and a new passagio or covered technique must be eventually learned for this new top register (c^1 to c^2). However, until such a time as the voice is settled and a certain stability is evident (senior high years), this new passagio register and technique must be avoided in favor of a modified approach using only the pure upper voice from approximately pitches e^1 to c^2 (Example 3.6). Continued use of the upper register through this part of the range will maintain its strength, so that later it can again be coordinated with the chest voice for a new passagio register.

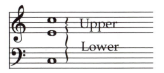

EXAMPLE 3.6. Adolescent Tenor Registers (junior high school).

It must be stressed again that the vocal production being recommended for the pure upper register of the male changing voice is not a falsetto registration. The falsetto voice is a "false" voice, in that it is a product of strained vocal technique in which the larynx rises and cuts out the laryngeal resonator, resulting in a weak and unsupported sound. Every effort must be made to avoid a falsetto sound. The pure upper voice in the male changing and changed voice will sound much like the prepubertal boy's voice in the octave from c^2 to c^3. It will be fuller and freer than the falsetto sound.

Boys with changing voices often fall into the same register trap that girls do: they sing everything in a mixed voice. As adolescent boys sing below middle C, they often will carry their unchanged mixed-register quality into the chest-voice range (middle C and lower). This results in a rather weak and undefined sound—neither man nor boy. Males with changing voices should be taught to find the pure lower register and to use it for the lower two-thirds of the male vocal range (great C to middle C). Unfortunately, many boys never hear a good model of a lower register sound and do not know that it is possible to sing in that voice. The following story by F. Mayer and J. Sacher illustrates this point:

> In a summer camp where Dr. Mayer recently conducted the junior high school chorus, there was one twelve-year-old boy singing soprano and five boys singing alto on the advice of their teachers. When tested, the boy soprano proved to be exactly that. . . . The five altos, when first tested, were capable of reaching about A below middle C, but, when they were introduced to the use of the lower register in their voices, three of them were immediately capable of singing D below middle C. One sang to E-flat and the other maintained a bottom pitch of A. . . . The following morning, during the demonstration, the boy soprano performed as expected, but the five "altos" all sang with ease to D below middle C. These voices did not develop overnight, but, by finding the use of the lower register, which was already a reality when the boys first came to the camp, they were able to sing about a fifth lower in a day's time [1964, p. 11].

Boys whose voices are changing are not necessarily limited to a small vocal range. It is true that at any given time there may be a spot in the vocal range in which no pitches sound. This is a matter of working out a register problem: "Developing voices are always capable of expression in a much wider range than is now held possible, and . . . the practice of limiting the range for these voices to an octave or less is in itself harmful and improper" (Mayer and Sacher, 1964, p. 8). Frederick Swanson, who for many years was the director of the Moline Boys Choir in Moline, Illinois, advocated that boys should continue to exercise the pure upper register while developing the lower register. Swanson (1977) and Herman (1988) agree that the eighth-grade bass exists. All adolescent males should be encouraged to develop the lower voice while maintaining a well-supported upper register, which, when later combined with the chest register, becomes the true passagio.

Boys with changing voices need to abandon their prepubertal mixed voices in favor of a two-register production: lower from approximately d^1 downward and upper from approximately e^1 upward to c^2 (Example 3.6). If both registers are well supported and firmly established, the adolescent boy will shift easily between these voices, without the strain so often noted in the top voice. The upper register must be sung lightly, but not as a falsetto. Boys with a strong c below middle C (and lower) will most likely become basses; baritones should be able to sing down to d, and tenors will not have much range below f. (These labels should not be confused with those used for mature male voices, but adolescent boys do like to be labeled with the terms used for their older male counterparts.) All voices, however, should be exercised in both register productions, lower and upper.

The adolescent tenor begins to emerge in the ninth grade. If the upper voice has been kept actively exercised, the true passagio, or incremental sharing of registers, will begin at approximately middle C (Example 3.5). This is a difficult technique to master, as it requires a covered quality, accomplished through lowering the larynx and narrowing the vowel vestibule (i.e., to produce a "closed vowel"). Appelman states, "All transitions into the upper voice by the male singer are made with a closed vowel. The back vowels [u] and [o] and the central [ʌ] are vowels that make this transition automatic" (1967, p. 92). Tenors must have a good vocal teacher if they are to master this technique correctly.

Mature tenors, who in high school are rare, must learn to master the upper end of the top voice (pitches g^1 to c^2). This requires more and more upper-adjustment quality until only a small amount of the lower vibratory pattern remains in the high C. It also requires a loud dynamic level; tenors who are required to sing softly in the topmost part of the range abandon the lower register and sing only on the inner edges of the vocal folds— upper register exclusively. While this is often referred to as falsetto singing, it should not be a false voice. This is a case where the pure upper voice, well supported, is still functional. It is not, however, the dramatic tenor sound associated with professional singers. High school tenors are not advised to try for the "big" sound from g^1 to c^2, but should switch registration to a pure upper voice (Example 3.7), with more incremental sharing of registers between c^1 and g^1. This will result in an ease of production with less strain. The tenor voice matures late and should not be rushed.

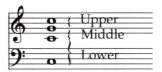

EXAMPLE 3.7.   Senior High School Tenor Registers.

Mature basses and baritones also will need to develop a passagio if they are to learn to sing in tune and without strain above middle C. For the bass, the incremental sharing of registers begins at approximately the pitch f. The baritone will begin to "mix in" the upper register at approximately the pitch g (Example 3.8). Basses should be expected to sing in this passagio register as high as e^1, and baritones can be expected to sing as high as f^1 or g^1.

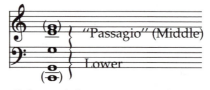

EXAMPLE 3.8.   Adult Baritone and Bass Registers.

The topic of vocal registers is a complex one and cannot be learned without hearing the differences associated with each vocal timbre. Teachers of singing need to avail themselves of instruction that will help them to comprehend aurally the concepts presented in this section on vocal registers.

QUALITY

The quality of the singing voice is a very subjective vocal parameter. It is influenced by cultural norms and expectations, and what is accepted in one environment may be totally unacceptable in another. The following guidelines for young singers are presented in terms of what has been called the "American school of singing."

William Ross identified the "general American quality" as one having bell or nasal-pharyngeal resonance. "It is a ringing-resonant quality, which makes use of the pharynx as the primary resonator and enunciator, amplified or modified by the nasal passages and the mouth" (1948, p. 11). This quality of "full-throated" singing is advocated in the present method. Specific exercises attempt to relax the larynx, jaw, tongue, and pharyngeal constrictors so as to maximize pharyngeal resonance and the "open throat" feeling. "It is, essentially, pharyngeal speech balanced with the resonators of mouth and nose. Properly established it creates in the singer an illusion of singing above the throat and high in the soft palate, as if one sang without any throat at all" (p. 12).

Pharyngeal resonance is lacking in the voices of most young singers. Faulty technique results in an elevated larynx, which eliminates much of the resonating space in the laryngopharynx (area above the larynx and below the tongue). It is pharyngeal resonance that gives depth to the voice; too much of this quality creates an overly dark, hooty sound, while too little results in a thin, colorless, overly bright quality. When the pharynx serves as the primary resonator, balanced with the resonators of mouth and nose, a "natural" quality appears, one that has a free and easy production. With uniform vowel enunciation, support, and focus, the young voice can produce a quality of great beauty.

Vocal quality is very much influenced by vocal registers. Singing only in the chest register will result in a far different vocal quality than singing only in the upper register or in a combination of the two. The present method teaches the development of two distinct registers (lower and upper) that overlap in the middle to form a third, shared register. While each of these registers has a particular resonance, it is possible to develop the voice so that it sounds like a single vocal line from top to bottom.

Child Vocal Quality

Untrained children's singing voices tend to be either loud and boisterous, or thin and whisperish. The former quality is a result of forced, loud singing all in the chest voice (the *Annie* sound). The latter quality is a result of unsupported upper-register production. Both of these qualities originate in faulty vocal technique and are most undesirable. Teachers who advocate a one-register chest-voice sound to let students "sing out" do not understand the damage they may be causing to young singers' voices. Similarly, those who tolerate falsettoish singing may be equally in danger of teaching poor vocal production. The American Academy of Teachers of Singing has stated, "We believe that the practice of inducing young people to sing in a way commonly and inaccurately described as 'soft,' which should be termed 'devitalized,' will result in the presence rather than in the absence of strain; therefore, children and adolescents should be taught the vitalization and coordination of the body in singing" (Roe, 1970, p. 366).

The well-produced child's voice is clear and flutelike in the upper register (c^2 to c^3), much like the traditional choirboy model. Boys and girls voices are capable of producing a well-supported, ringing sound in this octave, especially by the intermediate years. While this sound is best developed through softer singing in the primary years, the intermediate child can be expected to sing in this octave at a mezzo forte level.

Both very loud and very soft dynamic levels should be avoided throughout childhood; both call for a vocal technique beyond the maturity of most children. It often becomes necessary to revise adult expectations of children's voices—the "big" sound is not the best sound. A dynamic range of mezzo piano to mezzo forte is rather limited, but essential to the development of an ideal children's quality.

When the upper and lower registers are permitted to combine in the middle register (c^1 to c^2), the child's vocal quality will be perhaps slightly breathy, yet full and robust. Given the correct balance of registers above and below the critical f$^{\#1}$ pitch, the quality will be neither too thin nor too heavy. This is the most difficult quality to achieve, as children naturally tend to sing in either one register or the other (upper or lower). Exercises and vocalises must begin from the upper register down, permitting the natural emergence of the lower voice. Later, the voice must be exercised from the bottom up so as to teach the subtle shifting to the upper adjustment on ascending vocal lines.

The lower or chest-voice register, when sung in its pure form below middle C, will have a warm, vital quality *if sung easily*. The chest voice should never be pushed; the resulting sound is always harsh and undesirable. An ease of production, however, produces a quality that is distinct, warm, and vital.

In any discussion of the quality of the child voice, it is important to remember that children's voices cannot, and should not, sound like mature voices; the instrument is just too small and immature. However, greater warmth and richness are possible when children learn to keep the larynx at rest, maximizing the pharyngeal resonator. Children need not sing with monochromatic voices; greater warmth and beauty are possible when quality results from proper vocal production and registration.

Adolescent Vocal Quality

Adolescent singers are capable of a far greater richness of sound than is commonly heard. As in the case of children, improper vocal technique results in an elevated larynx and lack of pharyngeal resonance. Pop culture provides a strong model for a thin, breathy vocal production, and adolescents are hesitant to sound "mature" for fear of sounding different. While a false maturity (depressed larynx) is undesirable, the adolescent voice can be cultivated to produce a free, resonant sound, with uniformity of vowels and projection.

Sally Herman (1988) has a wonderful technique for helping junior high singers realize the depth and potential quality of their new voices. She asks them to sing a familiar song as they might have sounded when they were in first grade: it sounds very thin and babyish. She repeats this procedure, asking the students to sing like third-graders and then fifth graders: the sound remains thin but grows more mature. Finally, she asks them to sing as mature junior high students. As adolescents have a great need to demonstrate their emerging adult status, the sound becomes fuller and richer, and the students soon realize that it is possible to change the quality of their voices by opening and relaxing the throat. Once students realize that they are not being "phony" by singing with a more mature quality, they will eagerly adopt this new sound as another sign of their emerging adult status.

Loud singing still must be avoided in the junior high years; vocal technique is too immature to prevent voice abuse, and the resultant quality of loud singing is often forced and harsh. By the high school years, students should be vocally advanced to where they can sing at forte or even occasional fortissimo levels without forcing the sound. A good rule to tell singers: Never sing louder than that level at which you feel vocally comfortable.

Some senior high students can sound very mature with the proper voice instruction. Care must be taken not to force upon these students literature that is beyond their technique. The new voice is still emerging and must be treated with great care. There are far too many stories of promising singers whose careers have been cut short by vocal burnout. The human voice is a delicate instrument, but capable of great endurance when treated with respect. The topic of vocal health is discussed in Chapter 5.

Teachers should use recordings of excellent child and adolescent singers as models of vocal quality for their own students. The pop culture is pervasive, and most young singers have no idea of the sound they are capable of producing when vocal technique is properly balanced with good literature. Developing students' vocal quality is as much a challenge to training their ears as it is their throats.

The teacher's voice also should serve as a good model for young singers. Vocal music teachers must be competent singers. This is not to say that students should strive to copy the sound of their teacher, but a model that is free, resonant, and capable of projecting easily is an asset in teaching children to sing. While males and females cannot provide accurate models for the opposite genders, using other students or teachers as models is recommended. Students must have every opportunity to hear and experience good vocal models, whether live or recorded.

Finally, a beautiful vocal quality is one that is enhanced by an even vibrato. The slight even pulsing of the voice is a natural product of good vocal technique and should be encouraged as technique matures. Even elementary children with finely balanced voices can sing with a vibrato, although it must never be artificially encouraged or produced. Vibrato in the voices of high school students is the norm when good vocal technique is taught. Students who sing without vibrato sing with too much throat pressure (pressed voice) as a result of too little breath pressure. Relaxing the larynx and throat frees the vibrato.

RANGE AND TESSITURA

The vocal parameter of "range" refers to the number of pitches, or distance, between the highest and lowest pitches a person can sing. A more accurate definition relates two types of range: physiological and musical. Physiological frequency range is "the range from the very highest frequency the child can reach, even though it may be quite unmusical, down to the lowest physiological frequency range that can be analyzed," while musical frequency range is "the range from the highest musical tone a child can sing down to the lowest musical tone he can match accurately" (Wilson, 1978, pp. 9–10). It is musical frequency range that concerns teachers, and this is the topic of discussion in this chapter.

The term *tessitura* refers to the general lie of a vocal part, whether high or low in its average pitch. While the range of a song may be within the compass of the young singer, the tessitura must be checked to determine if the majority of pitches remain either too high or too low. The adolescent tenor who is called upon to sing at length above the register break will tire quickly and may strain his voice. Similarly, females who sing a lower harmony part and are asked to sing lines that remain in the chest-voice register are likely to develop a harsh, unbalanced vocal quality. Vocal teachers must monitor the comfortable tessituras of singers at various ages to pick appropriate literature.

Research on Vocal Range

"The vocal range and/or tessitura of young singers has probably been the focus of more research than any other single vocal concept for children" (Stafford, 1987, p. 42). While this is true, the findings of such research are often in conflict. Do young children have a small vocal range, or are they capable of singing the wider ranges found in some basal series textbooks and early twentieth-century songbooks? Is an emphasis on lower ranges warranted?

Studies indicate that young children's spontaneous singing ranges are wider than traditionally reported (Jersild and Beinstock, 1931, 1934; Moorhead and Pond, 1941; Wassum, 1979). The median number of pitches sung by eight-year-old children is given as fifteen by Jersild and Bienstock (1934), and sixteen for nine- and ten-year-olds. The median adult score was twenty. The authors report, "As early as the age of four years, individual children may be able to reproduce as many tones as the average adult, although the child at this age may not be as capable as the adult in singing tones in series or in utilizing them in songs" (p. 501). A more recent study found that preschoolers consistently used larger vocal ranges in echoing pitch patterns than in singing songs (Flowers and Dunne-Sousa, 1990).

A summary review of research concerning children's vocal ranges concludes that "young children's songs should be pitched in a limited range (c'–a') which gradually expands as the children mature" (Apfelstadt, 1982, p. 4). The author concurs with Jersild and Bienstock that although a child may vocalize a large range of pitches, he or she may not be able to sing all the pitches comfortably in structured songs.

Why do young children sing spontaneously with wider ranges than they appear to be capable of singing in song literature? One answer may be found in the previous discussion of physiological and musical frequency ranges. It seems that in spontaneous singing and play, young children may be capable of ranges up to two octaves. When put into a musical context, however, the song defines specific pitches and patterns that may not be in the young singer's vocabulary. Early childhood specialists offer this insight.

> According to Davidson (1985), children tend to establish "contour schemes" when singing—"tonal territories" characterized by a defined intervallic boundary of pitches—which they "fill in" with leaps and steps. The young child who attempts to reproduce a song with intervals not yet manageable will very likely squeeze or expand the intervals to fit into the contour scheme. Teachers should be aware of this way of processing melodic material so as not to expect intervallic accuracy before contour schemes have become stabilized enough to permit attention to precise interval reproduction. It would appear that choosing songs with limited ranges, small-sized skips, and prevalent descending melodic lines would accommodate this processing procedure [McDonald and Simons, 1989, pp. 92–93].

Another reason for the difference between physiological and musical frequency ranges may be that young children cannot attend to words and pitch simultaneously. McDonald and Simons report, "Although some young children use an extensive range of pitches in their spontaneous singing, they maneuver most successfully in a more limited range when words are added to the melodies" (p. 92). Goetze (1985) reports that children in kindergarten and first grade more accurately sing in tune on a neutral syllable such as *loo* than on words, which appear to be stumbling blocks to young children's singing. Other studies (Levinowitz, 1987; Sims, Moore, and Kuhn, 1982; Smale, 1987) report no significant difference in singing accuracy when young children use words or neutral syllables for singing songs. Goetze, Cooper, and Brown conclude, "Although there may be theoretical reasons to think text might distract young children's attention from the singing process, there are no consistent findings to confirm that children learn to sing in tune most effectively without text" (1990, p. 26).

A final reason for a limited musical frequency range, especially among older children, may be lack of training, especially in upper-register singing. "Research on vocal range indicates that young children sing more comfortably in lower ranges than higher ones, and that range expands with age, experience, and training. Voice production may be the link between research studies which support low range and those which stress higher ranges" (Apfelstadt, 1982, p. 4).

Most studies that have investigated children's singing ranges have not taken into account the influence of vocal registration on range. One study that has considered this interaction was made by C. J. Brown (1988), who investigated the effects of self-selected pitch and prescribed pitch with a model on the vocal range of children in the first, third, and fifth grades. In the first assessment, the students were asked to sing a familiar song at a pitch level of their own choosing. Range was then measured, ascending and descending, from the final pitch of the song. In the second assessment, the investigator provided a vocal model in the head register and guided the students with vocal activities (speech to song) that helped them to locate their upper voices. The students then repeated the familiar song, beginning on the pitch b^1. Range was then measured as before, beginning this time on the pitch g^1, the last note of the song. Results for vocal range showed a significantly wider range for singing in the higher vocal register. When permitted to choose their own singing level, the students, as a group, chose a lower range and register for singing. When exposed to a higher vocal register, the students were able to make the transition quickly to this new voice, resulting in a wider vocal range. Had the students not been instructed in the use of the head register, the results of the vocal-range assessment would have been quite different—that is, lower. The study did not limit range assessment to one register, and therefore, the results were more reflective of the true vocal range of the children.

Early advocates of child vocal training (Behnke and Browne, 1885; Howard, 1895; Johnson, 1935) all warned against the chest-voice range and recommended use of the upper register. Song ranges were commonly found to go as high as f^2 and g^2 for fifth- and sixth-graders. Later in the century, such writers as James Mursell stated, "Since children naturally sing on a lower pitch level, they should be allowed to do so" (1956, p. 146). This was the same time at which the song approach was replacing vocal exercises and vocalises as a regular part of the general music curriculum. Even though Mursell warned against omitting specific vocal exercise, it was too late: vocal technique was a thing of the past, and most children were not instructed in upper-register production. This resulted in the song literature of the time being too high for children to sing and a call for the general lowering of song ranges.

Children should exercise both lower and upper registers, thus making possible a full vocalise range of two octaves (g to g^2) by the sixth grade. While the initial singing range of children may be limited, proper vocal technique should provide the basis for an ever-expanding vocal range. Mary Goetze recommends that

> pitch-matching exercises be done in the range of second space A to the C above on the treble staff; this necessitates the children's responding in their singing voices rather than in the lower speaking range. Commonly

suggested for young children's songs, however, is the range of D to A above middle C. It may be that for singing prescribed limited-range songs accurately, that is indeed most comfortable for inexperienced children; on the other hand, teachers need to enable children to cultivate the head voice register so that the range can expand to its full potential [Apfelstadt, 1988, p. 30].

Child Vocal Ranges and Tessituras

The vocal ranges shown in Examples 3.9–3.14 are designed for consideration when choosing song literature for the grades indicated. The tessituras given are the comfort zones in which the majority of pitches should be written. These ranges and tessituras do not follow the trend of lowering song ranges, especially for the primary grades, where pure chest-voice singing (below middle C) is to be avoided. Rather, the limited vocal range in the primary grades is gradually raised and lowered until a full two octaves is used in the sixth grade. This is, of course, based upon the assumption that the three-register concept and the necessary vocal techniques are taught in order to permit students to learn to sing an ever-expanding range throughout the elementary grades.

EXAMPLE 3.9.   First-Grade Range and Tessitura.

EXAMPLE 3.10.   Second-Grade Range and Tessitura.

EXAMPLE 3.11.   Third-Grade Range and Tessitura.

EXAMPLE 3.12.   Fourth-Grade Range and Tessitura.

EXAMPLE 3.13.   Fifth-Grade Range and Tessitura.

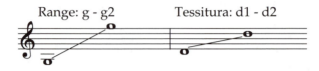

EXAMPLE 3.14.   Sixth-Grade Range and Tessitura.

Adolescent Vocal Ranges and Tessituras

The vocal ranges shown in Examples 3.15–3.21 are designed for consideration when choosing song literature for the grades indicated. These ranges represent an attempt to synthesize the research and information given by a number of leading adolescent-voice specialists (Cooksey, 1986; Cooper and Kuersteiner, 1965; Herman, 1988; Mayer and Sacher, 1964; McKenzie, 1956; Roe, 1983, Swanson, 1977; Thompson, 1982). The tessituras given are the comfort zones in which the majority of pitches should be written. The label *junior high* refers generally to seventh- and eighth-graders, although ninth-grade ranges may overlap between junior high and senior high.

    Junior High Treble I and II (male and female).   Most junior high females and those boys (unchanged voices) who feel very secure in their singing have a similar vocal quality and can sing within the soprano range (Example 3.15). It is best not to use the labels *soprano* and *alto* early on, and to encourage both treble I and II to sing alternately melody and harmony parts. These students may be arbitrarily divided into two sections, and as definable voice types emerge, students should be placed in the appropriate sections.

EXAMPLE 3.15.   Junior High Treble I and II.

    Junior High Tenor I (unchanged voice).   Most boys with unchanged voices (Example 3.16) are insecure and do not want to sit with the girls in the treble I or II section. For these boys, it is best to call them "first tenors" (not to be confused with the "real" tenor voice), seat them near the treble IIs, and have them sing the part as written with the treble II section.

EXAMPLE 3.16. Junior High Tenor I (unchanged voice).

Junior High Tenor II (changing voice). The eighth grade is usually the year of the most noticeable voice change for boys, although voice change may begin much earlier or much later; each boy's biological clock is different. Adolescent-voice specialists do not agree upon the rate of change of boys' voices; some say the change is slow and gradual, while others note boys who can sing bass in the seventh grade. The range given for the tenor II (again, not to be confused with the mature tenor voice) is for the boy whose voice changes rather slowly and gradually (Example 3.17). The label *tenor II* is used because it is acceptable terminology and appeals to the growing maturity of adolescent boys.

The tenor whose voice is changing may sing the alto part of SSA music, a limited tenor part in SATB music, a high baritone part in SAB music, a part written especially for the changing voice (e.g., cambiata), the tenor part in some TB or TTB music, and the soprano part down an octave in two-part music.

EXAMPLE 3.17. Junior High Tenor II (changing voice).

Junior High Tenor (newly changed voice). Some boys' voices tend to change more quickly and find the chest-voice registration that permits them to sing lower at an earlier point in puberty (Example 3.18). While this voice is closer to the mature tenor in range and quality, it remains a young voice capable of yet more change. It may be found in the seventh and eighth grades, and is common by the ninth grade. The new tenor will sing a higher tenor part in SATB music, may join with the tenor II on some music, and may join the baritone part on occasion.

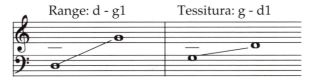

EXAMPLE 3.18. Junior High Tenor (newly changed voice).

Junior High Baritone (changing voice). The junior high baritone (not to be confused with the mature baritone) has a narrower and lower range than the tenor II (Example 3.19). This is a middle changing voice, with little top or bottom range. In two-part music, it may sing the soprano part down an octave, or it may pivot between tenor II and bass voice parts. This voice is more commonly found in the seventh and eighth grades, and usually has settled to a deeper baritone by the ninth grade.

Range: d - d1   Tessitura: g - c1

EXAMPLE 3.19.   Junior High Baritone (changing voice).

Junior High Bass (changing voice). Some boys' voices do change quickly and often exhibit a lower range, an upper range, and no middle! This voice (Example 3.20) is sometimes found in the seventh grade, but more commonly in the eighth and ninth grades, and presents a real problem to teachers. In two-part music, this voice can sing the alto part an octave lower. The range is limited, and as with all changing voice parts, the boys should be told to "fake" the notes that are not present in their voices (move their mouths with no sound). Work this voice from the top down (pure upper to lower registers) to bridge the gap between registers.

Range: B♭ - f; a1 - c2   Tessitura: c - e

EXAMPLE 3.20.   Junior High Bass (changing voice).

Junior High Bass-Baritone (newly changed). Some boys acquire a bass-baritone quality and range as early as the eighth grade, and it is commonly found by the ninth grade (Example 3.21). The mature bass quality is nonexistent at this age, but low ranges can occur when properly produced. The bass-baritone will sing the bass part of SATB music that is not too low and the baritone part of SAB music that is not too high. This voice also may sing the alto or soprano parts an octave lower in two-part music.

Range: A - d1   Tessitura: c - g

EXAMPLE 3.21.   Junior High Bass-Baritone (newly changed voice).

The senior high vocal ranges shown in Examples 3.22–3.29 are a synthesis of those presented by adolescent vocal authorities (Heffernan, 1982; Robinson and Winold, 1976; Roe, 1983). The ranges given are for choral music and represent the average for each voice given. Note that each voice may be expected to use a range of an octave and a fifth.

Senior High Soprano I. The first soprano quality is light, especially in the upper range, flutelike and lyrical (Example 3.22).

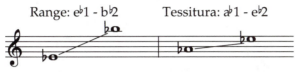

EXAMPLE 3.22. Senior High Soprano I.

Senior High Soprano II. The mezzo-soprano is more common at this age and has a quality that is fuller than the first soprano (Example 3.23).

EXAMPLE 3.23. Senior High Soprano II.

Senior High Alto I. The first alto has a quality similar to the mezzo-soprano, but lacks the top range (Example 3.24).

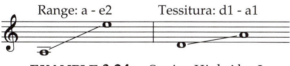

EXAMPLE 3.24. Senior High Alto I.

Senior High Alto II. The contralto voice is rare at the high school level (Example 3.25). The quality is somber, full, and rich, and maximizes pharyngeal resonance. Girls who sing this voice part usually do so because of a well-developed lower-register adjustment. They should be encouraged to develop the upper register for proper vocal coordination.

EXAMPLE 3.25. Senior High Alto II.

Senior High Tenor I.   The tenor voice is the last to mature (Example 3.26). This voice is characterized as light and lyric. A fully developed passagio is not possible, and boys singing this part should be encouraged to shift into the pure upper register at pitch e^2.

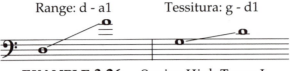

EXAMPLE 3.26.   Senior High Tenor I.

Senior High Tenor II.   This vocal part is similar to the tenor I, but the range is less high, with a more clearly defined lower adjustment (Example 3.27). The quality is still light, but closer to the baritone in fullness.

EXAMPLE 3.27.   Senior High Tenor II.

Senior High Baritone.   Most high school basses are actually baritones (Example 3.28). The quality is full, but often lacks real depth.

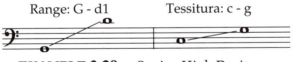

EXAMPLE 3.28.   Senior High Baritone.

Senior High Bass.   The senior high bass has a heavy, dark quality. While a boy may have the range (Example 3.29), the true, deeper quality is usually lacking at this age.

EXAMPLE 3.29.   Senior High Bass.

STUDY AND DISCUSSION QUESTIONS

1. What is a vocal register? How are changes in registers produced physiologically and perceived aurally?
2. Discuss the three-register approach as it applies to children's voices. What are the transitional pitches and quality changes associated with each register?
3. Compare the American pop style of registration for singing with the English choirboy model. What are the advantages and disadvantages of each style, and what is suggested as a solution to either extreme?
4. What type of vocalise encourages the blending of registers in the middle octave between c^1 and c^2? What is the objective of such a technique?
5. Compare the growth of the larynx of pubertal males and females. What are the effects of the voice change on the singing voice for each gender?
6. How can the problem of breaks in the vocal range of adolescents be resolved by means of proper registration?
7. Why is a limited vocal range of an octave or less not always appropriate for boys with changing voices?
8. What is the "passagio" register and how is it developed in the mature male singer?
9. What are the characteristics of the "general American quality" of singing? Is this quality nationally accepted by music educators and the general public? Explain.
10. What are the characteristic vocal qualities found among untrained child and adolescent singers? What are the sources of these qualities and how can vocal quality be improved?
11. How would you respond to a school administrator or parent who complained that the elementary choir could sing louder than your junior high ensemble?
12. Discuss the property of vocal vibrato and its appropriateness for child and adolescent voices.
13. Why do young children often sing spontaneously with wider vocal ranges than they appear to be capable of singing in song literature? How would this knowledge influence the ranges that you would choose for appropriate vocalises and song literature?
14. What may be the answer to research studies that support lower song ranges and those that support higher song ranges for children's singing?
15. What may be the expected vocal range of sixth-graders who have had a sequential program of vocal instruction? Relate the various parts of this range to correct vocal registration.

References

ALDERSON, R. (1979). *Complete handbook of singing.* New York: Parker.

APFELSTADT, H. (1982). Children's vocal range: Research findings and implications for music education. *UPDATE: The Applications of Research in Music Education, 1*(2), 3–7.

APFELSTADT, H. (1988). What makes children sing well? *UPDATE: The Applications of Research in Music Education, 7*(1), 27–32.

APPELMAN, R. D. (1967). *The science of vocal pedagogy: Theory and application.* Bloomington: Indiana University Press.

BEHNKE, E., & BROWN, L. (1885). *The child's voice.* Boston: Oliver Ditson.

BROWN, C. J. (1988). *The effect of two assessment procedures on the range of children's singing voices.* Unpublished master's thesis, Indiana University, Bloomington.

COOKSEY, J. (1986). The adolescent voice. Handout from a presentation for the Iowa Choral Directors Association Summer Symposium, Mason City, Iowa.

COOPER, I., & KUERSTEINER, K. O. (1965). *Teaching junior high school music.* Boston: Allyn and Bacon.

DANN, H. (1936). *Hollis Dann song series: Conductor's book.* Boston: American Book Co.

DAVIDSON, L. (1985). Preschool children's tonal knowledge: Antecedents of scale. In J. Boswell (Ed.), *The young child and music: Contemporary principles in child development and music education: Proceedings of the music in early childhood conference* (pp. 25–40). Reston, VA: Music Educators National Conference.

DAWSON, J. J. (1902). *The voice of the boy.* New York: E. L. Kellog.

FLOWERS, P. J., & DUNNE-SOUSA, D. (1990). Pitch-pattern accuracy, tonality, and vocal range in preschool children's singing. *Journal of Research in Music Education, 38*(2), 102–114.

GARCÍA, M. (1894). *Hints on singing.* New York: Schuberth.

GOETZE, M. (1986). Factors affecting accuracy in children's singing (Doctoral dissertation, University of Colorado, 1985). *Dissertation Abstracts International, 46,* 2955A.

GOETZE, M., COOPER, N., & BROWN, C. J. (1990). Recent research on singing in the general music classroom. *Bulletin of the Council for Research in Music Education, 104,* 16–37.

HEFFERNAN, C. W. (1982). *Choral music, technique and artistry.* Englewood Cliffs, NJ: Prentice-Hall.

HERMAN, S. (1988). *Building a pyramid of musicianship.* San Diego: Curtis Music Press.

HINES, J. (1982). *Great singers on great singing.* Garden City, NY: Doubleday.

HOWARD, F. E. (1923). *The child-voice in singing* (rev. ed). New York: H. W. Gray. (Original work published 1895.)

JERSILD, A. T., & BIENSTOCK, S. F. (1931). The influence of training on the vocal ability of three-year-old children. *Child Development, 2,* 272–291.

JERSILD, A. T., & BIENSTOCK, S. F. (1934). A study of the development of children's ability to sing. *Journal of Educational Psychology, 25,* 481–503.

JOHNSON, C. E. (1935). *The training of boys' voices.* Boston: Oliver Ditson.

KAHANE, J. C. (1978). A morphological study of the prepubertal and pubertal larynx. *American Journal of Anatomy, 151,* 11–20.

LEVINOWITZ, L. M. (1987). An experimental study of the comparative effects of singing songs with words and without words on children in kindergarten and first grade (Doctoral dissertation, Temple University). *Dissertation Abstracts International, 48,* 863A.

MAYER, F. D., & SACHER, J. (1964). The changing voice. *American Choral Review, 6*(2), 8, 10–12.

McDONALD, D. T., & SIMONS, G. M. (1989). *Musical growth and development, birth through six.* New York: Schirmer Books.

McKENZIE, D. (1956). *Training the boy's changing voice.* New Brunswick, NJ: Rutgers University Press.

MILLER, R. (1977). *English, French, German and Italian techniques of singing: A study in national tonal preferences and how they relate to functional efficiency.* Metuchen, NJ: Scarecrow Press.

MOOREHEAD, G., & POND, D. (1978). *Music of young children,* vols. 1–4. Santa Barbara, CA: Pillsbury Foundation for Advanced Music Education. (Original work published in 1941.)

MURSELL, J. L. (1956). *Music education, principles and programs.* Morristown, NJ: Silver Burdett.

ROBINSON, R., & WINOLD, A. (1976). *The choral experience.* New York: Harper's College Press.

REID, C. L. (1983). *A dictionary of vocal terminology: An analysis.* New York: Joseph Patelson Music House.

ROE, P. F. (1970). *Choral music education.* Englewood Cliffs, NJ: Prentice-Hall.

ROE, P. F. (1983). *Choral music education* (2nd. ed.) Englewood Cliffs, NJ: Prentice-Hall.

ROSS, W. E. (1948). *Sing high, sing low.* Bloomington: Indiana University Press.

SIMS, W. L., MOORE, R. S., & KUHN, T. L. (1982). Effects of female and male vocal stimuli, tonal pattern length and age on vocal pitch-matching abilities of young children from England and the United States [Special Issue]. *Psychology of Music,* 104–108.

SMALE, M. J. (1988). An investigation of pitch accuracy of four- and five-year-old singers (Doctoral dissertation, University of Minnesota, 1987). *Dissertation Abstracts International, 48,* 2013A.

STAFFORD, D. W. (1987). Perceptions of competencies and preparation needed for guiding young singers in elementary music classes (Doctoral dissertation, The Florida State University). *Dissertation Abstracts International, 48*(3), 591A.

SWANSON, F. J. (1977). *The male voice ages eight to eighteen.* Cedar Rapids, IA: Ingram.

THOMPSON, D. (1982). *Dick Thompson choral system: Teacher's manual.* Morristown, NJ: Silver Burdett.

WASSUM, S. (1979). Elementary school children's vocal range. *Journal of Research in Music Education, 27*(4), 214–224.

WILSON, D. K. (1978). An overview of vocal maturation from infancy through adolescence. In B. Weinberg and Van Lawrence (Eds.), *Transcripts of the Seventh Symposium: Care of the Professional Voice* (Pt. 2). New York: The Voice Foundation.

4

THE CHILD AND ADOLESCENT SINGER

The methodology in the second part of this text is prescribed for students in grades 1–12. It is in these years that some type of formal voice instruction is appropriate. The present chapter addresses vocal development during these years. However, music educators are becoming more and more aware that early success in the skill of singing is begun at the preschool level. Scott has stated that "infants and preschoolers have more capacity for music learning and responding than we have thought" (1989, p. 31). Therefore, this chapter begins with a brief discussion of singing in early childhood.

CHARACTERISTICS OF VOCAL DEVELOPMENT

The Preschool Singer

McDonald and Simons state, "As infants are 'programmed to learn,' they might also be described as 'programmed to sing' " (1989, p. 88). The authors note that babies soon begin to sort out the sounds they themselves can make as separate from the sounds of the environment. The result is a type of imitation in which children engage in vocal play, or what Gordon (1985) has called "musical babble." Greenberg (1979) states that first vocalizations such as cries and coos soon develop into musical babbles that have definite pitches, frequently repeated in small intervals. McDonald and Simons note that such vocal explorations should be encouraged and responded to by adults, "for it is through the responses of those around them that infants learn to attach meaning to their sounds" (p. 89).

The initial period of vocal play and experimentation is followed by what Greenberg calls a period of "approximation of singing" (eighteen months to three years). By the age of two, children may produce "songs" consisting only of the rhythmic repetition of a word or phrase, with undulating pitch inflection close to the pitch of speech, and by the age of two and a half, preschoolers will have begun to imitate familiar songs in rhythm and contour, but not the precise intervals (Davidson, 1985; Davidson, McKernon, and Gardner, 1981; Greenberg, 1979; Moog, 1968; Ramsey, 1983). This suggests that early singing experiences should include such speech activities as vocal chants and rhymes.

During this "approximation of singing" stage, a repertoire of tonal patterns is being developed and tonal memory is being shaped. These are important psychological parameters for the development of the singing voice in the young child. "Unfortunately, the heavy emphasis on language development at this time may result in inattention to the development of the child's singing voice" (Swears, 1985, p. 27). Therefore, children need an environment rich in musical experiences, including singing by and with adults.

> Instruction in singing for all preschoolers means singing to them, with them, and for them. A child who has heard much singing will produce parts of songs by age two; at age three, many children are tuneful singers who possess quite an extensive repertoire of songs. The preschool years are the ones when language skills are developing rapidly; singing skills, another form of language, should develop as well [McDonald and Simons, 1989, p. 89].

Children who have had many singing experiences will begin to sing accurately in a range from about d^1 to g^1 by about age three (Greenberg, 1979). Following their natural inclinations, many children will sing in their speaking, or chest, voices (lower adjustment). In fact, young children often cannot distinguish between their speaking and singing voices and thus sing in a kind of speaking drone. Children should be encouraged from a young age to explore the upper, or head, voice (upper adjustment) and to employ this voice for singing tasks as much as possible. The dynamic level must be kept soft, for loud singing automatically engages the laryngeal muscles that produce the chest voice. The following is a suggested procedure for discovering or learning to use the upper-adjustment voice:

1. Direct the children in a simple two-line chant or rhyme in the lower adjustment (speaking voice).

2. Move to rhymes with a place where the children can leap to the upper adjustment (e.g., "Jack be nimble, Jack be quick; Jack jump *over* [leap to upper voice] the candlestick").

3. Move to rhymes where a whole phrase can be said high (e.g., "Who's been eating my porridge?" as said by the baby bear in "The Three Bears").

4. Move to rhymes with two or three places for high voice.

5. Move to very short songs (two phrases), all in the upper voice. Keep the dynamic level soft, and pitch the song phrases above middle C, preferably around g^1 or a^1.

Many children become trapped in their lower voices at an early age and never learn to sing on the inner edges of their vocal folds (i.e., the upper voice). Therefore, it is recommended that young children be led to discover and sing in the upper voice for a time without attempting to combine it with the lower register. The upper voice will then become stronger and can be worked down into, and combined with, the lower voice in the elementary grades. Nevertheless, even with vocal exploration and good vocal models, many preschool children may be inclined to sing exclusively in their lower voices. These fledgling singers should not be discouraged from singing. They should be encouraged to sing lightly, to do much individual singing so as to hear their own voices, and to continue to explore the upper register through speech and song activities.

The type of song literature used with young children is an important consideration for vocal success. Songs generally should be short and contain much repetition of melodic and rhythmic patterns. Both pentatonic and diatonic melodic patterns are appropriate (Jarjisian, 1983), and half steps are not to be avoided in the melodic patterns of three-to-five-year-old children (Sinor, 1984). In a review of literature on singing in the general music classroom, Goetze, Cooper, and Brown report that "simple melodic material presented with reinforcement appears to be the condition most conducive to successful performance. We also conclude that descending as opposed to ascending intervals are sung with greater accuracy" (1990, p. 25). The descending interval of a minor third has had a traditional place in the melodic patterns and song literature of preschool children. In addition, successful performance is enhanced by the use of visuals, movement, and instruments.

The preschool years are tremendously important years for the foundation of musical learning. Unfortunately, these are the years most often neglected for regular music instruction. Scott concludes:

In a society where, increasingly, the television has become the main source of stimulation, and parents of all economic classes have less time to spend with their children and seemingly less confidence in how to make music with them, we in music education have a leadership role to play. After all, who knows better than we do the intrinsic value of music and the joy of community that comes from shared music making! [1989, p. 31]

The Elementary Singer

The first grade is the time to begin instruction in vocal technique. Some attention to the parameters of posture and breathing, phonation, tone production, diction, and expression is quite possible at this age. The mere singing of songs is not a complete singing program. Without proper instruction in the process of singing, children develop bad habits that become ingrained for life. Like any other skill that must be mastered, singing requires practice. Daily use of the singing voice is prescribed, and the regular classroom teacher should be expected to lead singing activities in the absence of the regular music specialist.

Many children are singing accurately by the first grade. Those who are not will be helped by a developmental program of vocal education. Maturity is a major factor, and boys, especially, may have trouble in coordinating the vocal mechanism. Fortunately, most children love to sing at this age and will do so enthusiastically. It is the job of the music teacher to channel the energy of these young people into constructive vocal habits that will produce accurate and confident singers.

Graham Welch (1986a, 1986b), from his own research and that of others, has hypothesized a "developmental continuum of singing ability," which is characterized by five stages from out-of-tune to in-tune singing. These stages are as follows:

Stage 1. The words of the song appear to be the initial center of interest rather than the melody. Often there is very little variation in sung pitch, perhaps because some children find it impossible to attend to more than one parameter of the song at any one time, and words are, for them, the dominant feature. In response to a pitch stimulus, children appear to choose a comfortable vocal pitch rather than attempt to match the target. There is some evidence, however, that the comfortable pitch is frequently consonant with the pitch target.

Stage 2. Some variation in sung pitch may occasionally coincide with the target. There is a growing awareness that vocal pitch can be a conscious process and that changes in pitch are controllable.

Stage 3. A more active attempt is made to control vocal pitch by making the voice jump intervals toward the target. More individual pitches are matched correctly. Melodic outline follows the general contours of the target melody. Vocal range continues to expand.

Stage 4. Children are now able to perform some fine-tuning of pitches. The melodic shape and composite pitches are mostly correct, but some changes of tonality may occur if the pitch targets become uncomfortable or outside the still relatively limited vocal range.

Stage 5. No major pitch or melodic errors are made. There is a high level of pitch-matching ability. Vocal range is both higher and lower than previously [Welch, 1986b, pp. 299–300].

The above stages are not definitive and not meant to be exclusive, but suggest that children's singing can be thought of as a developmental process and that teaching strategies should account for these stages. Research and practical experience indicate that children will exhibit singing behaviors somewhere along the continuum and that with help singing may be improved. Welch concludes, "The teacher's role involves a recognition of the complexity of this singing development. A child who shows evidence of being at one of the less skilled stages should be regarded as a client for development, rather than necessarily revealing an irretrievable lack of ability in music" (1986b, p. 300).

The Singing Voice Development Measure was developed by Rutkowski (1990) for studying the singing responses of kindergarten children. The five categories are very similar to those proposed by Welch:

1. **Pre-singers:** Children who do not sustain tones; their singing response resembles chanting in the speaking voice range.
2. **Speaking-range singers:** Children who sustain tones and exhibit some sensitivity to pitch but remain within the speaking voice range. . . .
3. **Uncertain singers:** Children who sustain tones but often waver between a speaking-voice range and a singing-voice range. When in singing voice, they utilize a range up to approximately . . . [$f^{\#1}$]
4. **Initial-range singers:** Children who have use of the singing-voice range up to the register lift, usually to . . . [a^1].
5. **Singers:** Children who are able to sing over the register lift, $b^{\flat3}$ [$b^{\flat1}$] and above, and have full use of their singing voices [Rutkowski, 1990, p. 92].

Children in the primary grades may fall into any of the five stages given by Welch and Rutkowski. Without the proper help, those in the early stages will never become accurate or confident singers. Teachers should use—along with the techniques given in this method—songs and games for chanting and echoing, in individual as well as group singing. Children at this age need to experience singing in unison with other voices and, most important, need to exercise the upper register downward, with a light head-tone production. The lower register should not be suppressed as it naturally emerges, but the singing should be kept light so as to minimize its predominance. The range of songs must be kept above middle C, below which the chest voice takes over.

The third grade appears to be a pivotal year in the life of children. Third-graders are no longer babies, and boy-girl distinctions become ever clearer. Boys no longer want to play with girls at recess, and if the music teacher is not careful, singing will be perceived by many boys as a girls' activity. Children who once eagerly participated in singing often become self-conscious and resist participation. If left unchecked, such attitudes will harden, and by the intermediate years, many children will have ceased to enjoy singing. Some teachers capitulate and do little singing; general music becomes music "appreciation." Others form so-called select elementary choirs for those students who want to continue singing. Unfortunately, many children are discouraged from singing only by a misdirected attitude, and not being chosen for the select choir only adds to their confusion. Teachers must do everything possible to assure children that singing knows no gender bias and is something that everyone can *learn* to do. This issue must be addressed head-on in the third grade if many children are to be spared the inevitable consequences of insecurity masked by indifference.

By the fourth grade, students who have experienced good vocal instruction and many opportunities to sing will begin to show evidence of that beautiful quality associated with fine children's singing. A more demanding song literature with longer phrases and wider ranges is possible, and more attention can be paid to detail in musical expression. Singing in harmony should be established, with all students singing alternately melody and harmony parts in different selections. The dynamic level for singing may be increased, but never beyond "mezzo forte." Those children who fail to match pitch should be given individual remedial help. It is likely that some part of the motor coordination process is not working properly and needs the individual attention of the music teacher.

Vocal development and beauty peaks in the child's voice in the fifth, sixth, and seventh grades. A range of up to two octaves (g to g^2) is possible, which results in a flutelike upper register, a warm lower register (below middle C) and a middle register (c^1 to c^2) that brings into balance the head and chest timbres. A developing vocal technique should be evidenced in habitual attention to posture, breath management, pitch accuracy, resonance, and diction, and greater attention to the meaning and mood of song texts. Children should be encouraged to participate in solo singing and to make discriminating judgments concerning correct vocal technique and vocal quality. Dynamics may be increased to an occasional forte, but the beauty of the tone must never be sacrificed for loud singing.

Children who continue to sing inaccurately should be given remedial help. Musical aptitude tests may help to determine if the inaccuracy is the result of psychological or motor problems. Physical coordination may be helped by posture and breathing exercises, but medical consultation is recommended for students who exhibit vocal problems at the laryngeal level (i.e., chronic huskiness or hoarseness).

Finally, students at this age should be prepared for the voice change experienced in adolescence by open and frank discussions of the psychological and physiological changes that children experience on their way to adulthood, changes that some students already may be experiencing. This is a crucial time to allay the fears and misconceptions that students often have concerning puberty. The junior high years are too late to discuss adolescence.

The Adolescent Singer

The adolescent period in human development is generally considered to begin in the seventh grade, or when the student is approximately twelve years old. It is a time of passage from childhood to adulthood, a period of maturation that can be fraught with insecurity as physiological and psychological changes require new ways of dealing with life. The adolescent temperament is often mercurial, characterized by rapid and unpredictable changeableness of mood. The desire to become an independent adult is often at odds with the anxiety of leaving the safety and security of childhood. At one moment, adolescents can act silly and immature, but in the next can be serious and thoughtful.

The teacher of adolescents, especially in the seventh and eighth grades, must deal with a group of students that varies widely in physical size, personality, mental ability, and emotional stability—or instability, as is more often the case. Girls tend to be emotionally high-strung, while boys affect a more "cool" or passive attitude. Girls more willingly participate in classroom activities, while boys hold back and observe. The macho attitude of strength and stoicism is strong in adolescent males, and causes them to be more conformist than adolescent girls. Sports are important at this age, but more so for boys, who seek to establish their identities on the playing field. Girls, in general, are more mature, but both genders can be insensitive in the way they treat others. The adolescent boy who is small for his age may become the brunt of jokes, as can the girl who is not "developing." Adolescence is a most difficult period of life. It is a wonder anyone survives it!

Teaching music to adolescents requires great intuition and patience. Adolescents, by their very nature, are skeptical, and teachers must work to win over these students in ways that create a special bond. Talking down to, or embarrassing, adolescents in front of the class are two sure ways to alienate the teacher from the students. On the other hand, adolescents are not yet adults and require a great deal of guidance and encouragement. When that special bond is created between teacher and class, there is no one more dedicated and enthusiastic than a group of junior or senior high school students.

Maintaining boys' active interest in singing during the adolescent years is a major challenge to music educators. In some schools, sports programs so dominate young males' attention that music programs suffer. Establishing good relationships with athletic coaches can help bridge the gap between sports and music activities. In addition, young males are often embarrassed by the problems associated with the voice change. An open and honest discussion concerning the various parameters of vocal maturation is a necessity at this age. Some teachers choose to have separate music classes for boys and girls in the seventh and eighth grades. This permits teachers to work more effectively with the problems unique to each gender and lessens the embarrassment and tension between boys and girls at this age.

A most important consideration is that adolescent students must be kept singing throughout the early adolescent years. The senior high school choral program relies heavily upon the feeder system of the junior high or middle school. Generally, once students drop out of vocal music in the seventh or eighth grades, they do not return to it. For this reason, singing must be a component of the seventh- and eighth-grade general music curriculum. Often, this is the music teacher's last chance to convince these students of the value of singing.

Unfortunately, most singing that is done in general music classes is based upon the song approach. The music books are passed out, and students are expected to join in, whether they feel comfortable singing or not. This type of recreational activity often hardens already negative attitudes toward singing. It is just at this time that students should be made aware that singing is a learned behavior, a skill governed by a psychomotor process. A physiological approach, as advocated in this method, is most appealing to boys trying to deal with their changing bodies. Singing can be demonstrated to require the same types of physical coordination required for athletic participation. If the fundamental techniques for good singing have not been established prior to the adolescent years, then a program of voice development should commence in the seventh grade. It is never too late to teach young people that singing is something almost everyone can learn to do!

The texts of songs for adolescents are another important consideration for stimulating interest in singing. Texts of a sentimental or personal nature often will turn students off, as will texts they consider to be of the elementary-school type. Song texts must by chosen carefully to reflect the needs and interests of adolescents, and fun songs should not be ignored.

An adolescent male chorus is another means by which to keep interest in singing strong among pubertal boys. The esprit do corps that is established creates a bond beneficial to the entire music program. When boys participate in singing, the girls will be there! Some schools alternate days for boys and girls choruses at the same period, with a mixed chorus formed on one day, usually Friday. By whatever means, adolescents must be kept singing!

THE CHANGING VOICE

Male Voice Change

The male voice change is a well-documented (Kahane, 1978) phenomenon brought about by hormonal changes in the body during the adolescent years. This may begin as early as the intermediate years of elementary school (grades 4–6), but most often begins when a boy is approximately twelve years old and seems to peak in the eighth grade. Physiological indicators of the entrance into puberty include a growth spurt, physical awkwardness, the development of the sex organs, growth of body hair, and facial blemishes.

A change in the speaking voice is another indicator that physical change is taking place, especially in the thickening and growth of the larynx. The prepubertal boy who is about to enter into the voice change will often display a greater brilliance and power in both speaking and singing voices. Noticeable changes in speaking may include a temporary loss of control, or "cracking," and a heavy or husky quality.

Once the pubertal change begins, the vocal folds of boys increase in length and thickness. Kahane, in a study comparing the human prepubertal and pubertal larynx, reports that "the vocal folds in both sexes reached essentially their adult length by puberty; however, the absolute length of the male vocal folds had increased by over two times that of the female" (1978, p. 11). This overt increase in the length of the male vocal folds (approximately ten millimeters) accounts for the octave register drop between the voice of the boy and that of the adult male. It also accounts for the anterior protrusion of the male larynx at the thyroid notch, or what is popularly called the "Adam's apple."

The voices of boys change at different rates. Some boys never seem to experience a voice break. Their voices may change slowly, and often such boys become adult tenors. Other boys experience a radical and quick change; these most often become adult basses. The biological clock of each boy is different, and nature must take its own course in determining the rate of voice change. It is not uncommon for a boy in the ninth grade to have an unchanged voice. Such boys must be protected from ridicule and reminded that the change *will* happen because it's a fact of life!

Over the years a number of approaches have been recommended regarding the singing of boys during the adolescent years, and specifically during the voice-change period. This author's own recommendations are outlined in Chapter 3, along with suitable vocal ranges and tessituras for males in grades 7–12. However, a number of vocal authorities have written on the topic of the male voice change, and the most prominent of these are presented here as a basis of comparison.

Six Contemporary Approaches to the Male Changing Voice

Royal School of Church Music (Church of England). This approach (Johnson, 1935) continues the practice of the English choir tradition of training boys to sing for the Anglican church service. Boys with unchanged voices (trebles) are taught to sing the professional soprano range in the upper adjustment only. The sound is pure in quality, with little or no vibrato. Because the boys are not permitted to use any chest-voice quality, the range below e[1] is weak and almost unusable. For this reason, the alto part must be sung by male countertenors. Even during the voice change, boy trebles are kept singing in the pure upper voice. When the boys mature and it is no longer possible to sustain the soprano range of c[2] to c[3], the voice is quieted for a period of adjustment until the lower voice settles.

Critics claim that the English approach results in the voice break, which is often associated with the male changing voice. As noted in Chapter 3, John Dawson (1902) highly criticized this approach, and Richard Miller (1977) reports that some English choirmasters are now beginning to question the practice of a one-register technique for boys. Singing only in the upper voice does not prepare the young male for what should be a natural transition into the use of this lower register. However, this English approach does demonstrate that boys can continue to sing safely in the pure upper register through adolescence and that this voice need not be altogether abandoned.

Alto-Tenor Approach (Duncan McKenzie). The "alto-tenor" approach (McKenzie, 1956) says that the voice change is a gradual process in which the boy loses his upper register as he adds notes in his lower register. The term *alto-tenor* describes the boy's voice after it has lowered to the stage when the changed voice begins to develop. As a vocal part, the range designates one octave, from g to g[1]. The vocal quality is distinct (neither boy nor man), and light. All voices follow a gradual lowering process, with a corresponding change in quality. The change in the speaking voice is the most reliable indicator of the change in the singing voice. As the changed voice develops (from alto-tenor), the boy's voice disappears entirely, and lower tones are added to the range. After that, the voice may lose some of its bottom tones and add pitches in the upper range. This moving-up is characteristic of this approach. Only after this stage can one be assured that the voice has truly settled. (The moving-up process most often occurs in the high school years.) The longer the voice stays in the alto-tenor range (from a few months to a year), the more likely it will become a tenor when changed. The alto-tenor can sing the first-tenor part of four-part SATB music, but will not have the strength of the changed tenor voice to balance the other parts. McKenzie cautions against the boy in the voice change using either the upper or lower registers and maintains that a safe, middle, comfortable range is best.

The Cambiata Approach (Irvin Cooper and Don Collins). The Cambiata approach (Collins, 1981; Cooper, 1953; Cooper and Kuersteiner, 1965) has been among the most popular American approaches to handling the male changing voice. This approach prescribes four types of boys' voices that exist in grades 4–12: (1) boys unchanged, called trebles; (2) boys in the first phase of change, called "cambiata"; (3) boys in the second phase of change, called baritone; and (4) boys changed voices, called basses. Tenors in the true sense do not exist in these years, as the mature tenor voice does not emerge until the middle or late twenties.

The majority of boys will enter the process of the first change (cambiata) in grade 7. The boys' lower tones become richer and thicker, and the lower range extends down considerably. The range of the cambiata part is f to c^2, with a one-octave tessitura of a to a^1. The quality is rich and woolly. This first stage of voice change may last anywhere from a few months to two years. Care must be taken not to assign the cambiata to a part an octave lower, as this voice often will present an aural illusion of sounding lower.

The cambiata voice usually changes to baritone in the eighth grade, with little quality or volume in this second phase of change. Traditional four-part (SATB) music is inappropriate for the junior high boy as the tenor parts are too low and ignore the upper cambiata range; bass voices are rare and bass parts are too low for the baritones. Four-part compositions must be arranged: treble/soprano I and II (alto voice is not recognized at this age), cambiata, and baritone. (Publications of this type were rare until the founding of the Cambiata Press by Don Collins, a former student of Irvin Cooper.) Unison singing is difficult because of the small common range; the cambiata part lies at the lower end of the soprano tessitura and the upper part of the baritone tessitura.

The cambiata approach prescribes that 90 percent of all boys' voices change and lower according to a common pattern: first change to cambiata in seventh grade, and second change to baritone in eighth grade. Voices that change more quickly are liable to be mislabeled because of the aural illusion found in the voice-change process. Tenor and bass voices begin to appear in the ninth grade, but true tenors do not develop until later.

The Contemporary Eclectic Approach (John Cooksey). John Cooksey, like Don Collins, was a student of Irvin Collins and the cambiata concept. But Cooksey broke from his mentor's tradition, finding it too limiting in the classification of the changing male voice. Cooksey, in a series of four articles appearing in the *Choral Journal* (1977–1978), set forth what he has called a "contemporary eclectic theory" of the boy's changing voice, which, in essence, recognizes three changing-voice categories. Cooksey (1986a) has noted that Cooper's single classification of cambiata for the changing voice is too limiting and that boys actually pass through three definable stages of voice change.

Since the original publication of the ranges and tessituras for each of the voice parts as recognized by Cooksey, he has twice revised these ranges and tessituras (1981, 1986). The latest (1986) ranges and tessituras (in parentheses) for the three changing-voice classifications are as follows:

Stage I	Midvoice I	a^b to c^2 ($c^{\#1}$ to $a^{\#1}$)
Stage II	Midvoice II	f to a^1 ($g^\#$ to f^1)
Stage III	Midvoice IIA	d to $f^{\#1}$ ($f^\#$ to d^1)

Cooksey recommends that music teachers select music that matches in range and tessitura the various stages of the changing voice. He has noted (1986a), however, that little such music exists. In most music chosen for changing voices, the boys' changing voice parts will be collapsed to a single cambiata part. Thus, while the theory of three stages for the changing voice is documented by Cooksey's research, the practical application of such a theory is limited because of the unavailability of a literature with three changing-voice parts.

The contemporary eclectic theory asserts that maturation of the singing voice proceeds at various rates through a predictable, sequential pattern of stages. The majority of voices pass through the three stages given above to a "new baritone" stage and finally to a "settling baritone" stage. Tenors and basses at the junior high or middle school levels are rare. Teachers are admonished not to exercise register extremes in either direction, but to exercise the changing voices in the comfortable ranges as given earlier.

The Baritone-Bass Approach (Frederick Swanson).   Frederick Swanson (1973, 1977) spent his professional life working with adolescent boys, and his recommendations are quite different from those previously discussed. Swanson states that the rate of the voice change may be very rapid and that the voice can change over the summer or even within a few weeks. The voice drops at least an octave at the onset of maturation for 30–40 percent of eighth- and ninth-grade boys. Materials and techniques must be changed constantly to accommodate the ever-changing male voice.

Basses are quite common in junior high, but new basses have a limited range of A to g. Some boys will develop even lower ranges and become contrabasses, if encouraged. Many new basses also have their treble ranges intact, but in a significant number of cases there are blank spots or areas around middle C where no tones can be produced. When the boys try to sing in this area, their voices squeak or possibly break, and extreme strain occurs. This condition can last for as long as a full school year.

Boys in the seventh grade are usually still trebles and sing with girls on either the soprano or alto parts. The eighth grade is when the first change most often takes place, and this change can be unmanageable. It is best to separate the boys at this stage from the girls in order to give attention to the training these boys need. By the use of falsetto singing, vocalizing from treble tones down through the break area, the two registers of the newly changed voice can be merged with much practice. Some boys do not have this break between adjustments and can carry the falsetto into the chest register. These boys are assigned the baritone part. True tenors are rare, but not unknown.

Swanson recommends the establishment of a "bass-clef chorus" for those boys in the eighth and ninth grades who have changing voices. Special song materials are necessary for this group, as the traditional TTB music is not yet suitable. Newly emerging basses need to sing the melody to encourage their participation, and teachers should rearrange traditional music to include the melody in the bass with the baritone part harmonized a sixth above the melody. Boys in these junior high grades whose voices have not yet begun to change will probably feel discouraged singing with girls and should be included in a bass-clef chorus. They can be given a descant part in the alto range and moved gradually into the baritone or bass ranges as their voices change. The ranges for the three voice parts are as follows:

Boy alto: g to f^2
Baritone: d to e^2
Newly changed bass: A to g (or a)

A preparatory mixed choir where boys' voices have progressed to their approximate adult ranges is also recommended. Singing four-part music begins at approximately age fourteen, and by age eighteen students should be singing in more advanced mixed choirs.

Voice Pivoting Approach (Sally Herman). The voice-pivoting approach (Herman, 1988) says that the part sung by the adolescent male with changing voice be pivoted to other voice parts in order to keep him singing within his most comfortable range. The author advocates using quality multivoiced literature in which the male voices sing a combination of voice parts according to their present vocal ranges. "A singer may start out on a first tenor part for five measures, switch to second tenor for three measures, go back to first tenor, etc. The first tenor may even sing alto for a few measures" (Herman, 1988, p. 92). This requires knowing, and keeping a record of, the range for each male singer throughout the voice-change process.

Herman classifies the voices of young adolescent boys into four voice parts: first tenor, second tenor, baritone, and bass. She notes that these classifications are not to be confused with the adult or changed-voice counterparts. Herman (1988) states, "By classifying the boys with terminology associated with the male voice, I can alleviate some misconceptions about being macho and singing. I have mostly boy altos in the seventh grade, but they are not comfortable with being placed in the alto section, nor are they comfortable with being called an alto" (p. 87).

The general and most common ranges for each of the male voice parts are as follows:

First tenor: b♭ to a¹
Second tenor: a♭ to d¹
Baritone: f to c¹
Bass: G to c

Herman recommends that when these voice parts are seated, the second tenors and baritones be close to the sopranos so that they can sing the soprano part down one octave when using two-part literature. The first tenors and basses should be seated close to the altos. In two-part literature, the first tenors will sing the alto part as written and the basses will sing the alto part one octave lower.

Herman relates that adolescent boys who have the most difficulty matching pitch are those whose voices changed at a very early age or changed very rapidly. Very often these young men have only a three- or four-note range in the lower register and nothing in the middle! Teachers must reassure these singers that this condition is perfectly normal and can be helped by working their voices downward from the falsetto. "I often have my male singers sing in the soprano range to develop falsetto and head voice" (Herman, 1988, p. 92).

The use of male glee clubs is recommended by Herman to stimulate interest among adolescent males in singing and to help them with the unique problems they are dealing with in the voice change. "If you teach three- and four-part literature to the glee clubs, then the next year when you move that same student to your best choir, it is easy to sing six- and eight-part literature" (Herman, 1988, p. 95).

Female Voice Change

While little research or writing exists concerning the voice change of the adolescent female, the pubertal girl does experience a voice change. This is a topic that is gaining increasing interest among music educators (Gackle, 1987, 1991; Huff-Gackle, 1985; Maddox, 1986; May and Williams, 1989).

In general, puberty begins earlier for girls than boys. Girls experience the same growth spurt as boys, but usually enter into this time of rapid growth development when they are ten or eleven years old. At the midpoint of puberty (between 12.5 and 14.5 years) occurs the first menstruation, which has traditionally been considered the end of childhood and the beginning of adulthood.

Kahane (1978) has documented the growth of the female larynx during puberty. While the larynx of the female does not undergo as radical a change as that of the male, it does thicken and grow in a more lateral or rounded direction. The vocal folds of the female grow less than those of the male, averaging only a three-to-four-millimeter increase. This growth does result in a slight lowering of the speaking voice and lower extension of the singing range.

The growth of the female larynx results in certain weaknesses and thickenings of the laryngeal muscles, specifically those of the interarytenoids (located between the arytenoid cartilages, to which the vocal folds are attached posteriorly) and the thyroarytenoids (muscles within the vocal folds). The first sign of voice change for the girl is often evidenced in a huskiness or unsteadiness of the speaking voice and is caused by the increased thickening of the vocal folds. This may be accompanied by a certain amount of breathiness caused by air passing through what Vennard (1967) called the "mutational chink." This chink is a triangular gap that appears between the posterior ends of the vocal folds as a result of weakened interarytenoid muscles that fail to close the vocal folds completely for phonation. The flutelike quality of the child voice is replaced by the husky, breathy sound of the adolescent female, who has to be treated with care by the music teacher if a positive attitude toward singing is to continue.

One way of dealing with the adolescent female voice is to change the concept of tone from "loud and full" to an accepted "soft and pure" (Huff-Gackle, 1985, p. 15). Emphasis on good vocal technique and realignment of the voice will encourage young women to improve their singing and to understand the new sound as a temporary condition. Continued vocalization in the upper register is also recommended. It is at this age when many girls are labeled "altos" because they seem to lose their ability to sing high. Harris points out that "very few young female voices should be categorized as 'altos' or even mezzo-sopranos at such an early age" (1987, p. 21). He notes that after singing alto for an extended period of time, girls become convinced that they are altos and develop only the chest register for singing. Maddox found that female subjects in seventh and eighth grades who were classified as inaccurate singers responded to remedial training in head-voice technique with "significant gains in individual pitch accuracy and melodic contour as a total group" (1986, p. 124). Unstrained, light, upper-register vocalization is a must for all adolescent girls.

Gackle (1991), as a result of her work with adolescent female singers, has prescribed a model for classifying characteristic stages of development in the adolescent female voice. The three stages and various levels are as follows:

I. Stage I: Prepubertal: Ages 8–10 (11)
Singing voice: Light, flutelike quality; no apparent register breaks; soprano quality; flexible, able to manage intervallic skips; much like male voice at same age with the exception that the female voice is lighter in "weight" because the volume potential is generally not as great.

Depending on other physiological changes (i.e., breast development, menarche) this stage could continue through age 12 or 13.

II. Stage IIA: Pubescence/Pre-Menarcheal: Ages 11–12 (13)
First signs of physical maturation begin.
Singing voice: Breathiness in the tone due to appearance of mutational *chink*, an inadequate closure of the vocal folds as growth occurs in the laryngeal area; register break appears between G^4 [g^1] and B^4 [b^1]; if not using lower (chest) voice, there is apparent loss of lower range—around C^4 [middle C]. (Some girls have trouble producing chest voice at this time.)
Symptomatic signs: Difficulty or discomfort with singing; difficulty in achieving volume (especially in middle and upper range); breathy tone throughout upper range (head voice); fuller tone in lower/chest range; obvious "flip" into breathy, childlike, fluty voice at transition from lower to upper registers.

Stage IIB: Puberty/Post-Menarcheal: Ages 13–14 (15)
Peak of Maturation
Singing voice: Very critical time; after the Stage IIA, tessituras can move up or down or, sometimes, can narrow at either end, yielding basically a five- or six-note range of comfortable singing. Register breaks still apparent between G^4 [g^1] and B^4 [b^1], and also at D^5 [d^2] to F-sharp^5 [$F^{\#2}$]. At times, lower notes are more easily produced, yielding an illusion of an alto quality; singing in this range may be easier and can be recommended for short periods of time; singing only in the lower range for an indefinite period of time can be injurious to the young unsettled voice because of the tendency to overuse the lower (chest) register.

Vocalization should occur throughout the vocal range, always striving to avoid any unnecessary strain in the lower or upper range. Because the changes during this stage are sporadic and unpredictable, it is necessary to listen to individual voices frequently in order to assess vocal development.
Symptomatic signs: Hoarseness without upper respiratory infection; voice cracking; difficulty or discomfort with singing; lack of clarity in the tone.

Stage III: Young Adult Female/Post-Menarcheal: Ages 14–15 (16)
Singing voice: Overall range capabilities increase. (At times, range does not decrease during the time of mutation. One characteristic of a quality singing voice is that it encompasses a large range. This does not imply that any voice *is* an alto at age 15–16 simply because those tones are within the young singer's capability.) Greater consistency occurs between registers; voice breaks are more apparent at passaggio D^5 [d^2]–F-sharp^5 [$f^{\#2}$] (more typical of adult voice). Breathiness appears to decrease. Tone, though not as full as mature adult, is deeper and richer. Ease returns in the singing process. Vibrato appears in the voice. Volume, resonance, and vocal agility increase [Gackle, 1991, pp. 22–23].

Gackle (1987), in an experimental study involving adolescent females, attempted to improve the girls' tone quality and pitch perturbation (regularity of pitch) through systematic instruction in breath management, resonance, and vowel unification. Results showed that while pitch perturbation was significantly improved in the experimental group, the treatment did not significantly improve the breathy quality of the singing. Gackle reports that this may have been in part because of the shortness of the treatment period and recommends that future research study the problem over a longer period of time. This is an area in need of much continued research.

May and Williams, in a review of literature concerning the female changing voice, note that "how students feel about their voices during the mutation process has not been adequately addressed by the research community" (1989, p. 22). The authors believe that attitude may have an important influence on vocal development, interest, enjoyment, and willingness to participate in singing among adolescent females. They conclude:

> If the music teacher focuses exclusively on this student's [female with changing-voice difficulties] physical problems associated with her singing without attending to her psychological difficulties, then that teacher risks alienating or discouraging the student. The simplest solution for this child is to remove herself from the circumstances or drop out of music class. As a result, a budding talent is lost [p. 22].

This is certainly an area in which much research is needed, as is the entire topic of the adolescent female voice. Enough is known, however, for music teachers to recognize the importance of dealing with the singing problems experienced by both males and females in the adolescent years.

STUDY AND DISCUSSION QUESTIONS

1. Describe infant vocalization and suggest ways in which adults can encourage vocal exploration by infants.
2. What two psychological parameters are being developed during the "approximation of singing" stage? Why are these important?
3. In what year and in what vocal range may preschoolers be expected to become tuneful singers?
4. Suggest techniques for encouraging preschoolers to sing in their upper voices. How will singing in the upper voice influence the choice of song literature for preschoolers?

5. What element of a song appears to be of initial interest to young children? How does this affect tuneful singing?

6. What aspects of singing do children need to experience in the early elementary school years?

7. Why is the third grade a pivotal year for the young singer? What issue must be addressed head-on in the third grade?

8. Discuss the characteristics of vocal development during the fourth, fifth, and sixth grades. What dynamic level is most appropriate for singing at these grade levels?

9. Describe both the personal and vocal characteristics of adolescents.

10. What are some ways in which to keep boys actively interested in singing during the adolescent years, and why must adolescents continue to sing?

11. What are some textual considerations when choosing song literature for adolescents?

12. Describe the voice-change process for adolescent boys. At what age does this change usually begin, and what are some of the physiological indicators that signal the onset of puberty among boys?

13. State the basic tenet of each of the following approaches to the changing voice of the boy: (a) Royal School of Church Music; (b) altotenor of Duncan McKenzie; (c) cambiata of Irvin Cooper; (d) eclectic of John Cooksey; (e) baritone-bass of Frederick Swanson; (f) voice pivoting of Sally Herman.

14. Discuss the voice change of the adolescent female. When does puberty begin for girls in relationship to boys, and what vocal qualities are characteristic of the female during the voice change?

15. Suggest some techniques for helping the female singer during the voice change. What else besides techniques for vocal problems must music teachers monitor among adolescent females? Why?

References

COLLINS, D. L. (1981). *The cambiata concept.* Conway, AK: Cambiata Press.

COOKSEY, J. M. (October 1977–January 1978). The development of a contemporary, eclectic theory for the training and cultivation of the junior high school male changing voice. *The Choral Journal, 18*(2, 3, 4, 5), Pt. 1, 5–14; Pt. 2, 5–16; Pt. 3, 5–15, Pt. 4, 5–17.

COOKSEY, J. M. (1983). *A longitudinal investigation of selected vocal, physiological and acoustical factors associated with voice maturation in the junior high school male adolescent.* Unpublished manuscript.

COOKSEY, J. M. (1986). *The adolescent voice.* Unpublished manuscript from the Iowa Choral Directors Association Summer Convention and Symposium, Mason City, IA.

COOKSEY, J. M., BECKETT, R. L., & WISEMAN, R. A. (1981). A longitudinal investigation of selected vocal, physiological, and acoustical factors associated with voice maturation in the junior high school male adolescent. Report for the National American Choral Directors Association Convention, New Orleans, LA.

COOPER, I. (1953). *Changing voices in the junior high—letters to Pat.* New York: Carl Fischer.

COOPER, I. & KUERSTEINER, K. (1965). *Teaching junior high school music.* Boston: Allyn and Bacon.

DAVIDSON, L. (1985). Preschool children's tonal knowledge: Antecedents to scale. In J. Boswell (Ed.), *The young child and music: Contemporary principles in child development and music education: Proceedings of the Music in Early Childhood Conference* (pp. 25–40). Reston, VA: Music Educators National Conference.

DAVIDSON, L., MCKERNON, P., & GARDNER, H. E. (1981). The acquisition of song: A developmental approach. In R. A. Choate (Ed.), *Documentary report of the Ann Arbor Symposium: Applications of psychology to the teaching and learning of music* (pp. 301–315). Reston, VA: Music Educators National Conference.

DAWSON, J. J. (1902). *The voice of the boy.* New York: E. L. Kellog.

GACKLE, M. L. (1987). The effect of selected vocal techniques for breath management, resonation, and vowel unification on tone production in the junior high school female voice (Doctoral dissertation, University of Miami, 1987). *Dissertation Abstracts International, 48*(04), 862A.

GACKLE, M. L. (1991). The adolescent female voice: Characteristics of change and stages of development. *The Choral Journal, 31*(8), 17–25.

GOETZE, M., COOPER, N., & BROWN, C. J. (1990). Recent research on singing in the general music classroom. *Bulletin of the Council for Research in Music Education, 104,* 16–37.

GORDON, E. E. (1985). Research studies in audiation: I. *Bulletin of the Council for Research in Music Education, 84,* 34–50.

GREENBERG, M. (1979). *Your children need music.* Englewood Cliffs, NJ: Prentice-Hall.

HARRIS, R. L. (1987). The young female voice and alto. *The Choral Journal, 28*(3), 21–22.

HERMAN, S. (1988). *Building a pyramid of musicianship.* San Diego: Curtis Music Press.

HUFF-GACKLE, L. (1985). The young adolescent female voice (ages 11–15): Classification, placement, and development of tone. *The Choral Journal, 25*(8), 15–18.

JARJISIAN, C. S. (1983). Pitch pattern instruction and the singing achievement of young children. *Psychology of Music, 11*(1), 19–25.

JOHNSON, C. E. (1935). *The training of boys' voices.* Bryn Mawr, PA: Oliver Ditson.

KAHANE, J. C. (1978). A morphological study of the human prepubertal and pubertal larynx. *American Journal of Anatomy, 151,* 11–19.

MADDOX, D. L. (1986). A study for developing the head voice to improve pitch-singing accuracy of adolescent girls classified as non-singers. *Missouri Journal of Research in Music Education, 5*(3), 123–124.

MAY, W. V., & WILLIAMS, B. B. (1989). The girl's changing voice. *UPDATE: The Applications of Research in Music Education, 8*(1), 20–23.

MCDONALD, D. T., & SIMONS, G. M. (1989). *Musical growth and development: Birth through six.* New York: Schirmer Books.

MCKENZIE, D. (1956). *Training the boy's changing voice.* New Brunswick, NJ: Rutgers University Press.

MILLER, R. (1977). *English, French, German and Italian techniques of singing: A study in national tonal preferences and how they relate to functional efficiency.* Metuchen, NJ: Scarecrow Press.

MOOG, H. (1976). *The musical experience of the preschool child.* London: Schott. (Original work published 1968.)

RAMSEY, J. H. (1983). An investigation of the effects of age, singing ability, and experience with pitched instruments on preschool children's melodic perception. *Journal of Research in Music Education, 31*(2), 133–145.

RUTKOWSKI, J. (1990). The measurement and evaluation of children's singing voice development. *The Quarterly, 1*(1 & 2), 81–95.

SCOTT, C. R. (1989). How children grow—musically. *Music Educators Journal, 76*(2), 28–31.

SINOR, E. (1985). The singing of selected tonal patterns by preschool children (Doctoral dissertation, Indiana University, 1984). *Dissertation Abstracts International, 45,* 3299A.

SWANSON, F. J. (1973). *Music teaching in the junior high and middle school.* Englewood Cliffs, NJ: Prentice-Hall.

SWANSON, F. J. (1977). *The male singing voice ages eight to eighteen.* Cedar Rapids, IA: Ingram.

SWEARS, L. (1985). *Teaching the elementary school chorus.* West Nyack, NY: Parker.

VENNARD, W. (1967). *Singing, the mechanism and the technique.* New York: Carl Fischer.

WELCH, G. F. (1986a). Children's singing: a developmental continuum of ability. *Journal of Research in Singing, 9*(2), 49–56.

WELCH, G. F. (1986b). A developmental view of children's singing. *British Journal of Music Education, 3*(3), 295–303.

5

THE HEALTHY VOICE

Vocal-music teachers generally recognize that vocal abuse is a common occurrence among children and adolescents. The loud, boisterous yelling commonly found on the playground and at sports events is a way of life to which students have become accustomed. Little do students realize how delicate the vocal mechanism is or how much potential damage there is in misuse of the voice. Morton Cooper, speech therapist and expert in the field of voice training, writes:

> Children, who invariably receive no voice training, tend to yell and scream. When their voices go hoarse from this misuse and abuse, they just love to continue yelling and screaming even if they can no longer produce sound. Use good judgment if your children are prone to such excesses. Educate them gradually in the correct use of their voices. Without such guidance, children are susceptible to nodes and other growths on the vocal cords which might require surgical excision. They are particularly vulnerable to developing negative habits, unless otherwise instructed. Give them an advantage that you didn't have: a positive voice model and an education in the use of their voices [1984, pp. 166–167].

Part of the job of vocal-music instructors must be to communicate to students the need for proper vocal hygiene as it involves the proper use and care of both speaking and singing voices. The following two lessons on knowing your voice are for use in grades 5–8 and may be used in conjunction with, or independently of, the method in Part II of this text.

KNOWING YOUR VOICE

Goal: The student will gain an understanding of the basic structure, function, and proper care of the vocal mechanism (larynx) for the maintenance of healthy speaking and singing voices.

Session 1: Vocal Structure

Materials needed: large picture or model of the larynx, picture of the respiratory system (with lungs, trachea, larynx, and vocal tract), rubber band, chalkboard, and piano

Instructional objectives: By the completion of this unit of study, the student will have become acquainted with the following:

1. the larynx as the origin of phonation for both speaking and singing
2. the other functions of the larynx as a passageway for breathing and as an aid in keeping food and liquid from passing into the lungs, by closing the epiglottis
3. the voice as a wind instrument powered by the breath passing from the lungs, through the trachea and vocal folds, the latter set in motion (vibratory cycles) as the air passes between them
4. the three structural cartilages of the larynx as the thyroid, cricoid, and arytenoid, and the one bone as the hyoid
5. the two vocal folds (cords) as the source of sound-producing vibrations within the larynx, with regular vibratory cycles of the vocal folds producing pitch (e.g., $a^1 = 440$ Hz), which rises or falls according to the shape (thin or thick) and how fast the vocal cords vibrate
6. the brain as the source of a message to different muscles of the larynx, which respond automatically to close (for phonation) or open (for breathing) the vocal folds
7. the breath as the power source for phonation, without which the vocal folds cannot vibrate
8. too much pressure on the vocal folds in the form of loud yelling or harsh coughing as a cause of swelling of the delicate tissue, resulting in hoarseness, loss of voice, or even permanent vocal damage

9. how the larynx changes and grows during adolescence and the results that can be heard in the speaking and singing voices

10. the major structural parts of the larynx

INSTRUCTIONAL SEQUENCE

0.0:   Preclass activity: Write the word *larynx* on the chalkboard. The materials on laryngeal physiology in Chapter 8 should be studied as a basis for this lesson.

1.0:   Draw the students' attention to the word on the chalkboard. Ask if anyone knows how to pronounce the word they see. Depending upon the responses, affirm that the correct pronunciation is *lar-inks*, and not *lar-nix*.

1.1:   Direct students to repeat the correct pronunciation several times.

2.0:   Ask if anyone knows what a larynx is. Depending upon responses, the students should be led to understand the larynx as the "voice box," or physical structure from which sound originates.

2.1:   Direct students to touch their own larynges lightly with the fingertips of one hand. Note the position.

2.2:   Direct students to swallow and yawn alternately. Ask what happens. The larynx rises for swallowing and lowers for yawning.

2.3:   Direct students to produce a vocal drone, feeling the vibrations.

2.4:   Amplify upon the three functions of the larynx: (1) to produce sound, (2) to provide a passageway for air, and (3) to keep food and liquids from passing into the lungs, by closing the epiglottis.

3.0:   Show a picture of the human respiratory system. Note the positions of the lungs, bronchial tubes, trachea, larynx, and vocal tract.

3.1:   Explain the human voice as a wind instrument powered by the breath flowing from the lungs to the trachea and through the vocal folds, setting the latter in motion. The vocal tract above the larynx (throat, mouth, nasal passages, etc.) amplifies the sound and projects it from the oral cavity (mouth).

3.2:   Ask how the vocal sound is formed into language. Lead students to understand the role of the articulators (jaw, tongue, lips, teeth, soft palate, and hard palate) in producing speech.

4.0:   Direct students' attention to the model or picture of the larynx (see Figure 8–1 in Chapter 8). Explain how the larynx sits between the throat and the trachea and serves as a passage from one to the other. When you swallow, the epiglottis closes, sealing off the laryngeal passage into the trachea. If for some reason the epiglottis does not seal and permits food or liquid into the larynx, the sensitive tissue within the larynx reacts to the intrusion and a coughing reflex begins to rid the larynx of the foreign matter.

4.1:   Note the hyoid bone at the top of the laryngeal structure. This is the only bone of the body that is not attached to another bone. It is attached to the main structure of the larynx (thyroid cartilage) by horn-like structures on either side (superior cornu). The hyoid bone serves to position the larynx within the vocal tract. Certain muscles act upon it to raise and lower the larynx.

4.2:   Direct attention to the thyroid cartilage, which is the largest and most prominent of the cartilages. It is formed of two sides (laminae), which are joined in the front at the thyroid notch (also known as the Adam's apple). The thyroid cartilage is strong and serves to protect the vocal folds within from any damage, such as a blow to the throat area.

4.3:   Direct attention to the cricoid, or ring, cartilage, which sits on top of the trachea. This cartilage is difficult to see and is best shown from the back of the larynx. If using a model with separable parts, remove the thyroid cartilage to see the cricoid cartilage. The cricoid cartilage moves within the thyroid cartilage to change the length and tension on the vocal folds, which change pitch.

4.4:   Direct attention to the two arytenoid cartilages, which sit on top of the cricoid cartilage. To each of these pyramid-shaped cartilages is attached the rear portion of one vocal fold. When certain muscles act upon the arytenoid cartilages, they pivot and slide together, causing the vocal folds to close.

5.0:   Explain that there are two vocal folds within the larynx. These are folds of elastic tissue that stretch from the arytenoid cartilages in the rear to the front of the larynx, where they are joined at the thyroid notch. Draw a diagram of the folds.

5.1:   The vocal folds are the source of sound-producing vibrations within the larynx.

5.2:   Demonstrate the properties of a rubber band that is stretched and plucked. Listen for the rise of pitch as the band is stretched and for the lowering of pitch as the tension is lessened. Relate the analogy to the properties of the vocal folds.

5.3:   Note that air is forced between the vocal folds to set the folds vibrating. The thinner and longer the folds, the faster they vibrate and the higher the pitch. The thicker and shorter the folds, the slower they vibrate and the lower the resulting pitch.

6.0:   Illustrate the closed and opened positions of the vocal folds by holding the first two fingers up in the shape of a V. Demonstrate that the vocal folds are in an open V position for breathing and that they close (bring fingers together) for phonation.

6.1:   Note that the brain sends a message to different muscles of the larynx, which respond automatically to close or open the vocal folds as needed.

6.2: Play a pitch at the piano and direct the students to sing the pitch on a neutral vowel. This illustrates that the muscles of the larynx respond automatically to the brain as it calls for the given pitch to be produced vocally.

7.0: Ask what was necessary besides hearing the pitch to set the vocal cords vibrating. Amplify upon the need for an adequate flow of air through the vocal folds.

7.1: Direct students to sing high and low pitches, noting the difference in air pressure needed. Higher pitches require more air pressure, while lower pitches require less.

7.2: Direct students to sing loud and soft pitches, noting the difference in air pressure needed. Loud pitches require more air pressure, and soft pitches require less.

8.0: Ask if students have ever experienced a loss of voice. Under what conditions did this occur?

8.1: Note that too much pressure on the vocal folds in the form of yelling or harsh coughing can result in swelling of the delicate tissue, loss of voice, and even permanent damage.

8.2: Note that more will be learned about protecting the voice and ways to keep a healthy voice in the next lesson.

9.0: Explain that the laryngeal structure of boys and girls is the same, but once children begin to mature into adulthood, the laryngeal changes are different.

9.1: The larynx of the girl grows larger laterally, which sometimes causes interference in the vibratory cycle of the vocal folds. This is a temporary phenomenon and usually clears up with maturity and acquisition of a good vocal technique.

9.2: The larynx of the boy undergoes a greater change. It grows more from front to back, often causing the boy's larynx to protrude at the front of the neck. The place of the most noticeable protrusion is the Adam's apple.

9.3: Because the boy's larynx grows more than the girl's, the boy's vocal folds become longer and thicker. This results in a lowering of pitch of about one octave. This octave difference between the voices of males and females is most noticeable when both are singing in unison. Males will most often sing an octave lower.

9.4: The growth of the larynx and the resultant voice change are not to be feared. They are a natural part of growing to adulthood. Some voices grow more than others, but all voices, boys and girls, do grow and change in relation to the developing larynx.

10.0: Assign students the worksheet showing the larynx (Figure 5.1), asking them to label its parts.

Worksheet: Knowing Your Voice

Name: _____ Section: _____

I. True or False: Use T for true, F for false.

1. _____ Sound originates in the human trachea.

2. _____ The voice is a wind instrument.

3. _____ Each person has four true vocal folds.

4. _____ The vocal folds are located within the larynx.

5. _____ The breath sets the vocal folds to vibrating.

6. _____ The correct pronunciation of *larynx* is *lar-nix*.

7. _____ The larynx is a passageway for air to and from the lungs.

8. _____ Another name for the thyroid notch is the Adam's apple.

9. _____ The vocal folds close automatically for sound production.

10. _____ When the vocal folds are stretched longer, pitch becomes lower.

11. _____ The vocal folds close for breathing.

12. _____ During adolescence, boys' vocal folds grow longer than girls'.

13. _____ All voices experience a voice change during adolescence.

14. _____ Too much yelling may cause a swelling of the vocal folds.

II. Matching: Write the letter for each part of the larynx, as shown in the picture, in the blank provided below for each term.

15. _____ Arytenoid cartilage   18. _____ Hyoid bone

16. _____ Cricoid cartilage   19. _____ Adam's apple

17. _____ Thyroid cartilage   20. _____ Vocal folds

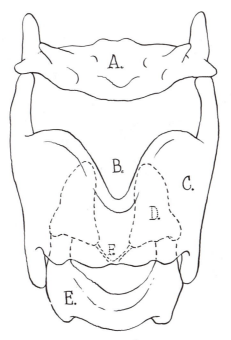

FIGURE 5–1. The Larynx.

Session 2: Vocal Health

Materials needed: chalkboard, picture or model of the larynx
Instructional Objectives: By the completion of this unit of study, the student will be able to recognize:

1. symptoms of voice disorders, such as pain or cramping in the throat or larynx, excessive throat clearing, laryngitis or loss of voice, breaks in phonation, and a vocal quality reflecting hoarseness, huskiness, breathiness, or harshness

2. three broad causes of voice disorders as being (1) organic (physical-genetic makeup), (2) external (pollution, allergy, viral infection), and (3) functional (overuse or abuse of the vocal mechanism)

3. functional causes of voice disorders as being (1) yelling and screaming, (2) loud and/or prolonged talking, (3) coughing and/or harsh clearing of the throat, (4) speaking on the wrong pitch (usually too low), (5) physical tiredness, and (6) the use of irritants such as drugs, alcohol, and tobacco

4. how the vocal folds react to misuse and abuse by (1) being slammed and rubbed together, causing irritation and swelling

of the vocal tissue, and (2) drying of the mucosa (wet surface of the vocal folds) as a result of drug, alcohol, or tobacco use

5. physical problems of the vocal folds that may result from prolonged voice abuse, such as (1) contact ulcers (ulcerations or sore spots caused by the forceful slamming together of the vocal folds), (2) polyps (a benign lesion of the vocal folds caused by irritants such as smoke), (3) vocal nodules, or nodes (callus-type growths caused by excessive rubbing together of the folds), and (4) bowed vocal folds (unnatural concavity of the vocal folds, resulting in too much air passing between the folds and a breathy quality)

6. the possibility that persistent vocal abuse may result in permanent damage to the vocal folds or may need correction through voice therapy or surgery

7. ten ways to protect the vocal folds and maintain a healthy voice: (1) eat a well-balanced diet of food and drink plenty of water; (2) avoid irritants such as drugs, alcohol, and tobacco; (3) get plenty of rest; (4) avoid harsh and excessive throat clearing; (5) avoid yelling and screaming; (6) avoid loud and/or prolonged talking; (7) speak on the correct pitch for your voice; (8) support vocal production with the breath; (9) sing in the proper vocal register(s); and (10) see a doctor if vocal problems persist

8. ways to handle occasional hoarseness, sore throat, or laryngitis: (1) rest the voice; (2) inhale steam for five minutes every three to four hours; (3) avoid aspirin-based medications (Tylenol® is permitted); (4) use glycerin-based lozenges (avoid mint, menthol, or medicated ones that dry the mucosa)

9. the viability of singing with a cold or allergy as long as the infection or irritation has not spread to the vocal folds, in which case the voice should be rested and used as little as possible

10. the close relationship of speaking and singing and the necessity of a proper vocal technique for safe and efficient use of the voice in both modes

INSTRUCTIONAL SEQUENCE

0.0: Begin with a review of laryngeal and vocal-fold structure.

1.0: Ask students if any of them have ever experienced any vocal discomforts, such as hoarseness or laryngitis. Explore the feelings associated with such disorders, and make a list of them on the chalkboard (throat pain or cramping, excessive throat clearing, loss of voice, breaks in phonation, hoarseness, breathiness, harshness, etc.).

1.1: Note that the larynx is a structure that serves us every day, but that it can show these signs of stress resulting in interference with speaking and singing.

1.2: State that by the end of this lesson, the students should be able to identify symptoms and causes of, and remedies for, vocal disorders.

2.0: Write on the chalkboard the three broad causes of voice disorders: (1) organic, (2) external, (3) functional.

2.1: Ask the students what they think an organic cause of voice disorder might be. This refers to a disorder caused by the physical or genetic makeup of the individual. An example is laryngeal papilloma, a disease that most often occurs in young children in which wartlike growths appear on the vocal folds and sometimes obstruct breathing. Such a disease must be treated medically by a doctor.

2.2: Ask the students what they think an external cause of voice disorder might be. This refers to a disorder caused by outside factors, such as air pollution, allergies, or viral infections that result in colds.

2.3: Ask for an example of air pollution. A smoke-filled environment is one. Note that smoke tends to dry and swell the vocal folds, often resulting in excessive throat clearing.

2.4: Ask students what they think a functional cause of voice disorder might be. This refers to abuse or overuse of the vocal mechanism.

3.0: Ask students in what ways people abuse or misuse their voices. Make a list that includes the following: (1) yelling and screaming, (2) loud and/or prolonged talking, (3) coughing and/or harsh clearing of the throat, (4) speaking on the wrong pitch (usually too low), (5) physical tiredness, and (6) the use of irritants such as drugs, alcohol, and tobacco.

3.1: Ask students to describe activities in which they might abuse their voices. Responses should include recess, sports events, talking over noise (e.g., in the cafeteria or on the bus), and music class!

3.2: Ask students how they can avoid abusing their voices in music class. (Answer: by using good vocal technique for proper vocal production.)

4.0: Make a sketch of the vocal folds on the chalkboard, showing the positions of the folds when vibrating in the lower register and the upper register (see Figure 8–6). Note that in the lower register or speaking voice, the folds make more contact than in the upper voice, where only the inner edges of the folds make contact.

4.1: Ask students if they think that the vocal folds would tire more easily in the lower or upper register. Guide the response to note that the greater contact of the folds in the lower voice results in more friction, which can cause swelling and hoarseness.

4.2: Note that the continual and forced slamming or rubbing together of the vocal folds through strain and poor vocal technique results in vocal-fold irritation, swelling, or even voice loss.

4.3: Ask students if they know the effect of drugs, alcohol, and tobacco on the vocal folds. Such irritants cause the mucosal membrane of the folds to dry, resulting in a raspy vocal quality and excessive clearing of the throat.

5.0: Relate that prolonged vocal abuse may result in physical damage to the vocal folds as follows: (1) contact ulcers (ulcerations or sore spots caused by the forceful slamming together of the vocal folds), (2) polyps (a benign lesion) of the vocal folds caused by irritants such as smoke), (3) vocal nodules, or nodes (callus-type growths caused by excessive rubbing together of the folds), and (4) bowed vocal folds (unnatural concavity of the vocal folds, resulting in too much air passing between the folds and a breathy quality). These physical problems interfere with the proper vibration pattern of the vocal folds.

5.1: Sketch on the chalkboard each of the above physical problems as each would appear on the vocal folds. The contact ulcer should appear as an open sore where the vocal fold joins to the arytenoid cartilage. The polyp may be drawn as a small sac protruding from the folds. The node should appear as a darkened hard spot on the edge of the fold. With line drawings, contrast straight vocal folds and bowed folds.

5.2: Ask students if they know or have ever known any person with any of the above conditions. Ask them to describe the vocal quality of the person. Answers should include *breathy, harsh, broken,* or similar terms. (If there is a child in the class with a vocal problem, avoid having the child become an example or the subject of embarrassment.)

6.0: Note that persistent vocal abuse may result in permanent damage to the vocal folds and may need correction through surgery.

6.1: Note that physical problems of the vocal folds often respond to rest and vocal therapy. Persons who suspect that they have a serious vocal disorder should see a medical doctor.

7.0: The following ten ways to protect the vocal folds and maintain a healthy voice should be listed on the chalkboard and discussed: (1) eat a well-balanced diet and drink plenty of water; (2) avoid irritants such as drugs, alcohol, and tobacco; (3) get plenty of rest; (4) avoid harsh and excessive throat clearing; (5) avoid yelling and screaming; (6) avoid loud and/or prolonged talking; (7) speak on the correct pitch for your voice; (8) support vocal production with the breath; (9) sing in the proper vocal register(s); and (10) see a doctor if vocal problems persist.

7.1: Note that many people speak too low, causing the vocal folds to make too much contact. Review the procedures for finding the optimal speaking pitch presented in Chapter 8.

8.0: List on the chalkboard and discuss the following eight ways to handle occasional hoarseness, sore throat, or laryngitis: (1) rest the voice; (2) inhale steam for five minutes every three to four hours; (3) avoid aspirin-based medications (Tylenol is permitted); (4) use glycerin-based lozenges (avoid mint, menthol, or medicated ones that dry the mucosa.)

8.1:   Ask if any student has ever had to be on prolonged vocal rest. What was, or would it be, like? How could you communicate? (By writing.)

9.0:   Ask students if they think it is permissible to sing if you have a cold. Relate that singing with a cold or allergy is permitted as long as the infection or irritation has not spread to the vocal folds, in which case the voice should be rested.

10.0:   Conclude the lesson by noting that speaking and singing are closely related and require proper vocal technique for safe and efficient use of the voice in both modes. Review the ten ways to protect and maintain a healthy voice presented in 7.0.

STUDY AND DISCUSSION QUESTIONS

The following questions may be used in constructing a student exam for the two lessons presented in this chapter.

1. What three functions does the larynx have?
2. What are the three major cartilages and the one bone of the larynx?
3. How many vocal folds does each person have, and where are these folds located? How are they attached?
4. How do the vocal folds produce sound? Are the vocal folds open or closed for normal breathing? Are they long and thin or short and thick at high pitches?
5. What is another name for the Adam's apple? What is the trachea?
6. At what stage of life does the larynx begin to grow rapidly, and how does the larynx grow in girls, as compared to boys?
7. Why do boys' voices sound an octave lower after the voice change?
8. What are three symptoms of voice disorder?
9. When wrong speaking pitch is a source of voice disorder, is it more likely to be too high or too low a pitch?
10. How do the vocal folds react to slamming or rubbing together and to drugs, alcohol, and tobacco?
11. Describe each of the following vocal problems: a contact ulcer, a polyp, and a vocal nodule. How can these problems be prevented?
12. Persistent vocal abuse may result in what condition?
13. What are ten ways to protect the vocal folds and maintain a healthy voice?
14. What are four ways to handle occasional hoarseness and sore throat?
15. When may a person sing with a cold?

References

APFELSTADT, H. (1988). Warning! Vocal danger ahead. *General Music Journal, 7*(1), 2–5.

COOPER, M. (1984). *Change your voice, change your life.* New York: Macmillan.

FEDER, R. J. (1990). Vocal health: A view from the medical profession. *The Choral Journal, 30*(7), 23–25.

MILLER, R. (1986). Healthy singing. In *The structure of singing: System and art in vocal technique* (Chapter 17). New York: Schirmer Books.

NILSON, H., & SCHNEIDERMAN, C. R. (1983). Classroom program for the prevention of vocal abuse and hoarseness in elementary school children. *Language, Speech, and Hearing Devices in Schools, 14*(2), 121–127.

SATALOFF, R. T. (1985). Ten good ways to abuse your voice: A singer's guide to a short career (Pt. 1). *The NATS Journal, 42*(1), 23–25.

SATALOFF, R. T. (1986). Ten more good ways to abuse your voice: A singer's guide to a short career (Pt. 2). *The NATS Journal 43*(1), 22–26.

WARE, C. (1988). Physical preparations. In *Voice adventures* (Chapter 3). Saint Paul: Harmony.

Part
II

VOCAL TECHNIQUE FOR YOUNG SINGERS

From the lips of children and infants you have ordained praise.
—Psalm 8:2

6

VOCAL-TECHNIQUE CURRICULUM

The curriculum for the vocal method in Part II of this text is introduced by a consideration of the philosophy underlying the curriculum. A statement of "why" should lead to "what" when considering curricular matters. Music educators need to consider carefully why singing is important to the school program and what the results of that philosophy should be. A clearly articulated rationale gives shape and meaning to what is planned and demonstrates to administrators and the community that singing is important in the music curriculum. The rationale is given here in the hope that a stronger philosophy for teaching children to sing will be adopted in the schools.

A RATIONALE FOR TEACHING CHILDREN TO SING

Singing is a basic means of human expression. From the spontaneous play songs of childhood to the polished presentations of concert artists, singing fulfills the human need to transmit both thoughts and feelings in a form that augments speech alone. Over the centuries, this form has become a standard vehicle for expressing and sharing the human experience. In its many forms, song permits people to experience life as others have found it and to share themselves with others in an expression that transcends the physical and psychological boundaries of life.

Through the singing of songs people are able to express themselves in a captivating form. Song is a powerful communicator, especially among the young.

Singing is a learned behavior; it is not some type of gift bestowed only upon a talented few. Children and adolescents can be taught to sing, and each person has the right to *learn* to sing in order that he or she may experience the joy of music as an active participant. The music curriculum provides for the development of singing as an important area of instruction for all young people.

Singing is a complex skill; it requires time to develop the coordination of both the psychological and motor responses needed for successful vocal production. Therefore, instruction in singing begins early in the career of students when other basic skills are being cultivated. Early confidence in singing lays the foundation for a successful music education.

The process of singing involves the three major forms of learning: cognitive (knowledge), psychomotor (skills), and affective (feelings and attitudes). Instruction in singing challenges students to grow in knowledge, to explore their feelings, and to learn expressive means of communicating thoughts and emotions.

Singing is a comprehensive art, that is, within its study students come into contact with other basic areas of the curriculum: math, science, social studies, languages, and physical education. While singing is a subject with its own special body of knowledge, its comprehensive nature serves as a foundation for a unified and comprehensive curriculum.

A student who sings learns about life. The transmission of cultural heritages, traditions, and beliefs are all part of the singing experience. In addition, the study of singing helps to reveal relationships to others and to our environment. To study singing is to study the world. Every student has a right to develop this skill; it is basic for an educated people who desire that each succeeding generation be led to develop a high degree of musical understanding.

THE CURRICULUM

Vocal technique for young singers (grades 1–12) consists of ninety sequential exercises through five areas of vocal development: respiration, phonation, resonant tone production, diction, and expression. Taken together, these exercises represent a comprehensive program of vocal technique for children and adolescents.

In this method instruction in vocal technique begins in the first grade with fifteen exercises, and each following year (grades 2–6), fifteen more exercises are taught, until all ninety exercises have been covered through the sixth grade. It is reasonable to expect that in a school year of thirty-six weeks, fifteen exercises in vocal technique can be taught and learned. This represents one new exercise approximately every other week.

If all the exercises have been covered by grade 6, high school teachers may then continue to develop, through review, the vocal skills outlined in this method. Constant monitoring of student progress will determine those areas that need remediation and review.

The ninety graded exercises of the method are arranged in three learning sequences. Sequence 1 is to be used when the method is begun in grades 1–6. This sequence follows the strict order of the ninety numbered exercises and consists of six levels of fifteen exercises each. When the method is begun in the second grade, it is necessary to cover both of the first two levels. If it is begun in the third grade, a more intense program will be required to cover the first three levels (forty-five exercises). This is not an unreasonable expectation, as third-graders are maturing to the point where they can handle larger amounts of material more quickly. After the third grade, the normal order of levels is followed through the sixth grade.

Sequence 2 is to be used when the method is begun in grades 4–6 or grades 7–9. This sequence consists of three levels of thirty exercises each. When begun in the fourth or seventh grades, thirty exercises will be introduced in each of the grade levels (4–6, 7–9). If begun in the fifth, sixth, eighth, or ninth grades, it is unreasonable to expect that sixty or ninety exercises can be covered in one year. In this case, the instructor should begin with the exercises in the first level and proceed accordingly as far as possible.

Sequence 3 is to be used when the method is begun in the high school grades 9/10–12. This sequence consists of two levels of forty-five exercises each. It is not unreasonable to expect students in these grades to learn forty-five exercises in one year, when choral groups rehearse from three to five times per week. If this is not possible, the instructor should proceed according to the sequence of exercises and begin the next year where the students ended the previous year (after a period of review).

A fourth alternative is possible. Instructors may choose to use the exercises as an "approach" rather than a "method." Well-established programs of vocal instruction exist in many schools, especially at the high school level, and the instructors may not need to start with the beginning exercises in vocal technique. In this case, the instructor is free to select those exercises that best supplement the program of voice development already in place. A review of all exercises may, however, point out gaps in existing programs.

Procedures for the proper execution of the ninety exercises are given detailed explanation in Chapters 7–11. The instructor will need to study and master each technique before class presentation. As the exercises are learned, the outlines presented in Chapter 12 will suffice for quick recall.

The vocal-production techniques in this method are meant for group instruction, and group mastery of each exercise needs to be monitored before instruction begins on a new exercise. Individual student progress should be evaluated as much as possible. Keep the progress rate moving while providing ample repetition of the exercises so that slow achievers can master the necessary steps at each level.

The pace at which the exercises are introduced and practiced has to be determined by the instructor on the basis of group mastery and achievement. Introduction and mastery of the ninety techniques in this method are not meant for a one-year plan of vocal development, especially at the primary and intermediate grade levels. Ideally, level I would be introduced in the first grade, with each successive level being introduced at each successive grade. In this way, all six levels will be covered by the end of the sixth grade (fifteen new exercises per year).

All exercises should be done by the students while standing, unless otherwise directed. Students must have enough room to avoid being crowded while standing. The directive to "move to your own space" will cue the students as to the proper standing position for vocal-development exercises.

It is helpful for the instructor to keep a record of the exercises and frequency of practice at each level. In this way, it will be easy to monitor the progress of the group, noting those exercises that have been practiced each session. A practice record is provided in Chapter 12.

The practice of vocal-production skills should be an enjoyable activity for students. The techniques have been given descriptive titles in order to stimulate student interest and bring about immediate recall of what is expected without a lengthy explanation each session. Do not spend too much time on any one technique, and keep variety in your planning. It is not necessary to do all of the exercises you plan for a session all at one time. In fact, it is better if you spread the exercises throughout the class time.

No more than five or six minutes per class should be spent on vocal technique at the elementary level. This method is not meant to be a comprehensive music program; it is a comprehensive vocal-production technique program, which is only one part of the total music curriculum. Spending too much time on vocal technique will bore students, and they will end up disliking the exercises. Use wise judgment and plan a vocal-technique segment for the class that is short and moves quickly.

Vocal-technique exercises should become part of the regular warm-up routine for high school choral rehearsals. The amount of time spent will be determined by the length of the rehearsal, but normally, no more than 15 percent of the total rehearsal time should be spent on vocal production. If, however, you wish to spend more time on vocal skills, this may be done early in the semester, when performance pressures are not as great. In this case, no more than a third of the class time should be spent on vocal technique.

If the vocal-music instructor has other exercises and vocalises that have been found to be effective, they most certainly may be used as a supplement to this program of vocal development. The fifteen subdivisions of the five main areas of this method are broad enough to include other exercises, as long as the objectives are similar.

BROAD CURRICULUM GOALS

Part I: Respiration Goals

Posture Development. The student will develop the technique of proper posture, through exercises involving physical conditioning (stretching and limbering), active body positioning, and mental alertness.

Breathing Motion. The student will develop the technique of correct breathing motion (the cycle of inhalation-exhalation), through exercises involving active use of the major breathing muscles.

Breath Management. The student will develop the technique of breath management, through exercises involving the support (energized air column) and control (slow emission of air) of the exhaled breath when applied to vocal production.

Part II: Phonation Goals

Lower Adjustment. The student will develop the technique of lower-adjustment (register) voice production through exercises involving vocal clarity, placement, and projection.

Upper Adjustment. The student will develop the technique of upper-adjustment (register) voice production as a means to finding and strengthening the upper adjustment for singing, through exercises involving vocal clarity, placement, and projection.

Adjustment Coordination. The student will develop the technique of vocal-adjustment coordination (middle register, c^1 to c^2) through exercises involving vocal clarity, placement, balance, and projection.

Part III: Resonant Tone Production Goals

Vocal Resonance. The student will develop the technique of vocal resonance through various exercises involving freedom, focus, and projection of the voice.

Uniform Vowel Colors. The student will develop the technique of uniform vowel colors for resonant singing, through exercises that involve shaping the vocal tract, increasing resonance, and achieving legato movement.

Vocal Coordination. The student will develop the technique of vocal-register coordination through various exercises involving pitch exploration and accuracy, register definition and coordination, increased resonance, and flexibility.

Part IV: Diction Goals

Vocal-Tract Freedom. The student will develop the technique of singing with an open throat, through vocal-tract conditioning exercises involving the relaxation and flexibility of the vocal articulators.

Word Pronunciation. The student will develop the technique of singing with accurate and intelligible word pronunciation, through exercises involving both enunciation of vowels and articulation of consonants.

Consonant Articulation. The student will develop the technique of singing with distinct articulation of consonants, through exercises involving flexible, rapid, and often exaggerated use of the vocal articulators.

Part V: Expression Goals

Phrasing. The student will develop the technique of expressive phrasing, through exercises involving the development of musical line as it relates to musical structure and overall musical performance.

Dynamic and Tempo Variation. The student will develop the techniques of both dynamic and tempo variation through exercises involving degrees of loudness-softness and fastness-slowness.

Agility and Range Extension. The student will develop the techniques of both agility and range extension through exercises involving increasing articulation demands (syllabic, neumatic, melismatic) over a gradually increasing vocal range.

SCOPE AND SEQUENCE, GRADES 1–6

Sequence 1 (when begun in grades 1–3)

Instructional Objectives for Grade 1. By the completion of grade 1 students will be able to do the following:

1. stretch and prepare the physical body as an instrument for singing (Exercise 1)

2. demonstrate a natural breathing motion in which the diaphragm contracts and abdominal muscles relax for inhalation,

and the diaphragm relaxes and abdominal muscles contract for exhalation (Exercise 2)

3. apply the breath to vocal production through mild contraction, or lifting, of the abdominal muscles upon exhalation for singing (Exercise 3)

4. demonstrate production of spoken sound in the three vocal registers: upper, lower, and middle (Exercises 4, 5, and 6)

5. sustain the voice on single pitches (d^1 to a^1) with proper humming production for a slow count of 4 (quarter note = 60) (Exercise 7)

6. correctly form and sing the [u] vowel with slightly flared lips and relaxed jaw on a series of sustained pitches (d^1 to a^1) (Exercise 8)

7. sing sustained pitches and short motivic patterns on and around the centers of the three vocal registers: g^1 (middle), c^1 (lower), and c^2 (upper) (Exercise 9)

8. demonstrate correct mouth (vertical opening) and jaw (relaxed) positions while singing (Exercise 10)

9. demonstrate flexibility of the vocal articulators for intelligible word pronunciation (Exercise 11)

10. demonstrate exaggerated production of voiceless plosive consonants (*p, t, k, ch*) as a consonant group drill and individually when applied to song texts (Exercise 12)

11. sing accurately a sustained descending five-note pattern (sol-fa-mi-re-do) on one breath (Exercise 13)

12. identify the six basic dynamic levels and vary the intensity of vocal production for both speaking and singing (Exercise 14)

13. sing accurately and with agility song motives that contain examples of two pitches per syllable (Exercise 15)

14. sing a variety of song literature in the range from c^1 to c^2 (tessitura of d^1 to a^1) with accurate pitch

15. sing a variety of song literature in the range from c^1 to c^2 with a light tone quality that is a combination of both upper and lower vocal registers.

INSTRUCTIONAL SEQUENCE FOR GRADE 1 (LEVEL 1)

Part I: Respiration

		Page
Exercise 1	Muscle Movers	153 (Posture development)
Exercise 2	Natural Breathing	200 (Breathing motion)
Exercise 3	Abdominal Lift	212 (Breath management)

Instructional Objectives for Grade 2. By the completion of grade 2, students will be able to do the following:

1. align and prepare the physical body as a singing instrument for both sitting and standing positions (Exercise 16)
2. demonstrate a deep-breathing motion for singing in which the lungs comfortably fill with air upon inhalation (Exercise 17)
3. control the breath stream as a continuous flow of air from the abdominal region to the vocal cords (Exercise 18)
4. demonstrate proper production of the speaking voice as to breath support and voice placement (Exercises 19, 20, and 21)
5. sing in the correct adjustment in the upper register (above c^2) and downward while maintaining a light, staccato production (Exercise 22)
6. sing in tune various tonal patterns using the basic solfège syllables within the range from d^1 to d^2 (Exercise 23)
7. demonstrate the skill of carrying the pure quality of the upper singing voice downward below pitch c^2 to produce a balanced

vocal production of upper and lower adjustments between pitches c^1 and c^2 (Exercise 24)

8. demonstrate correct mouth (vertical opening) and relaxed jaw positions while singing (Exercise 25)

9. demonstrate flexibility of the vocal articulators for intelligible word pronunciation of final consonants (Exercise 26)

10. demonstrate exaggerated production of voiced plosive consonants (*b, d, g, j*) as a group drill and individually when applied to song texts (Exercise 27)

11. sing complete song phrases on one breath (Exercise 28)

12. identify the six basic tempo markings and vary the tempo of vocal production for both speaking and singing (Exercise 29)

13. sing accurately and with agility song motives that contain examples of one to four pitches per syllable (Exercise 30)

14. sing a variety of song literature in the range from b to d^2 (tessitura of d^1 to b^1) with accurate pitch

15. sing a variety of song literature in the range of b to d^2 with a light tone quality that is pure upper voice above c^2 pure lower voice below c^1, and a balance of both voices between c^1 and c^2

INSTRUCTIONAL SEQUENCE FOR GRADE 2 (LEVEL 2)

Part I: Respiration

		Page
Exercise 16	Body Alignment	180 (Posture development)
Exercise 17	Deep Breathing	202 (Breathing motion)
Exercise 18	Breath Stream	212 (Breath management)

Part II: Phonation

Exercise 19	Voice Placement	236 (Lower adjustment)
Exercise 20	Marcato Thrust	243 (Upper adjustment)
Exercise 21	Woofers and Tweeters	247 (Adjustment coordination)

Part III: Resonant Tone Production

Exercise 22	Staccato Koo-koo	270 (Vocal resonance)
Exercise 23	Solfège Patterns	285 (Uniform vowel colors)
Exercise 24	Upper to Lower	295 (Vocal coordination)

Instructional Objectives for Grade 3. By the completion of grade 3, students will be able to do the following:

1. align and prepare the physical body as a singing instrument according to the seven principles of posture development (Exercise 31)
2. demonstrate the skill of holding or suspending the inhaled breath without closing the throat (Exercise 32)
3. manage breath articulation for greater support of vocal production (Exercise 33)
4. demonstrate proper production of the speaking voice as to breath support and voice projection (Exercises 34, 35, and 36)
5. demonstrate the skill of correct vocal attack for the beginning of vocal production (Exercise 37)
6. sing the five primary vowel colors with increased resonance using a flared lip position and relaxed jaw (Exercise 38)
7. demonstrate the skill of singing from the lower register to the upper register with accuracy and breath support (Exercise 39)
8. sing with an open (unconstricted) and relaxed throat (Exercise 40)
9. demonstrate flexibility of the vocal articulators for intelligible word pronunciation of hissing sibilants (Exercise 41)
10. demonstrate exaggerated production (*f, th*) and nonexaggerated production (*s, sh*) of voiceless sibilants as a group drill and individually when applied to song texts (Exercise 42)
11. sing song phrases either separated with a properly executed "catch breath" or extended by "staggered breathing" techniques (Exercise 43)
12. identify the two basic tempo markings *accelerando* and *ritardando* and vary the tempo of vocal production for both speaking and singing (Exercise 44)

13. sing accurately and with agility tonic triad arpeggios over the range from b^b to e^{b2} (Exercise 45)

14. sing a variety of song literature in the range from b^b to e^{b2} (tessitura of d^1 to c^2) with accurate pitch

15. sing a variety of song literature in the range from b^b to e^{b2} with a light tone quality that is pure upper voice above c^2, pure lower voice below c^1, and a balance of both voices between c^1 and c^2

INSTRUCTIONAL SEQUENCE FOR GRADE 3 (LEVEL 3)

Part I: Respiration

		Page
Exercise 31	Posture Practice	183 (Posture development)
Exercise 32	Breath Suspension	202 (Breathing motion)
Exercise 33	Breath Articulation	213 (Breath management)

Part II: Phonation

Exercise 34	Energized Speech	238 (Lower adjustment)
Exercise 35	Staccato Bump	244 (Upper adjustment)
Exercise 36	Voice Inflectors	248 (Adjustment coordination)

Part III: Resonant Tone Production

Exercise 37	The Attack	271 (Vocal resonance)
Exercise 38	Vertical Vowels	287 (Uniform vowel colors)
Exercise 39	Octave Lift	296 (Vocal coordination)

Part IV: Diction

Exercise 40	Pharyngeal Openers	317 (Vocal-tract freedom)
Exercise 41	Hissing Sibilants	321 (Word pronunciation)
Exercise 42	Voiceless Sibilants	331 (Consonant articulation)

Part V: Expression

Exercise 43	Breath Techniques	343 (Phrasing)
Exercise 44	Accelerando and Ritardando	348 (Tempo variation)
Exercise 45	The Arpeggio	354 (Agility, range extension)

Instructional Objectives for Grade 4. By the completion of grade 4, students will be able to do the following:

1. align and prepare the physical body as a singing instrument with added emphasis on facial mobility (Exercise 46)

2. demonstrate increased coordination of the breathing motion with a faster-paced inhalation-exhalation cycle (Exercise 47)

3. demonstrate increased coordination of breath articulation for greater support and control of vocal production (Exercise 48)

4. demonstrate active breath-pulsing support for speech production in all three vocal registers (Exercises 49, 50, and 51)

5. demonstrate active breath-pulsing support for singing production in all three vocal registers (Exercise 52)

6. sing with an increasing legato line (Exercise 53)

7. demonstrate the skill of singing from the lower voice to the upper voice with an increasing upper quality in the vocal production (Exercise 54)

8. sing with an open throat, characterized by a relaxed and forward tongue (Exercise 55)

9. demonstrate flexibility of the vocal articulators for correct articulation of the consonant *r* (Exercise 56)

10. demonstrate prolonged production of tuned continuants (*m, n*) and rapid production of tuned continuants (*l, r*) as a group drill and individually when applied to song texts (Exercise 57)

11. sing songs with increased vocal expression based upon an understanding of word meaning and mood (Exercise 58)

12. identify the two basic dynamic terms *crescendo* and *decrescendo* and increase the dynamic variations of vocal production for both speaking and singing (Exercise 59)

13. sing accurately and with agility a vocalise of ever-expanding vocal range, up to and including g^2 (Exercise 60)

14. sing a variety of song literature in the range from a to e^2 (tessitura of d^1 and d^2) with accurate pitch

15. sing a variety of song literature in the range from a to e^2 with a light, yet more resonant tone quality that is pure upper voice above c^2, pure lower voice below c^1, and a balance of both voices between c^1 and c^2

INSTRUCTIONAL SEQUENCE FOR GRADE 4 (LEVEL 4)

Part I: Respiration

		Page
Exercise 46	Face Lift	190 (Posture development)
Exercise 47	Breath Rhythm	206 (Breathing motion)
Exercise 48	Breath Pulse	215 (Breath management)

Part II: Phonation

Exercise 49	Lower Wheelie	239 (Lower adjustment)
Exercise 50	Upper Wheelie	244 (Upper adjustment)
Exercise 51	Spiral Wheelie	248 (Adjustment coordination)

Part III: Resonant Tone Production

Exercise 52	Rolling Pulse	271 (Vocal resonance)
Exercise 53	Legato Movement	290 (Uniform vowel colors)
Exercise 54	Lighten Up	296 (Vocal coordination)

Part IV: Diction

Exercise 55	Forward Tongue	317 (Vocal-tract freedom)
Exercise 56	The Three Rs	321 (Word pronunciation)
Exercise 57	Tuned Continuants	331 (Consonant articulation)

Part V: Expression

Exercise 58	Meaning and Mood	344 (Phrasing)
Exercise 59	Crescendo and Decrescendo	349 (Dynamic variation)
Exercise 60	Agility and Range 1	354 (Agility, range extension)

Instructional Objectives for Grade 5. By the completion of grade 5, students will be able to do the following:

1. align and prepare the physical body as a singing instrument, with added emphasis on active posturing (Exercise 61)
2. demonstrate increased coordination of the breathing motion with a regular but slow-paced inhalation-exhalation cycle (Exercise 62)

3. demonstrate increased breath control through slow emission cf the air column upon exhalation (Exercise 63)

4. demonstrate active application of breath support and control for speech production in all three vocal registers (Exercises 64, 65, and 66)

5. demonstrate the accurate singing of intervals (ascending and descending) from a variety of pitches (Exercise 67)

6. sing the short-vowel colors with relaxed jaw and vertical positioning (Exercise 68)

7. sing in the middle voice (c^1 to c^2) with increased resonance and proper balance of vocal registers (Exercise 69)

8. demonstrate techniques for releasing muscle tension in the face and jaw (Exercise 70)

9. sing the words of songs with greater attention to proper pronunciation and intelligibility (Exercise 71)

10. demonstrate exaggerated and production of voiced continuants (*v, z, th, zh*) as a group drill and individually when applied to song texts (Exercise 72)

11. sing songs with increased expression using expressive movement (Exercise 73)

12. identify the dynamic terms *subito piano, subito forte,* and *sforzando* and increase the dynamic variations of vocal production for both speaking and singing (Exercise 74)

13. sing accurately and with agility vocalise of ever-expanding vocal range and articulation, up to and including g^2 (Exercise 75)

14. sing a variety of song literature in the range from a^b to f^2 (tessitura of d^1 to d^2) with accurate pitch.

15. sing a variety of song literature in the range of ab to f^2 with a light, yet more resonant tone quality that is pure upper voice above c^2, pure lower voice below c^1, and a balance of both voices between c^1 and c^2

INSTRUCTIONAL SEQUENCE FOR GRADE 5 (LEVEL 5)

Part I: Respiration   Page

		Page
Exercise 61	Active Posturing	191 (Posture development)
Exercise 62	Tired Dog Pant	207 (Breathing motion)
Exercise 63	Breath Extension	215 (Breath management)

Part II: Phonation

Part III: Resonant Tone Production

Part IV: Diction

Part V: Expression

Instructional Objectives for Grade 6. By the completion of grade 6, students will be able to do the following:

1. align and prepare the physical body as a singing instrument with added emphasis on mental posturing (Exercise 76)
2. demonstrate increased coordination of the breathing motion with a regular, fast-paced inhalation-exhalation cycle (Exercise 77)
3. demonstrate increased breath management through rib (costal) control and slow emission of the air column upon exhalation (Exercise 78)
4. demonstrate active application of breath support and control for speech production in choric speaking, soundscapes, and vocal glissando (Exercises 79, 80, and 81)
5. demonstrate the application of breath management and vocal production techniques to warm-up tunes (Exercise 82)
6. sing diphthong vowel combinations with correct production

and attention to primary and vanishing vowel colors (Exercise 83)

7. sing with increased resonance and support throughout the vocal range (Exercise 84)

8. demonstrate techniques for releasing tension in the tongue and swallowing muscles (Exercise 85)

9. demonstrate an understanding of the International Phonetic Alphabet symbols for vowels and increasing awareness of vowel uniformity (Exercise 86)

10. demonstrate production of aspirates (*h* and voiced *wh*) as a consonant group drill and individually when applied to song (Exercise 87)

11. demonstrate a knowledge of expressive phrasing by singing the musical peaks of song phrases with greater energy (Exercise 88)

12. identify the dynamic term *messa di voce* as an expressive device and employ it in singing to increase the dynamic and expressive quality of the song literature (Exercise 89)

13. sing accurately and with agility a vocalise of ever-expanding melismatic articulation (Exercise 90)

14. sing a variety of song literature in the range from g to g^2 (tessitura of d^1 to d^2) with accurate pitch and a light, yet ever-increasing resonant tone quality that is pure upper voice above c^2, pure lower voice below c^1, and a balance of both voices between c^1 and c^2

15. sing a variety of song literature demonstrating correct vocal technique for respiration, phonation, resonant tone production, diction, and expression

INSTRUCTIONAL SEQUENCE FOR GRADE 6 (LEVEL 6)

Part I: Respiration

		Page
Exercise 76	Mental Posturing	192 (Posture development)
Exercise 77	Hot Dog Pant	207 (Breathing motion)
Exercise 78	Costal Control	216 (Breath management)

Part II: Phonation

Exercise 79	Choric Speech	240 (Lower adjustment)
Exercise 80	Soundscape	245 (Upper adjustment)
Exercise 81	Vocal Glissando	249 (Adjustment coordination)

Part III: Resonant Tone Production

Part IV: Diction

Part V: Expression

SCOPE AND SEQUENCE, GRADES 4–6 OR 7–9

Sequence 2 (when begun in grade 4 or 7)

Instructional Objectives for Grade 4 or 7. By the completion of grades 4 or 7, students will be able to do the following:

1. stretch, prepare, and align the physical body as a singing instrument for both sitting and standing positions (Exercises 1 and 16)
2. demonstrate a deep-breathing motion in which the diaphragm contracts and abdominal muscles relax for inhalation and the diaphragm relaxes and abdominal muscles contract for exhalation (Exercises 2 and 17)
3. apply the breath to vocal production through mild contraction, or lifting, of the abdominal muscles upon exhalation for singing (Exercise 3)
4. control the breath stream as a continuous flow of air from the abdominal region to the vocal cords (Exercise 18)
5. demonstrate production of spoken sound in the three vocal registers: upper, lower, and middle (Exercises 4, 5, and 6)

6. demonstrate proper production of the speaking voice as to breath support and voice placement (Exercises 19, 20, and 21)

7. sustain the voice on single pitches (d^1 to a^1) with proper humming production for a slow count of 4 (quarter note = 60) (Exercise 7)

8. sing in the correct adjustment in the upper register (above c^2) and downward while maintaining a light, staccato production (Exercise 22)

9. correctly form and sing the [u] vowel with slightly flared lips and relaxed jaw on a series of sustained pitches (Exercise 8)

10. sing in tune various tonal patterns using the basic solfège syllables within a suitable range (Exercise 23)

11. sing sustained pitches and short motivic patterns on and around the centers of the three vocal registers: g^1 (middle), c^1 (lower), and c^2 (upper) (Exercise 9)

12. demonstrate the skill of carrying the pure quality of the upper singing voice downward below pitch c^2 to produce a balanced vocal production of upper and lower adjustments between pitches c^1 and c^2 (Exercise 24)

13. demonstrate correct mouth (vertical opening) and jaw (relaxed) positions while singing (Exercises 10 and 25)

14. demonstrate flexibility of the vocal articulators for final consonants and intelligible word pronunciation (Exercises 11 and 26)

15. demonstrate exaggerated production of voiceless plosive consonants (*p, t, k, ch*) and voiced plosive consonants (*b, d, g, j*) as group drills and individually when applied to song texts (Exercises 12 and 27)

16. sing accurately a sustained descending five-note pattern (sol-fa-mi-re-do) and other complete song phrases on one breath (Exercises 13 and 28)

17. identify the six basic dynamic levels and vary the intensity of vocal production for both speaking and singing (Exercise 14)

18. identify the six basic tempo markings and vary the tempo of vocal production for both speaking and singing (Exercise 29)

19. sing accurately and with agility song motives that contain examples of one to four pitches per syllable (Exercises 15 and 30)

20. sing a variety of song literature in the appropriate ranges with a light tone quality that is pure upper voice above c^2, pure lower voice below c^1, and a balance of both voices between c^1 and c^2

INSTRUCTIONAL SEQUENCE FOR GRADE 4 OR 7 (LEVELS 1–2)

Part I: Respiration

		Page
Exercise 1	Muscle Movers	153 (Posture development)
Exercise 2	Natural Breathing	200 (Breathing motion)
Exercise 3	Abdominal Lift	212 (Breath management)
Exercise 16	Body Alignment	180 (Posture development)
Exercise 17	Deep Breathing	202 (Breathing motion)
Exercise 18	Breath Stream	212 (Breath management)

Part II: Phonation

Exercise 4	Animal Farm	235 (Lower adjustment)
Exercise 5	Animal Farm	243 (Upper adjustment)
Exercise 6	Animal Farm	247 (Adjustment coordination)
Exercise 19	Voice Placement	236 (Lower adjustment)
Exercise 20	Marcato Thrust	243 (Upper adjustment)
Exercise 21	Woofers and Tweeters	247 (Adjustment coordination)

Part III: Resonant Tone Production

Exercise 7	Sustained Humming	268 (Vocal resonance)
Exercise 8	The Model Vowel	278 (Uniform vowel colors)
Exercise 9	Pitch Exploration	293 (Vocal coordination)
Exercise 22	Staccato Koo-koo	270 (Vocal resonance)
Exercise 23	Solfège Patterns	285 (Uniform vowel colors)
Exercise 24	Upper to Lower	295 (Vocal coordination)

Part IV: Diction

Exercise 10	Jaw Flex	316 (Vocal-tract freedom)
Exercise 11	Tongue Twisters	320 (Word pronunciation)
Exercise 12	Voiceless Plosives	330 (Consonant articulation)
Exercise 25	Jaw Prop	316 (Vocal-tract freedom)
Exercise 26	Final Consonants	321 (Word pronunciation)
Exercise 27	Voiced Plosives	330 (Consonant articulation)

Instructional Objectives for Grade 5 or 8. By the completion of grade 5 or 8, students will be able to do the following:

1. align and prepare the physical body as a singing instrument according to the seven principles of posture development and facial expression (Exercises 31 and 46)

2. demonstrate the proper breathing motion phases while employing a faster-paced inhalation-exhalation cycle (Exercises 32 and 47)

3. demonstrate increased coordination of breath articulation for greater support and control of vocal production (Exercises 33 and 48)

4. demonstrate proper production of the speaking voice as to breath support and voice projection (Exercises 34, 35, and 36)

5. demonstrate breath-pulsing support for activating vocal production in all three vocal registers (Exercises 49, 50, and 51)

6. demonstrate the skill of correct vocal attack for the beginning of vocal production (Exercise 37)

7. sing the five primary vowel colors with increased resonance using a flared lip position and relaxed jaw (Exercise 38)

8. demonstrate the skill of singing from the lower register to the upper register with accuracy, breath support, and an increasing upper quality of vocal production (Exercises 39 and 54)

9. demonstrate active breath pulsing support for singing production in all three vocal registers (Exercise 52)

10. sing with an increasing legato line (Exercise 53)

11. sing with an open (unconstricted) throat and relaxed and forward tongue (Exercises 40 and 55)

12. demonstrate flexibility of the vocal articulators for intelligible word pronunciation of hissing sibilants (Exercise 41)

13. demonstrate exaggerated production (*f, th*) and nonexaggerated production (*s, sh*) of voiceless sibilants as a group drill and individually when applied to song texts (Exercise 42)

14. demonstrate flexibility of the vocal articulators for correct articulation of the consonant *r* (Exercise 56)
15. demonstrate prolonged production of tuned continuants (*m, n*) and rapid production of tuned continuants (*l, r*) as a group drill and individually when applied to song texts (Exercise 57)
16. sing song phrases either separated with a properly executed catch breath or extended by staggered-breathing techniques (Exercise 43)
17. identify the two basic tempo markings *accelerando* and *ritardando* and vary the tempo of vocal production for both speaking and singing (Exercise 44)
18. sing accurately and with agility arpeggios and a vocalise of ever-expanding range (Exercises 45 and 60)
19. sing songs with increased vocal expression based upon an understanding of word meaning and mood (Exercise 58)
20. identify the two basic dynamic terms *crescendo* and *decrescendo* and increase the dynamic variations of vocal production for both speaking and singing (Exercise 59)
21. sing a variety of song literature while demonstrating correct vocal technique for respiration, phonation, resonant tone production, diction, and expression

INSTRUCTIONAL SEQUENCE FOR GRADE 5 OR 8 (LEVELS 3–4)

Part I: Respiration

		Page
Exercise 31	Posture Practice	183 (Posture development)
Exercise 32	Breath Suspension	202 (Breathing motion)
Exercise 33	Breath Articulation	213 (Breath management)
Exercise 46	Face Lift	191 (Posture development)
Exercise 47	Breath Rhythm	206 (Breathing motion)
Exercise 48	Breath Pulse	215 (Breath management)

Part II: Phonation

Exercise 34	Energized Speech	238 (Lower adjustment)
Exercise 35	Staccato Bump	244 (Upper adjustment)
Exercise 36	Voice Inflectors	248 (Adjustment coordination)
Exercise 49	Lower Wheelie	239 (Lower adjustment)
Exercise 50	Upper Wheelie	244 (Upper adjustment)
Exercise 51	Spiral Wheelie	248 (Adjustment coordination)

Part III: Resonant Tone Production

Part IV: Diction

Part V: Expression

Instructional Objectives for Grade 6 or 9.   By the completion of grade 6 or 9, students will be able to do the following:

1. align and prepare the physical body as a singing instrument with added emphasis on active and mental posturing (Exercises 61 and 76)

2. demonstrate increased coordination of the breathing motion with slow- and fast-paced inhalation-exhalation cycles (Exercises 62 and 76)

3. demonstrate increased breath management through rib (costal) control and slow emission of the air column upon exhalation (Exercises 63 and 78)

4. demonstrate active application of breath support and control for speech production in all three vocal registers (Exercises 64, 65, and 66)

5. demonstrate active application of breath support and control for speech production in choric speaking, soundscapes, and vocal glissando (Exercises 79, 80, and 81)

6. demonstrate the accurate singing of intervals (ascending and descending) from a variety of pitches (Exercise 67)

7. sing the short-vowel colors with relaxed jaw and vertical positioning (Exercise 68)

8. sing throughout the vocal registers with increased resonance and breath support (Exercise 69)

9. demonstrate the application of breath management and vocal production techniques to warm-up tunes (Exercise 82)

10. sing vowel combinations with correct production and attention to primary and vanishing vowel colors (Exercise 83)

11. sing with flexible breath support throughout the vocal range (Exercise 84)

12. demonstrate techniques for releasing muscle tension in the face, tongue, jaw, and swallowing muscles (Exercises 70 and 85)

13. sing the words of songs with greater attention to proper pronunciation and intelligibility (Exercise 71)

14. demonstrate exaggerated production of voiced continuants (*v, z, th, zh*) and aspirates (*h* and voiced *wh*) as consonant group drills and individually when applied to song texts (Exercises 72 and 87)

15. demonstrate an understanding of the International Phonetic Alphabet symbols for vowels and increasing awareness of vowel uniformity (Exercise 86)

16. sing songs with increased expression using expressive movement and phrase-sculpting techniques (Exercises 73 and 88)

17. identify the dynamic terms *subito piano, subito forte,* and *sforzando* and increase the dynamic variations of vocal production for both speaking and singing (Exercise 74)

18. sing accurately and with agility a vocalise of ever-expanding range and increasingly complex articulation (Exercise 75)

19. identify the dynamic term *messa di voce* as an expressive device and employ it in singing to increase the dynamic and expressive quality of the song literature (Exercise 89)

20. sing accurately and with agility a vocalise of ever-expanding melismatic articulation (Exercise 90)

21. sing a variety of song literature while demonstrating correct vocal technique for respiration, phonation, resonant tone production, diction, and expression

INSTRUCTIONAL SEQUENCE FOR GRADE 6 OR 8 (LEVELS 5–6)

Part I: Respiration

		Page
Exercise 61	Active Posturing	191 (Posture development)
Exercise 62	Tired Dog Pant	207 (Breathing motion)
Exercise 63	Breath Extension	215 (Breath management)
Exercise 76	Mental Posturing	192 (Posture development)
Exercise 77	Hot Dog Pant	207 (Breathing motion)
Exercise 78	Costal Control	216 (Breath management)

Part II: Phonation

Exercise 64	Accented Pulse	240 (Lower adjustment)
Exercise 65	Sustained Howl	245 (Upper adjustment)
Exercise 66	Sustained Bleat	249 (Adjustment coordination)
Exercise 79	Choric Speech	240 (Lower adjustment)
Exercise 80	Soundscape	245 (Upper adjustment)
Exercise 81	Vocal Glissando	249 (Adjustment coordination)

Part III: Resonant Tone Production

Exercise 67	Intonation	272 (Vocal resonance)
Exercise 68	Short Vowels	290 (Uniform vowel colors)
Exercise 69	Midvoice Balance	297 (Vocal coordination)
Exercise 82	Warm-up Tunes	274 (Vocal resonance)
Exercise 83	Diphthongs	292 (Uniform vowel colors)
Exercise 84	Ho-ho Choruses	298 (Vocal coordination)

Part IV: Diction

Exercise 70	Chin-facial Massage	319 (Vocal-tract freedom)
Exercise 71	Song Études	322 (Word pronunciation)
Exercise 72	Voiced Continuants	331 (Consonant articulation)
Exercise 85	Tongue Flex	319 (Vocal-tract freedom)
Exercise 86	IPA Studies	324 (Word pronunciation)
Exercise 87	Aspirates	331 (Consonant articulation)

SCOPE AND SEQUENCE, GRADES 9/10–12

Sequence 3 (when begun in grade 9 or 10)

Instructional Objectives for Grade 9 or 10.   By the completion of grade 9 or 10, students will be able to do the following:

1. stretch, prepare, and align the physical body as a singing instrument for both sitting and standing positions according to the seven principles of posture development (Exercises 1, 16, and 31)

2. demonstrate a natural deep-breathing motion for singing in three phases: (1) inhalation, (2) suspension, and (3) exhalation (Exercises 2, 17, and 32)

3. manage the breath for singing by controlling for a continuous flow of air while supporting with a mild contraction, or lifting, of the abdominal muscles upon measured exhalation (Exercises 3, 18, and 33)

4. demonstrate production of spoken sound in the three vocal registers: upper, lower, and middle (Exercises 4, 5, and 6)

5. demonstrate proper production of the speaking voice using breath support and voice placement (Exercises 19, 20, and 21)

6. demonstrate proper production of the speaking voice as to breath support and voice projection (Exercises 34, 35, and 36)

7. sustain the voice on single pitches with proper humming production for a slow count of 4 (quarter note = 60) (Exercise 7)

8. correctly form and sing the primary vowels with slightly flared lips and relaxed jaw on a series of sustained pitches and in solfège patterns (Exercises 8, 23, and 38)

9. sing sustained pitches and short motivic patterns both descend-

ing and ascending throughout the vocal range while maintaining proper vocal quality in each of the registers (Exercises 9, 22, 24, and 39)

10. demonstrate the skill of correct vocal attack for the beginning of vocal production (Exercise 37)

11. demonstrate correct mouth (vertical opening), jaw (relaxed), and throat (open) positions while singing (Exercises 10, 25, and 40)

12. demonstrate flexibility of the vocal articulators for intelligible word pronunciation of tongue twisters, final consonants, and hissing sibilants (Exercises 11, 26, and 41)

13. demonstrate correct production of voiceless plosives (*p, t, k, ch*), voiced plosives (*b, d, g, j*), and voiceless sibilants (*f, s, th, sh*) as group drills and individually when applied to song texts (Exercises 12, 27, and 42)

15. sing phrases on one breath, extended phrases with staggered breathing, and catch breaths between phrases (Exercises 13, 28, and 43)

16. identify the six basic dynamic levels and vary the intensity of vocal production for both speaking and singing (Exercise 14)

17. sing accurately and with agility melodic lines that contain examples of two to four pitches per syllable (Exercises 15 and 30)

18. identify eight basic tempo markings and vary the tempo of vocal production for both speaking and singing (Exercises 29 and 44)

19. sing accurately and with agility arpeggios and a vocalise of ever-expanding range (Exercise 45)

20. sing a variety of song literature with accurate pitch and proper quality for the three vocal registers

INSTRUCTIONAL SEQUENCE FOR GRADE 9 AND 10 (LEVELS 1–3)

Part I: Respiration	**Page**
Exercise 1 Muscle Movers	153 (Posture development)
Exercise 2 Natural Breathing	200 (Breathing motion)
Exercise 3 Abdominal Lift	212 (Breath management)
Exercise 16 Body Alignment	180 (Posture development)
Exercise 17 Deep Breathing	202 (Breathing motion)

Instructional Objectives for Grades 11–12.   By the end of the grade 12, students will be able to do the following:

1. mentally and actively align the physical body as a singing instrument with increased emphasis on facial mobility (Exercises 46, 61, and 76)

2. demonstrate the proper breathing motion phases while employing slow- and fast-paced inhalation-exhalation cycles (Exercises 47, 62, and 77)

3. demonstrate increased coordination of breath management for greater support and control of vocal production (Exercises 48, 63, and 78)

4. demonstrate breath-pulsing support for activating vocal production in all three vocal registers (Exercises 49, 50, and 51)

5. demonstrate active application of breath support and control for speech production in all three vocal registers (Exercises 64, 65, and 66)

6. demonstrate active application of breath support and control for speech production in choric speaking, soundscapes, and vocal glissando (Exercises 79, 80, and 81)

7. demonstrate active breath-pulsing support for singing production in all three vocal registers (Exercise 52)

8. sing with an increasing legato line (Exercise 53)

9. demonstrate the skill of singing from the lower register to the upper register with accuracy, breath support, and an increasingly upper-voice quality of production (Exercise 54)

10. demonstrate the accurate singing of intervals (ascending and descending) from a variety of pitches (Exercise 67)

11. sing the short-vowel colors with relaxed jaw and vertical positioning (Exercise 68)

12. sing throughout the vocal registers with increased resonance and breath support (Exercise 69)

13. demonstrate the application of breath management and vocal production techniques to warm-up tunes (Exercise 82)

14. sing vowel combinations with correct production and attention to primary and vanishing vowel colors (Exercise 83)

15. sing with increased flexibility throughout the vocal range (Exercise 84)

16. demonstrate techniques for releasing tension in the tongue and swallowing muscles (Exercises 55, 70, and 85)

17. demonstrate flexibility of the vocal articulators for correct articulation of the consonant *r* (Exercise 56)

18. demonstrate prolonged production of tuned continuants (*m, n*), rapid production of tuned continuants (*l, r*), and exaggerated production of voiced continuants (*v, z, th, zh*) and aspirates (*h,* voiced *wh*) as group drills and individually when applied to song texts (Exercises 57, 72, and 87)

19. demonstrate an understanding of word pronunciation in song literature through use of the International Phonetic Alphabet (Exercises 71 and 86)

20. sing songs with increased vocal expression based upon an understanding of phrasing, word meaning, and mood (Exercises 58, 73, and 88)

21. identify basic terminology for dynamics and vary the intensity of vocal production for both speaking and singing (Exercises 59, 74, and 89)

22. sing accurately and with agility a vocalise of ever-expanding vocal range and melismatic articulation (Exercises 60, 75, and 90)

23. sing a variety of song literature while demonstrating correct vocal technique for respiration, phonation, resonant tone production, diction, and expression

INSTRUCTIONAL SEQUENCE FOR GRADES 11–12 (LEVELS 4–6)

Part I: Respiration   Page

Exercise 46   Face Lift   191 (Posture development)
Exercise 47   Breath Rhythm   206 (Breathing motion)
Exercise 48   Breath Pulse   215 (Breath management)
Exercise 61   Active Posturing   191 (Posture development)
Exercise 62   Tired Dog Pant   207 (Breathing motion)
Exercise 63   Breath Extension   215 (Breath management)
Exercise 76   Mental Posturing   192 (Posture development)
Exercise 77   Hot Dog Pant   207 (Breathing motion)
Exercise 78   Costal Control   216 (Breath management)

Part II: Phonation

Exercise 49   Lower Wheelie   239 (Lower adjustment)
Exercise 50   Upper Wheelie   244 (Upper adjustment)
Exercise 51   Spiral Wheelie   248 (Adjustment coordination)
Exercise 64   Accented Pulse   240 (Lower adjustment)
Exercise 65   Sustained Howl   245 (Upper adjustment)
Exercise 66   Sustained Bleat   249 (Adjustment coordination)
Exercise 79   Choric Speech   240 (Lower adjustment)
Exercise 80   Soundscape   245 (Upper adjustment)
Exercise 81   Vocal Glissando   249 (Adjustment coordination)

Part III: Resonant Tone Production

Exercise 52   Rolling Pulse   271 (Vocal resonance)
Exercise 53   Legato Movement   290 (Uniform vowel colors)
Exercise 54   Lighten Up   298 (Vocal coordination)
Exercise 67   Intonation   272 (Vocal resonance)
Exercise 68   Short Vowels   290 (Uniform vowel colors)
Exercise 69   Midvoice Balance   299 (Vocal coordination)
Exercise 82   Warm-up Tunes   274 (Vocal resonance)
Exercise 83   Diphthongs   292 (Uniform vowel colors)
Exercise 84   Ho-ho Choruses   298 (Vocal coordination)

Part IV: Diction **Page**

Part V: Expression

EVALUATION

Since singing is a learned behavior, it is possible to evaluate for vocal-technique achievement. This may be done individually (especially at the high school level), in small groups, or in a group setting. The evaluation of students' singing technique should be an ongoing process, whether carried out formally or informally. However, at least two written evaluations should be made each year (at the end of each semester), and they should be shared with students and parents. The results of these evaluations should be a contributing factor in student grading.

The assessment of students' singing technique by the classroom instructor must be, by its very nature, a rather subjective evaluation. Without sophisticated laboratory equipment to measure breathing, pitch accuracy, resonance, and the like, the instructor has to rely on measures that reflect judgment rather than objective quantification. Nevertheless, some type of objectivity can be possible when a structured evaluation form is used in the assessment process.

The following vocal-technique evaluation forms for grades 1–6 and 7–12 may be used for all grade levels as shown, and one form may be used for each student as he or she passes from one grade level to the next. A scale of 1 (lowest) to 5 (highest) is used for each assessment statement, and a corresponding number is placed in each box. The fifteen statements may be summed and the average figured for an overall assessment. Not all areas need to be assessed each evaluation period.

The assessment form for grades 7–12 is especially helpful for private voice study or when making initial vocal evaluations for audition purposes. It is more detailed in its prescriptors.

Vocal Technique Evaluation Form

Grades 1–6

Name_____

Grade: 1st: _____ 2nd: _____ 3rd: _____ 4th: _____
5th: _____ 6th: _____

Evaluation Scale: 1 = minimal or no achievement
2 = below-average achievement
3 = average achievement
4 = above-average achievement
5 = superior achievement

GRADE LEVELS

VOCAL TECHNIQUES	1	1	2	2	3	3	4	4	5	5	6	6
Date of Evaluation:												
1. Posture development												
2. Breathing motion												
3. Breath management												
4. Lower adjustment												
5. Upper adjustment												
6. Adjustment coordination												
7. Vocal resonance												
8. Vowel uniformity												
9. Vocal coordination												
10. Open/relaxed throat												
11. Pronunciation												
12. Consonant production												
13. Phrasing												
14. Dynamic/tempo variation												
15. Agility/range												

Vocal Technique Evaluation Form

Grades 7–12

Name_____

Grade: 7th _____ 8th _____ 9th _____ 10th _____
              11th _____ 12th _____

Evaluation Scale: 1 = minimal or no achievement
                                 2 = below-average achievement
                                 3 = average achievement
                                 4 = above-average achievement
                                 5 = superior achievement

GRADE LEVELS

VOCAL TECHNIQUES	7	7	8	8	9	9	10	10	11	11	12	12
Date of evaluation:												
1. Posture development												
2. Breathing motion												
3. Breath management												
4. Lower adjustment												
5. Upper adjustment												
6. Adjustment coordination												
7. Vocal resonance												
8. Vowel uniformity												
9. Vocal coordination												
10. Open throat												
11. Pronunciation												
12. Consonant production												
13. Phrasing												
14. Dynamic/tempo variation												
15. Agility/range												

Vocal Technique Evaluation Form

Private Study or Audition

Name_____ Date: _____

RESPIRATION

Posture
1. Poor: lack of seven postural elements
2. Below average: stands/sits upright with little vitality
3. Average: awareness demonstrated for correct posture
4. Above average: most postural elements correct
5. Superior: all seven postural elements correct

Breathing Motion
1. Poor: inverted chest breathing
2. Below average: correct inhalation but incorrect exhalation
3. Average: correct motion under conscious control
4. Above average: correct motion with fast, reflexive control
5. Superior: correct motion used habitually in singing

Breath Control
1. Poor: 10"-tone sustained
2. Below average: 15"-tone sustained
3. Average: 20"-tone sustained
4. Above average: 30"-tone sustained
5. Superior: 40"-tone sustained

Breath Support
1. Poor: no use of abdominal musculature
2. Below average: some use of abdominal musculature
3. Average: shows tendency to use abdominal musculature consciously
4. Above average: use of abdominal musculature becoming a habit
5. Superior: habitual use of abdominal musculature

RESONANT TONE PRODUCTION

Laryngeal Position
1. Poor: moves to a high position in all registers
2. Below average: varies in position as to vocal demands
3. Average: remains down in lower register but rises in upper
4. Above average: remains relatively down throughout registers
5. Superior: remains down consistently throughout registers

Vibrato
1. Poor: absent—straight tone
2. Below average: some—very uneven
3. Average: present but uneven
4. Above average: present consistently with slight variation
5. Superior: present consistently with no variation

Clarity
1. Poor: lack of clarity in all registers
2. Below average: some clarity in middle register
3. Average: clarity varies over registers
4. Above average: mostly clear in all registers
5. Superior: very clear in all registers

Pitch
1. Poor: accurate matching below 50 percent
2. Below average: accurate matching of at least 50 percent
3. Average: accurate matching of at least 75 percent
4. Above average: accurate matching of at least 90 percent
5. Superior: accurate matching of at least 99 percent

Registers
1. Poor: use of lower adjustment only
2. Below average: strong lower with weak upper adjustment
3. Average: use of both adjustments with register break between
4. Above average: use of both adjustments with no break between
5. Superior: upper, middle, and lower adjustments equally balanced

Resonance
1. Poor: indistinguishable quality
2. Below average: some distinguishable quality
3. Average: distinguishable quality
4. Above average: quality distinguished by fullness and depth
5. Superior: quality distinguished by fullness, depth, uniformity

Projection
1. Poor: very weak
2. Below average: weak
3. Average: some projection
4. Above average: projects well but lacks ring
5. Superior: projects fully with characteristic ring

DICTION

Flexibility of Articulators (tongue, lips, teeth, jaw)
1. Poor: very rigid muscle interference
2. Below average: much muscle interference
3. Average: some muscle interference

4. Above average: relaxed production free of tension
5. Superior: agile production with distinct articulation

Position of Articulators
1. Poor: grooved tongue, tight jaw, small mouth opening
2. Below average: stiff tongue, tense jaw, small mouth opening
3. Average: relaxed tongue, tense jaw, medium mouth opening
4. Above average: forward tongue, relaxed jaw, medium mouth opening
5. Superior: forward tongue, relaxed jaw, wide mouth opening

Word Intelligibility
1. Poor: garbled
2. Below average: poor vowel formation, lazy consonants
3. Average: some vowel uniformity, slow consonants
4. Above average: vowel uniformity, crisper consonants
5. Superior: vowel uniformity, exaggerated and rapid consonants

EXPRESSION

Phrasing
1. Poor: unable to sustain minimal phrases
2. Below average: sustains short phrases
3. Average: sustains medium phrases
4. Above average: sustains long phrases
5. Superior: sustains extended phrases

Range
1. Poor: less than one octave
2. Below average: one octave
3. Average: one octave and a fifth
4. Above average: two octaves
5. Superior: three octaves

Dynamic Variation
1. Poor: p–p–p; no < >
2. Below average: p–mp–p; minimal < >
3. Average: p–mf–p; average < >
4. Above average: pp–f–pp; above average < >
5. Superior: pp–ff–pp; superior control < >

Agility and Tempo Variation
1. Poor: unable to sing short melismatic phrase at slow tempo
2. Below average: sings short melismatic phrase at slow tempo
3. Average: sings short melismatic phrase at medium tempo
4. Above average: sings medium melismatic phrase at medium tempo
5. Superior: sings long melismatic phrase at fast tempo

Meaning and Mood
1. Poor: expressionless
2. Below average: minimal expression
3. Average: some textual contrast evident
4. Above average: reflects general meaning and mood
5. Superior: reflects accurate meaning and mood

COMMENTS

_____

_____

_____

_____

_____

_____

_____

_____

STUDY AND DISCUSSION QUESTIONS

1. Why is it important that vocal-music teachers be able to articulate clearly a rationale for the inclusion of singing in the music curriculum?
2. What does singing contribute to the (a) education of the student and (b) overall academic program?
3. The study of singing involves learning in what three domains? What types of learning do each of these domains represent?
4. Why should instruction in singing begin early? What are the likely consequences of early education that does not include singing?
5. Discuss the ways in which vocal techniques are to be taught as to (a) the number of techniques to be taught per year in the normal sequence, (b) the two ways the techniques may be used, (c) the need for ample repetition and pacing, and (d) the ideal implementation schedule for introducing the techniques.

6. Describe the vocal-technique experience as to (a) standing versus sitting position, (b) record keeping, (c) two important directives, and (d) the amount of time to be spent on vocal-technique development at the elementary and high school levels.
7. What attitude must the instructor stress from the beginning when teaching vocal skills? Why?
8. What are the five main areas of vocal technique presented in the methods part of this text? Define each of these areas.
9. For each of the five main parts of the methodology, state each of the subareas, and be able to summarize the goal for each.
10. Why should evaluation of vocal technique be a contributing factor to a student's grade in music?

References

LEHMANN, P. R. (1987). *Music in today's schools: Rationale and commentary.* Reston, VA: Music Educators National Conference.

LEONARD, C. (1985). *A realistic rationale for teaching music.* Reston, VA: Music Educators National Conference.

Music Educators National Conference (1986). *The school music program: Description and Standards.* Reston, VA: Music Educators National Conference.

National Endowment for the Arts (1988). *Toward civilization.* Washington, DC: NEA.

PHILLIPS, K. H. (1985). Training the child voice. *Music Educators Journal, 72*(4), 19–22, 57–58.

PHILLIPS, K. H. (1986). Back to basics: Teaching children to sing. *The Choral Journal 27*(3), 34–36.

7

RESPIRATION ℘≶

Goal: The student will develop the skill of habitual, abdicostal (abdominal-diaphragmatic-costal) breathing, through exercises directed to posture development, breathing motion (natural breathing), and breath management (support and control).

Classroom music teachers should be concerned with the act of breathing almost as much as the studio voice teacher, for proper respiration serves as the basis of good singing. In most cases, especially at the elementary and secondary levels, the only training a student may receive in breath management will be from the classroom music teacher. But this important area of vocal development is usually neglected in the training of young singers. This lack of concern stems from the mistaken belief that children will breathe correctly if they are musically "inspired," allowed to breathe naturally, or instructed only in proper posture. Research on children's breathing has shown none of these to be accurate (Phillips, 1985a). In fact, most children will begin to breathe incorrectly for singing as early as the primary years. Chest heaving and collarbone breathing soon become the norm for young singers, habits that are detrimental to good singing and difficult to change once established.

It is the purpose of this chapter to instruct classroom vocal-music teachers and choir directors in a developmental approach to respiration that takes into account the psychomotor process involved in breathing. Teaching proper breathing for singing is not an easy task. It does not just happen, but requires much patience and endurance on the part of both teachers and students. A definite sequence of motor activities must be mastered in order to habituate a correct and lasting breathing response. There are no shortcuts to such mastery, but the rewards gained result in a solid foundation for confident singing.

The exercises in Part I (Respiration) of this method involve no phonation or vocalization. As such, they are developmental, not an end in themselves. Respiration exercises that are not eventually applied to the act of phonation (speaking voice) or singing are worthless. But these exercises cannot be omitted, as they are foundational to the entire sequence. Until a student makes proper "breathing motion" (natural movement of the body wall for regular breathing) habitual, it is unlikely that the proper type of breath will be taken automatically for singing. As the various exercises in Part I are mastered, phonation and resonant tone production will be added in the proper sequence, allowing for the application of one to the other. It is this learning according to a well-defined process of psychomotor activities that makes this developmental sequence different from the typical song approach. As the students progress through each level of the five parts, it will not be necessary to return to all of the exercises in Part I each time the students meet. One or two silent breathing exercises will suffice. Proper application of the breath to the voice is the ultimate objective of all respiration training.

Begin Early

At what age can such respiration training begin? It can start as early as the first grade or at any age thereafter in which improved singing is desired. A long-range study of the child's singing voice in Russia was begun in the 1940s and reported in 1962 by Gembizkaja. Of note in this study is the finding that the lungs of first-grade children are not fully developed and therefore not capable of full, deep breathing. It is stated that deep breathing develops in the child during the second grade, accompanied by a broadening vocal range and greater accuracy of intonation. Phillips (1985b) has also shown that respiration training is appropriate with children as early as grade 2. The present method, however, begins preliminary breathing exercises in the first grade as a means of establishing a natural breathing motion for life, speaking, and singing. Overt management of the breath is delayed until the second grade when the lungs are more developed and better able to be used in the "support" (energizing of the air column) process.

Respiration Training

The hesitancy of music teachers to teach breathing may result from a lack of understanding of the physical aspects of the breathing process.

This is compounded by the lack of agreement found among vocal authorities as to the proper mode of breathing for singing. The author has researched this topic from the viewpoint of successful vocal pedagogues, scientific studies of respiration and its relationship to singing (both with adults and children), and doctoral dissertations on the topic of breathing for singing and instrumental playing. The breathing recommended in this method represents an approach taught by leading vocal instructors and one substantiated by research. Its success has been demonstrated with both children and adolescents. The study of breathing for singing is often a highly subjective one, but all attempts have been made to remain as objective as possible.

It is not necessary for the music instructor to have an in-depth knowledge of all the physiology involved in the respiration act. This information is readily available in such sources as Gray (1977) and Campbell (1958). What must be understood are the three major muscle groups (abdominal, diaphragmatic, and costal) and the ways in which they should function and interact with one another.

Abdominal-Diaphragmatic-Costal Breathing

Teaching children and adolescents to support and control the breath through abdominal-diaphragmatic-costal (abdicostal) interaction is the major goal of respiration training. This training involves three basic areas: posture development, breathing motion (natural breathing), and breath management (support and control). The interaction of these three areas provides the basis for proper vocal production. Without the habituation of properly developed respiration techniques, the student will not have a solid foundation for singing.

The exercises in this method are generally intended for use with students in grades 1–12 (ages seven to eighteen). Where exercises are more appropriate for certain levels than others, they are designated "primary" (grades 1–3), "intermediate" (grades 4–6), or "adolescent" (7–12).

The outline of Part I contains three divisions: posture development, breathing motion, and breath management. Each division comprises six sequential exercises, for a total of eighteen exercises in respiration training. This outline is given for teacher-training purposes only and is not intended as the total sequence for group instruction. To teach respiration apart from the other areas of vocal development (phonation, resonant tone production, diction, and expression) is not the intention of this outline. The purpose here is to give the teacher an overview of the entire development of the respiration process. Only three respiration exercises actually appear in each of the six sequence levels.

PART I. RESPIRATION-TRAINING OUTLINE

Posture Development

1. Muscle Movers
2. Body Alignment
3. Posture Practice
4. Face Lift
5. Active Posturing
6. Mental Posturing

Breathing Motion

1. Natural Breathing
2. Deep Breathing
3. Breath Suspension
4. Breath Rhythm
5. Tired Dog Pant
6. Hot Dog Pant

Breath Management

1. Abdominal Lift
2. Breath Stream
3. Breath Articulation
4. Breath Pulse
5. Breath Extension
6. Costal Control

POSTURE DEVELOPMENT

Correct posture for singing, whether standing or sitting, is the first requirement in the respiration process. Children and adolescents must be trained in the elements of good posture, and this training should begin in the primary grades. The postural habits instilled in children at this early age will endure for the years to follow. Once poor postural habits are permitted to develop, it will take increased effort on the part of the instructor to change the students' manner of sitting and standing for singing. Admonishing children to "sit up" or "stand tall" usually avails little when poor posture has become habitual. Students need to be taught and exercised in the components of posture so as to habituate them to the correct stance. The seven requirements for a good singing posture are as follows:

1. feet on the floor, one foot slightly ahead of the other
2. knees slightly relaxed
3. spine lifted up and out of the hips
4. shoulders slightly back and down
5. sternum up throughout the act of singing
6. head level and held high
7. hands and arms down and back at the sides

For standing posture, the weight of the body should be distributed evenly on both legs toward the balls of the feet. One foot should be slightly ahead of the other to maintain balance, and the legs should be relaxed slightly at the knees (Figure 7–1). For sitting posture, students should sit on the front half of the seats with feet flat on the floor, one foot slightly ahead of the other (Figure 7–2). Where students' feet do not touch the floor, they may sit as far back in the seats as possible (sitting in the angle between the chair seats and backs), while hooking their feet on the front rung of their chair. Care should be taken that the spinal stretch is maintained and that no slumping or swayback positions are permitted. If necessary, primary children may sit on the floor, but should sit up tall for singing.

It is not good to keep a group of students sitting for an entire class period. In some cases, instructors rehearse students in a standing position for the duration of the class. This is not recommended for elementary students. Alternate sitting and standing positions frequently. Standing posture is better for singing and helps to revitalize the body after a time of sitting. Posture exercises should always be practiced in the standing position, except when giving definite instructions for sitting posture.

Exercises for postural development include concentration on the following physical areas: feet and legs/knees, hips and spine, shoulders, sternum and rib cage, neck and head, and arms and hands. Sets of "muscle movers" begin each practice period for two basic reasons: (1) to call attention to the fact that singing is a physical act and requires physical coordination (boys, especially, will be drawn to the physical nature of posture development exercises), and (2) to condition and prepare the body for good singing. Also, physical exercises at the beginning of a music class help to channel unharnessed energy into a positive activity, which will be beneficial to students' singing! Such a routine can function as a cool-down technique. These and other posture exercises are necessary to establish a habitual singing posture that is conducive to good singing.

FIGURE 7–1.   Posture for Standing: (a) Standing Tall, Front View.

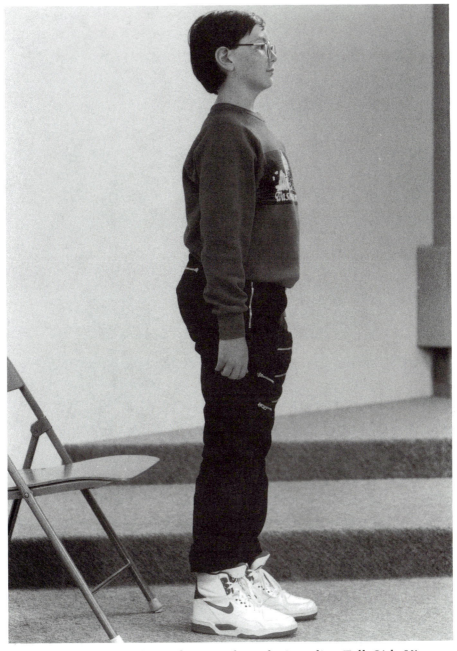

FIGURE 7–1. Posture for Standing: (b) Standing Tall, Side View.

FIGURE 7–2.   Posture for Sitting.

POSTURE-DEVELOPMENT EXERCISES

Goal: The student will develop the technique of proper posture through exercises involving physical conditioning (stretching and limbering), active body positioning, and mental alertness.

Nagging singers about poor posture usually avails little. Students who do not stand or sit properly have not learned to habituate themselves to the proper positions and must be trained to do so. Posture exercises should be practiced regularly until the spoken directives "standing position" or "sitting position" bring about the desired responses. Thereafter, posture exercises should be returned to on occasion for review or when the group begins to show signs of poor posture. "Muscle movers" should always be used at the beginning of each class as a physical warm-up. Direct students to find their own space (spread out) as they enter the room so as not to interfere with one another's movements.

Level 1: Muscle Movers (Exercise 1)

The following stretching and limbering exercises are intended to invigorate and prepare the physical body for the act of singing. Do the four exercises of each set as a sequence. Do not stop after each exercise, but flow from one to the other, giving verbal cues for each successive exercise. Begin each class or rehearsal with a different set, and repeat as needed throughout the session when students show signs of sagging. Move quickly through each sequence of four exercises, which should not take more than a minute from beginning to end. Create your own sets of muscle movers and/or direct students to independently use those stretches that most benefit them. This latter technique is especially good at the high school level. For younger singers, a student director or students at random may be chosen to lead the class in these physical exercises.

Notice that these muscle movers do not involve aerobic-type exercises such as jumping jacks. The emphasis should be on stretching, expanding, and limbering—not on huffing and puffing!

SET 1 (MUSCLE MOVERS)

1. Spinal Stretch (torso expansion). In a standing position, extend the arms straight forward, interlocking the fingers of both hands, palms inward. Turn the hands over to palms outward and gently push forward (bending at the hips), then upward over the head (standing tall), forward again, and then, bending at the hips, down to the floor. Note the stretch in the back as it opens and elongates (Figure 7–3). Warning: All

FIGURE 7–3. Muscle Mover—Spinal Stretch: (a) Outward.

FIGURE 7–3.   Muscle Mover—Spinal Stretch: (*b*) Upward.

FIGURE 7–3. Muscle Mover—Spinal Stretch: (*c*) Downward.

stretches must be done slowly and held slightly in each position before proceeding to the next move. Sudden or jerky movements may tear muscle fiber. Always move slowly and deliberately.

2. Shoulder Roll (shoulder conditioning-limbering). The arms are extended loosely with elbows out to the sides. Roll the shoulders three times with a gentle backward circular motion. Stress a gentle motion to avoid muscle cramps. Repeat with a forward motion. Make big, lazy circles with the arms and shoulders. Be sure that the elbows are away from the body (Figure 7–4). With younger children it is necessary to set the pace of the exercise by saying, "Roll, roll, roll," for each revolution desired. This will prevent a rotation that is too fast and counterproductive. Finish this exercise by gently shaking the arms and hands.

3. Head Roll (neck and head conditioning-limbering). Drop the head gently to the chest. Roll the head in a gentle circular motion from the chest to one side, then to the other side and down again. Repeat in the opposite direction (Figure 7–5). Do not roll the head too far back when passing from side to side. Some doctors advise against this extreme position. With younger children it is best to speak the directives slowly (side, across, side, down, etc.) so as to keep the students from rushing and creating muscle strain.

4. Knee Flex (leg and feet conditioning-limbering). With arms extended forward parallel to the floor and hands hanging limp, gently bounce the body like a rag doll by flexing the knees. Alternate lifting and dropping the arms in a light, floating manner (Figure 7–6). Straighten the legs and lock the knees. Warn students against using this type of standing position. Repeat the knee flex and return to a standing position where the knees and legs are slightly relaxed.

SET 2 (MUSCLE MOVERS)

1. Side Stretch (torso expansion-stretch). Stand with hands on hips and feet apart ("at ease"). Count, "1 stretch, 2 stretch, 3 stretch," up to a count of four. Students stretch each time to alternating sides on "stretch," returning to the upright position on each spoken number (Figure 7–7). Be clear about the direction in which the students are to begin the stretch (left or right), so as to avoid the collision of bodies!

2. Shrug (shoulder conditioning-limbering). Lift the shoulders vertically, and hold taut for a count of two, releasing them on the third count. Do the same with individual shoulders alternating, and repeat with both shoulders (Figure 7–8). Direct students to let the shoulders fall in a relaxed state. Caution against pushing the shoulders down. Do the "wave" by alternating shoulder shrugs quickly, left to right and then right to left.

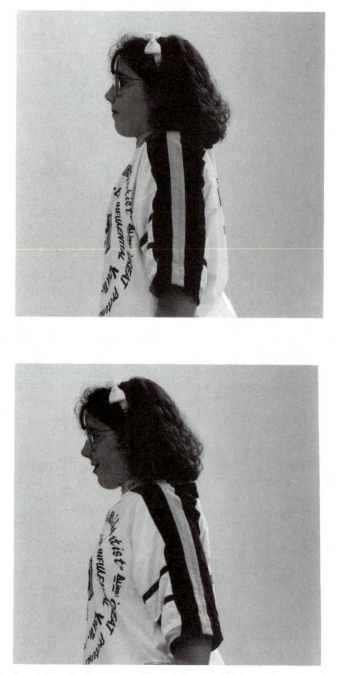

FIGURE 7–4. Muscle Mover—Shoulder Roll: (*a*) Elevate Shoulders, and (*b*) Roll Shoulders Back, Down, and Forward.

FIGURE 7–5. Muscle Mover—Head Roll: (*a*) Drop Head to Chest, (*b*) Roll Head Gently to One Side, and (*c*) Roll Head Gently to Opposite Side.

FIGURE 7–6. Muscle Mover—Knee Flex: (*a*) with Arms Loosely Extended, Flex Knees Easily as a Rag Doll.

FIGURE 7–6. Muscle Mover—Knee Flex: (*b*) Flop Arms while Continuing to Flex Knees.

FIGURE 7–7.   Muscle Mover—Side Stretch: (*a*) Stretch to the Right and Hold.

FIGURE 7–7. Muscle Mover—Side Stretch: *(b)* Stretch to the Left and Hold.

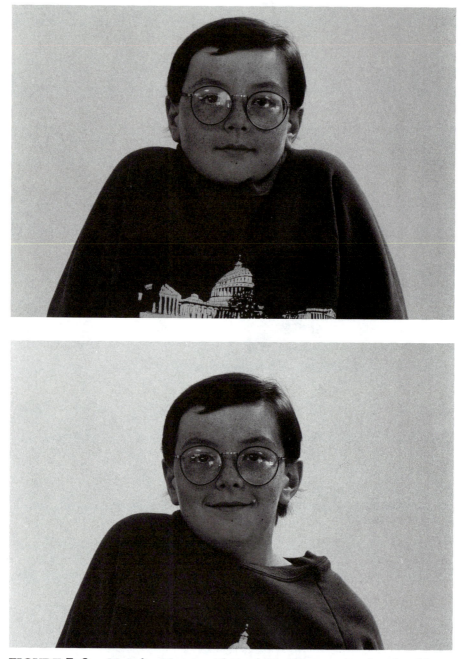

FIGURE 7–8.   Muscle Mover—Shrug: (*a*) Elevate Both Shoulders, Hold, and Drop; (*b*) Elevate Alternate Shoulders, Hold, and Drop.

3. Yes and No (neck and head conditioning-limbering). Move the head slowly up and down (nodding) on the "yes" command, and alternately to the left and right on the "no" command. Direct students to move the head slowly so as to prevent a muscle cramp (Figure 7–9). With younger students it is fun to say, "Yes yes yes no no no," in different tones of voice (approval and disapproval) as the exercise is being done.

4. Toe Jam (leg and feet conditioning-limbering). Direct students to wiggle their toes inside their shoes to stimulate blood flow and to relax their feet and legs. "Give your feet a massage!" This exercise is especially helpful when students must stand for a long time. It can be done during concerts without audience detection. You need but silently mouth "Toe jam" to note the looks of satisfaction on the faces of the singers!

SET 3 (MUSCLE MOVERS)

1. Back Stack (torso expansion-stretch). Stand, bend at the hips and knees in a sagging half-crouch. Extend the arms forward in line with the lower-back level, with one fist vertically over the other (Figure 7–10). Explain that each fist represents a vertebra and that the fists should not actually touch because the vertebrae have thin pads between them. In the crouched position, however, the vertebrae are not separated as much as possible, but are crunched together. As the instructor begins to count slowly, the students stand slowly upright, alternately placing one fist over the other as a visual representation of separating the vertebrae in a tall and upright "back stack." The stacking motion should continue through the neck-head level so as to bring about a stretched condition of the spine from the lower back to the top of the head. Caution against raising the chin. Lift the head from the crown and by stretching the cervical vertebrae upward.

2. Trap Stretch (shoulder conditioning-limbering). Stretch the head alternately to the right and left so as to touch the ear to the shoulder. Do not elevate the shoulders. As you count, "1 stretch, 2 stretch," and so on, move the head to one side on "stretch" (hold) and return to the upright position on each count. Repeat on the opposite side, stretching the trapezius muscles (Figure 7–11).

3. Up Periscope (neck and head conditioning-limbering). The head should be level and drawn upward very slightly from its normal resting position. It should feel as if it sits directly on top of the spinal column, as a periscope is positioned on top of a submarine. Direct students to lower the periscope (neck and head) by pulling the head downward in a cramped manner. Note the tension in this position. Now raise the peri-

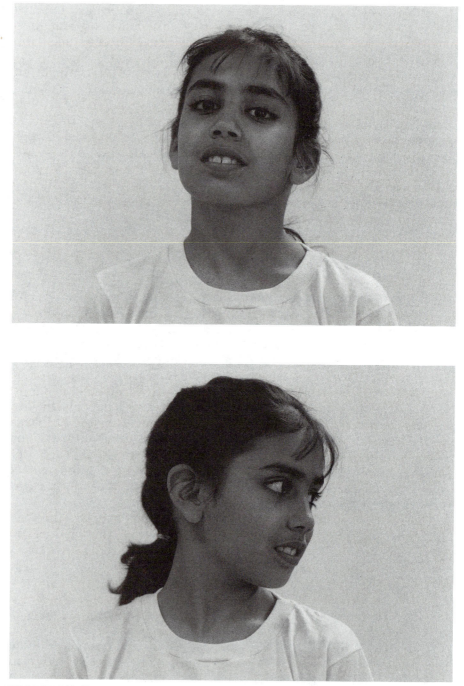

FIGURE 7–9.   Muscle Mover—Yes and No: (*a*) Raise and Lower Head for "Yes"; (*b*) Rotate Head Back and Forth for "No."

FIGURE 7–10. Muscle Mover—Back Stack: (*a*) Crouch and Collapse the Spinal Column.

FIGURE 7–10.   Muscle Mover—Back Stack: (*b*) Vertebrae upon Vertebrae, Straightening Up.

FIGURE 7–10. Muscle Mover—Back Stack: (*c*) Standing Tall with Spinal Stretch.

FIGURE 7–11.   Muscle Mover—Trap Stretch: (*a*) Stretch the Trape-zius Muscles to the Left; (*b*) Stretch the Trapezius Muscles to the Right.

scope by elevating the head upward (not outward). Note the feeling of stretch in the neck. Rotate the head slowly from side to side (looking for enemy submarines) while maintaining the feeling of the raised periscope (Figure 7–12).

4. Heel March (leg and feet conditioning-limbering). Standing in place, march slowly by alternately lifting one heel and then the other (do not lift toes from floor). Relax each knee deeply as the heel is lifted. Keep a bounce or spring in the movement when alternating from heel to heel (Figure 7–13).

SET 4 (MUSCLE MOVERS)

1. Torso Twist (torso expansion-stretch). Stand with fists together (downward) and arms extended parallel to the floor; feet should be in the at-ease position. Rotate the torso to each side alternately four times (Figure 7–14). For maximum benefit, rotate as far as possible in each direction (comfortably), keeping the feet flat on the floor.

2. Shoulder Flex (shoulder conditioning-limbering). Flex the shoulders forward and backward alternately several times (Figure 7–15). As an additional exercise for high school students, direct students to turn sideways in one direction and gently massage the shoulders of the student in front. Alternate with gentle karate-chop motions. Reverse the direction of students so that all benefit from the exercise; otherwise, people at the ends of rows may be excluded.

3. Neck Stretch (neck and head conditioning-limbering). Stretch the neck and chin upward and forward and then downward and backward, noting the tension placed on the muscles of the neck in both of these positions (Figure 7–16). Now relax these muscles and gently change the position of the head by elevating it from the rear while lowering the chin. Rock the head forward and up and then down and back alternately in a gentle manner, coming to rest with a feeling of relaxation in the neck muscles. Follow with the head roll. Warn students against excessive raising or lowering of the head, because not only does this create tension in the neck, which is not conducive to good singing, but it also can change the pitch by placing undue pressure on the larynx.

4. The Lunge (leg and feet conditioning-stretching). Taking one step forward, bend the knee of the forward leg while keeping the rear leg straight. Note the stretch in the rear leg as the forward leg bends. Alternate several times. Keeping hands on hips will aid balance during this exercise (Figure 7–17).

Mix and Match. Combine the twelve exercises in the four sets into new sets. Keep a variety so that the routine will not become boring. Also, as breathing exercises are introduced, combine the breathing

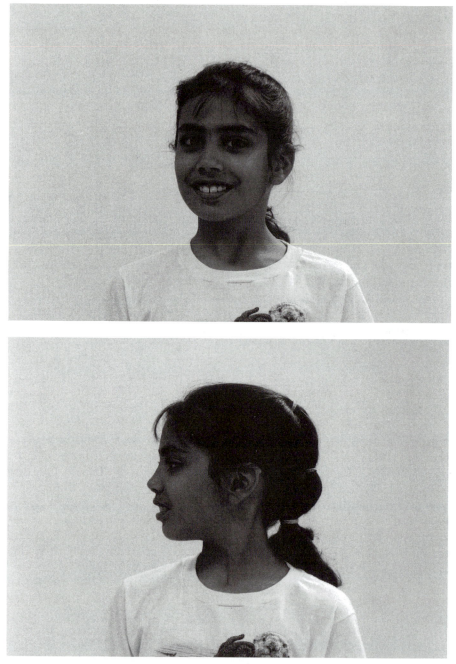

FIGURE 7–12. Muscle Mover—Up Periscope: (*a*) Elevate the Head High from the Crown; (*b*) Look for Enemy Submarines to the Left and Right.

FIGURE 7–13. Muscle Mover—Heel March.

FIGURE 7–14.   Muscle Mover—Torso Twist: (*a*) Fists Pressed Together in Front.

FIGURE 7–14. Muscle Mover—Torso Twist: (*b*) Twist to Alternate Sides and Hold.

FIGURE 7–15. Muscle Mover—Shoulder Flex: (*a*) Flex Shoulders Forward.

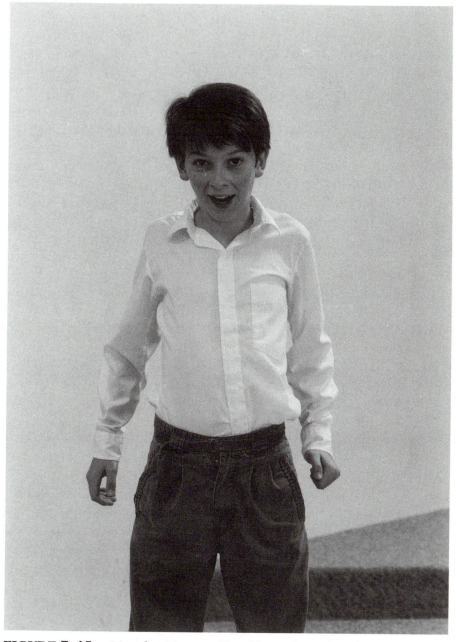

FIGURE 7–15. Muscle Mover—Shoulder Flex: (*b*) Flex Shoulders Back.

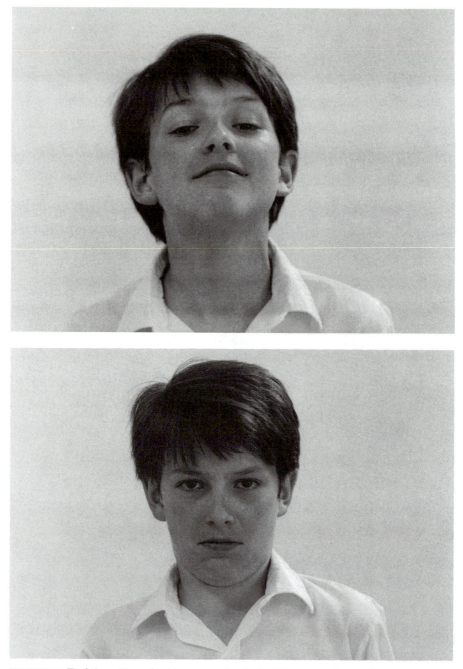

FIGURE 7–16. Muscle Mover—Neck Stretch: (*a*) Stretch Neck Muscles Upward; (*b*) Stretch Neck Muscles Backward.

FIGURE 7–17. Muscle Mover—The Lunge.

exercises with the muscle movers. This will save class time and is a natural extension of respiration development. Posture and breathing are interdependent.

Level 2: Body Alignment (Exercise 16)

The body-alignment exercises concentrate on the characteristics of good singing posture. Explain and provide a model posture for singing, and have the students practice this model posture through exercises directed toward a balanced stance.

Model Posturing (standing and sitting). Explain and model for students the proper posture for singing, both standing and sitting. Use the seven guidelines for model posture presented in the introduction to this chapter under "Posture Development" (see Figures 7–1 and 7–2). While it will take some practice for students to habituate themselves to proper posture, this brief demonstration should serve as a model to which to return regularly for comparison purposes. Draw attention to the career of the professional model and the training necessary to become one. Stress the importance of good posture in the business world. Note also that people are often judged on the basis of posture. Good posture is associated with self-confidence.

Balanced Stance. The following exercises draw the students' attention to the physical balance that is foundational to both athletics and singing. A stance reflecting spinal stretch, elevated sternum, proper head carriage, and weight evenly distributed on the balls of the feet should be stressed. This type of exercise is especially good for primary students who have trouble learning posture from a more direct approach.

1. Diving Position. Imitate the stance of an Olympic diver preparing to dive into a pool. Balance the body weight on an imaginary diving board with legs relaxed, sternum elevated, head erect, and arms extended out horizontal to the floor. Raise the body on the toes, hold, and return to full foot support. Lower arms to sides keeping the sternum high (Figure 7–18). Note the energized feeling of this type of balanced posture, which is necessary for singing.

2. Balance Beam. Imitate the stance of a gymnast on a balance beam that is four inches wide. With spinal stretch and elevated sternum, extend the arms to the sides, placing one foot directly in front of the other (Figure 7–19). Take four steps forward, alternately placing one foot in front of the other. Repeat taking four steps backward, alternately placing one foot behind the other. Do not look down! Note the energized feeling of this type of balanced stance. Maintain this position for singing activities.

Posture Cues. The following cues (gestures) may be used to help

FIGURE 7–18. Posture for Diving Position.

FIGURE 7–19.   Balance-Beam Posture.

students remember proper posture and stand up or sit down together and quietly.

1. Sitting Tall. The teacher's gesture of both hands extended forward with palms up may be used as a visual cue for students to come forward on the front halves of their chairs while seated. Both hands up in the stop position, pushing out to the students, signals sliding back into the chair for an at-rest position. Practice bringing students forward into singing position and backward into an at-rest position with these two visual cues (Figure 7–20).

2. Standing Tall. The "thumbs up" gesture may be used as a visual cue to remind students to stand tall.

3. Sitting to Standing. Cue the students by extending the hands forward, palms up. The students should respond by moving forward in their chairs, placing one foot slightly ahead of the other. Complete the cue by making a full circle with the hands (preparation) and a final upward or standing gesture. The students respond by standing together on the upward lift of your hands. This may be thought of as "ready" (palms out), "get set" (circle of hands), and "stand" (upward lift of hands). Direct the students to elevate the body by pushing with the back foot, coming up onto the forward foot as quietly as possible (Figure 7–21).

4. Standing to Sitting. Cue the students by extending the hands forward, palms downward. Complete the cue by circling the hands upward and then downward, while the students respond by sitting on the downward sweep of the hand. This may be thought of as "ready" (palms out and down), "get set" (upward lift) and "sit" (downward gesture). Direct students to sit first on the front half of the chairs before sliding back into the chairs. This should help keep the noise level down. Practice standing and sitting on cue so as to make as little noise as possible when moving. The shifting of body weight is important to the correct execution of this exercise.

Level 3: Posture Practice (Exercise 31)

This third level of posture development presents a synthesis of the model posture in "The Posture Rap." This "rap" will enable the students to remember the seven characteristics of good singing posture. The elements of posture are then practiced separately through various exercises, as a means of habituating students to proper posture for singing.

The Posture Rap. Direct students to memorize the following rap as a way of learning the seven basic elements of good singing posture. Say the rap together while concentrating on each element for proper execution. The meter is common time. The rhythm should be spoken with syncopation, as is common to all rapping.

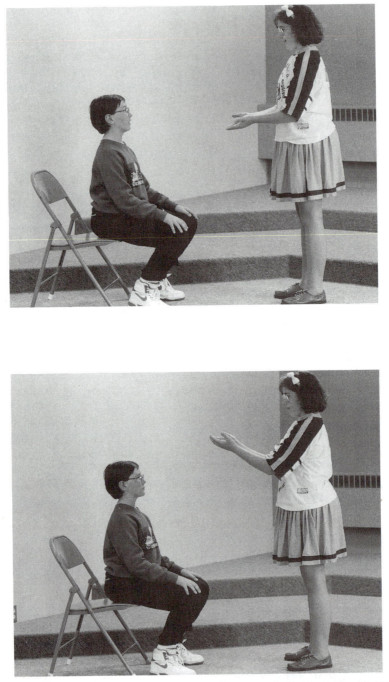

FIGURE 7–20.   Posture Cues: (*a*) Hands Extended, "Get Ready," Move Forward on Chair; (*b*) Hands Up, "Stand."

FIGURE 7–20.　Posture Cues: (*c*) Palms Out "Sit Back."

THE POSTURE RAP

Kenneth Phillips

Feet on the floor, one slightly ahead,
Relax those knees, don't lock them dead!
Hips rolled under, stretch your spine so tall,
Sternum up, don't let it fall!
Shoulders should be back and down,
Head is high, don't wear a frown!
Keep your hands down at your sides,
Let the seamlines be your guide!
This is how you stand to sing,
If you want your voice to ring!

Posture Exercises.　Once "The Posture Rap" is learned, select one of the following exercises each time to conclude the muscle-mover segment of the physical warm-up. These exercises will help to concentrate the practice of the individual posture elements.

1. The Slide. Direct students to slide one foot slightly forward of the other, distributing the weight toward the balls of the feet. Draw the foot back and slide forward again. Repeat several times.

FIGURE 7–21. Sitting to Standing, Push Down on Back Foot while Coming Up on Front Foot.

2. The Knee Lock. Direct students to lock their knees, noting the tension in such a position. Warn students against locking the knees for singing. Relax the knees and alternate locking and relaxing.

3. The Hip Roll. Direct students to place the hands on the hips with thumbs forward on the hipbone. Rotate the hips by relaxing the knees and turning the buttocks under, with the thumbs moving backward and the abdomen flattening. Relax the hips forward and repeat the rotation. Note the lift in the spinal column as the hips are rotated (Figure 7–22).

4. Sternum Stretch. Place the palms of the hands together directly in front of the body with elbows extended to the sides (praying position). Separate the hands by drawing the elbows backward until the open palms are in line with the shoulders. Note the stretch upward and forward of the sternum, as well as the rib-cage extension (Figure 7–23). Combine this movement with a slow sip of air. Lower the hands and arms outward to the sides and down without dropping the sternum. Place lowered hands on the seam line. Drop the sternum and repeat the exercise. Advise students that the sternum is raised before inhalation, maintaining this high position throughout the act of singing for maximum vocal efficiency.

5. Shoulder Rotation. Rotate each shoulder individually upward, backward, and down in one continuous motion. It should feel as if the shoulder is being set into a groove. Let the shoulders drop forward, and repeat the rotation with both shoulders simultaneously (see Figure 7–4). Care must be taken not to assume a rigid, military stance. The shoulders must be relaxed in a downward and backward position (see Figure 7–1).

6. Extended Neck Stretch. Stretch the neck and chin upward and forward, noting the tension placed on the muscles of the neck (see Figure 7–16). Sustain a vocal drone and hear the drop in pitch while the neck is moving upward. Stretching the neck upward will cause the vocal folds to loosen, thus lowering the pitch. Sustain a vocal drone and lower the chin to the chest. Note again that the pitch level is lowered because of interference with the laryngeal mechanism. Remind students to keep the head high and level for singing.

7. Hand Placement. Direct students to touch the seams of their pant legs with the index finger of each hand. Carrying the hands back a little more than usual in this manner will help to keep the shoulders back and down (see Figure 7–1). Keep the hands open and to the sides. Do not permit students to clasp their hands in front of them or behind their backs. This can cause tension in the arms, which is in turn carried to the larynx. Students also may be permitted to practice with their hands on their hips as an alternate way of keeping the arms and hands at their sides. When arms and hands are permitted to hang naturally, they tend to fall forward, rounding the shoulders. Keeping the hands on the seam line will help to keep the shoulders back and down.

FIGURE 7–22. Posture Element—Hip Roll: (*a*) Hands on Hips with Thumbs Forward.

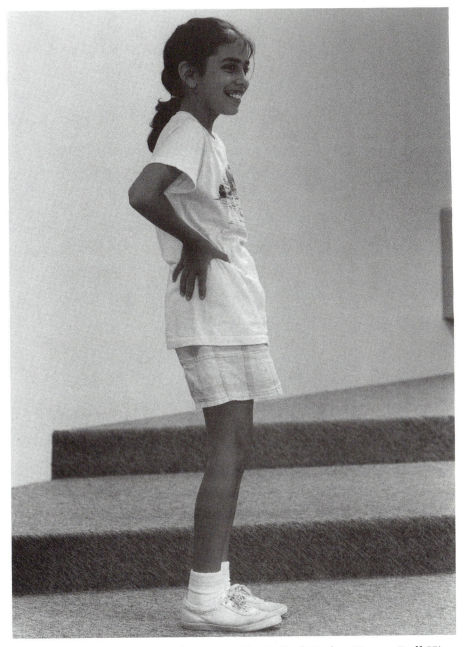

FIGURE 7–22. Posture Element—Hip Roll: (*b*) Relax Knees, Roll Hips Under.

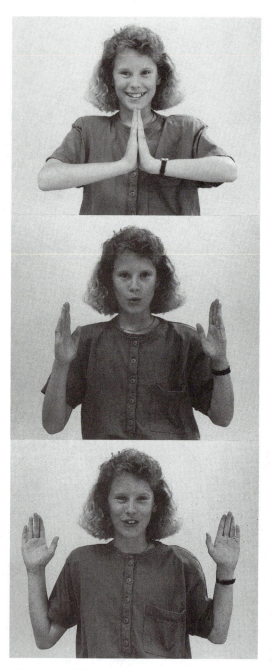

FIGURE 7–23. Posture Element—Sternum Stretch: (*a*) Place Hands Together in Praying Position; (*b*) Draw Hands to the Sides While Inhaling a "Slow Sip"; (*c*) Stop Movement at Sides, Feeling the Sternum Stretch.

Posture Jingle. This little jingle (adapted from Helen Kemp) is a good posture exercise for the primary grades:

Bend in the middle, hang down low,
Wiggle all your muscles loose to and fro,
Stand up tall, stretch your spine to the ceiling,
You should have a lively, kinda [spring on toes] bouncy feeling.
Take a deep breath, all the way around [breathe or slow sip],
But keep your shoulders down, now sing this sound.

Follow this with tonal-pattern echoes or a vocalise.

Level 4: Face Lift (Exercise 46)

This fourth level of posture development concentrates on facial expression. Most students sing with a dead expression. Learning to communicate effectively with facial animation does not come naturally to most people. The following exercises address this problem.

Eyebrow Sit-ups. Direct students to raise and lower their eyebrows alternately. Repeat with mouth open and jaw down, countering the slack jaw movement with elevated cheeks (zygomatic muscles) and eyebrows. Most music can be sung with a lifted face.

Surprise! Direct students to say "Aha!" (as in "Caught you!") with much facial animation (elevation of eyebrows and cheek muscles). Direct students to pretend that they have been splashed in the face with cold water.

Exaggerations. Direct students to (1) silently shout the alphabet, (2) make a "big face" (mouth and eyes wide open) and "little face" (lips pursed and eyebrows furrowed) with exaggerated facial expressions, or (3) mirror your actions. Use the face, hands, and arms. Call for instant response from students.

Level 5: Active Posturing (Exercise 61)

This fifth level of exercises concentrates upon the development of "energized" posture. Active postural response is characterized by a feeling of alertness, buoyancy, and stretch in the physical body. A "leaning-into" the music is called for as the phrase peaks so that the entire body is supporting the musical line. Direct students to sing with the whole body, from the feet upward, rather than from the neck upward. A certain amount of "vertical space" (forward-backward movement) is to be cultivated in this technique, but not a side-to-side movement (or sway). Students should feel free to move the body (leaning forward) in response to the music but not in such a way as to be detracting. A subtle physical movement is the desired response.

The Lean-to.   Standing with one foot ahead of the other, lean slightly forward on the forward-positioned leg, and then slightly backward on the back-positioned leg. Keep the knees flexed. Impress upon the students that this is their space in which they should feel free to move undetected.

Sing the triad pattern 1–3–5–3–1 (do-mi-sol-mi-do) on "ya-ha-ha-ah-ah" (staccato the first pitch and sustain the third and last pitches). Lean into the triad while singing with arms and hands extended palms up and slightly lifted in front of the body (Figure 7–24). Do not relax the forward extension and lift of the arms on the downward side of the arpeggio, but maintain the physical support throughout the exercise. Practice alternately with and without the arm movement, striving to maintain the same lift in the phrase even when the arms are at the sides. Encourage students to employ this leaning technique as the musical line moves to and from the peaks of phrases.

Stepping the Pulse.   To develop an internal buoyancy, direct students to step the pulse of the music in place or while walking. This may be refined further by the snapping of fingers on the offbeats.

Physical Gestures.   Direct students to conduct the music, using free-flowing diagonal curves to equate arm movement with pulse and flow of the music. Long, sweeping curves in front of the body may express phrase direction and extension. Circular motions may express building of the line or buoyancy. Slight upward and downward pulsing of arms and hands expresses the underlying pulse or meteric flow. Adapt various gestures that will help students to externalize the movement of the music.

For choral movement exercises developing other musical concepts, see references at the end of this chapter by Apfelstadt (1985), Gordon (1975), and McCoy (1986).

Level 6: Mental Posturing (Exercise 76)

The final phase of posture development involves the thought processes and how students should think about their physical actions for singing. These techniques are based upon the work of F. Matthius Alexander, a turn-of-the-century Australian actor and singer who kept losing his voice in performance. Alexander discovered that his posture was producing the muscular stress responsible for his voice loss. He then developed a sense of mental control over his bodily movements, and began to correct his posture in such a way as to alleviate his vocal problem. His approach has become known as the Alexander technique and is becoming increasingly popular throughout the world. The three basic Alexander orders are as follows: (1) let the neck be free (allow the tension in the muscles of the neck not to increase); (2) let the head go forward and up (do not allow it to be pulled back or down); and (3) let the torso widen

FIGURE 7–24. Active Posture—The Lean-to.

out and lengthen (do not allow it to be shortened and narrowed by arching the spine).

> These instructions are to be "ordered" or "directed" to the mind, and should be carried out, in Alexander's words, "one after another and all at once." It is important to stress that this single sensory experience, labeled **"primary control,"** does not constitute an act of passive relaxation, but is supposed to be an active process accompanying the execution of any movement [Duarte, 1981, p. 4].

The Alexander technique appears simple; it is not. It takes concentrated study to learn to apply its rudiments. It is not a set of exercises that one masters. In fact, one of the basic premises of the technique is that one does not do anything! It is all in the mental set. "The inception of the movements . . . occurs as a result of the correct mental order" (Alexander, quoted in Duarte, 1981, p. 5). Nevertheless, there are basic principles that will help students become more aware of their bodies and unnecessary tensions. The following exercises are given for the purpose of helping students develop a habitual mental attitude toward correct physical posturing. For those interested in further reading on the Alexander technique, refer to the reference section of this chapter for books by Barker (1978) and Stransky and Stone (1981).

Free Flight.   Lie on the back with eyes closed, legs and arms outstretched, palms up, and fingers relaxed. (If the room does not permit this position, sit comfortably in a chair.) Direct students to breathe deeply with the diaphragm, thinking of the breath as coming in on its own. Use a slow and continuous breathing motion as described in the next part of this chapter. After a short time of relaxed breathing, direct the students to free themselves mentally of bodily tensions by addressing specific body parts, such as "Relax your feet, now your knees, hips, back, shoulders." Speak slowly and allow time between each statement for concentrated relaxation of the entire body. Maintain this relaxed state of free flight for several minutes.

The Squeeze.   Direct students to tense or tighten the body in the following order: feet (curl toes), legs (lock knees), buttocks (squeeze), hands (make fists), arms (pull tightly to sides), shoulders and head (pull down). Hold this squeezed position for a count of five, release, and note the rush of relaxation as the tension is abandoned. Shake the limbs loose. Other variations include pursing the lips for five seconds and relaxing, frowning strongly for five seconds and then relaxing, and clenching the teeth for five seconds, followed by dropping the jaw.

Walking Tall.   Direct students to take a standing position and let the head float upward as the spinal column lengthens and the back widens. The shoulders should be relaxed down and back, and tensions in the arms and hands consciously discarded. Apply the correct breathing motion for slow, measured respiration. Now direct the students to walk in a circle, leading with the toes rather than the heels. Walk lightly with a sense of walking tall. Carry the body high with a mental set of floating. Stop, bend to pick something (imaginary) up without dropping the head or losing the feeling of spinal stretch (bend at the knees). Finally, bow from the hips without dropping the head; let the head move with the torso. Direct students to be kind to their bodies by developing a mental attitude toward posture that will result in less tension and greater freedom.

BREATHING MOTION

Before students can be taught to manage the breath for singing, they first must be instructed in the proper motion of breathing for regular respiration cycles (inhalation-exhalation). At a very early age, children tend to invert the breathing motion; that is, they inhale by lifting the upper chest, with a corresponding lowering of the chest upon exhalation. This type of clavicular breathing is too shallow for singing purposes, but often is used by the athlete or hard-playing child who is out of breath and needs to replenish the air supply quickly. When students are directed to take a big breath, their natural tendency is to lift the shoulders (clavicles) and inhale. For this reason, never instruct students to take a "big" breath; rather, use the terms "full" or "deep" when giving inhalation instruction. The correct breathing motion for singers of all ages is as follows (see Figure 7–25):

Inhalation: The diaphragm descends (contracts) and the lower ribs expand outward, with a corresponding enlargement of the body around the waistline.

Exhalation: The diaphragm ascends (relaxes) and the lower ribs contract inward, with a corresponding contraction of the body around the waistline.

The **lungs** are the primary organs of respiration. The tissue is porous, soft, and spongy. The lungs depend on the surrounding muscles for their expansion and contraction during the breathing cycle. They also assume the shape of their surroundings, which is called the thoracic cavity.

The **rib cage** protects the lungs from puncture. The ribs are attached to the spine, the lower end of which is fused into the pelvis. The ribs extend from the spine in a semicircular shape, and the upper ribs connect with the breastbone, or sternum, via the costal cartilages (Figure 7–26). The rotational axis of the ribs is through both the anterior

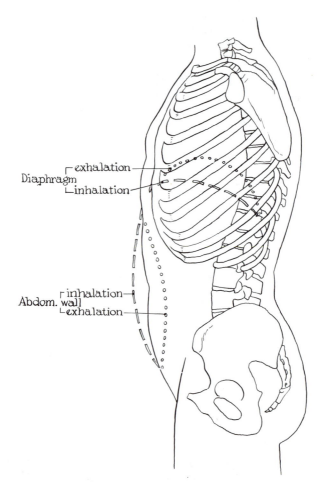

FIGURE 7–25.   Abdomen-Diaphragm
Displacement in Inhalation.

and posterior costovertebral articulations. The ribs move forward and upward with the sternum in a pump-handle fashion. The clavicles, or collarbones, are attached to the top of the sternum and to the shoulder blades on each side of the body (Figure 7–27).

The **diaphragm** is the major muscle of inhalation. It has a double-dome shape (the right dome being slightly higher than the left), and serves to separate the thoracic cavity from the abdominal cavity. It is attached to the lumbar (back) vertebrae, the costal (rib) margin, and the lower end of the sternum. Through the "central tendon" at its top pass the aorta, the vena cava, and the esophagus. It is a thin muscle like a large floor separating the torso into halves (see Figure 7–26).

When the muscle fibers of the diaphragm are contracted, the back

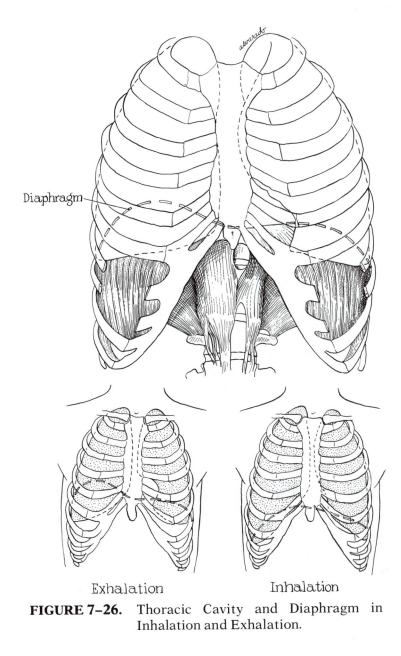

Diaphragm

Exhalation   Inhalation

FIGURE 7–26. Thoracic Cavity and Diaphragm in Inhalation and Exhalation.

part of the central tendon is drawn downward and forward, compressing the abdominal organs. The contraction and lowering of the diaphragm causes air to rush into the lungs. This is the result of the sudden decrease in atmospheric pressure brought about by the increase of room in the pleural (lung) cavity. The compression of the abdominal

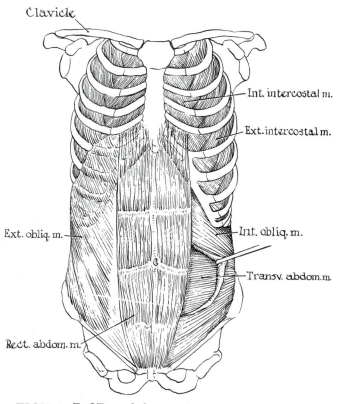

Clavicle

Int. intercostal m.

Ext. intercostal m.

Ext. obliq. m.

Int. obliq. m.

Transv. abdom. m.

Rect. abdom. m.

FIGURE 7–27.   Abdominal Muscles of Support.

area by the lowered diaphragm increases the circumference of the abdominal cavity around the waistline (see Figure 7–25).

The diaphragm is an "unpaired" muscle, that is, it has no paired muscle to reverse its action. Thus, the diaphragm only contracts during inhalation. In the breathing cycle, the diaphragm relaxes upward upon exhalation. The contraction of the abdominal muscles and muscles between the ribs (internal intercostals) exert pressure upon the diaphragm during exhalation. The diaphragm then returns to its dome-shaped position under the lungs, decreasing the size of the thoracic and pleural cavities and thereby causing air to flow out of the lungs.

During quiet breathing, the vertical excursion of the diaphragm amounts to approximately one-half inch. For deep breathing, the descent of the diaphragm is approximately four inches. In some cases, the diaphragm may be the only muscle that is really active during quiet breathing. As the diaphragm is an involuntary muscle (i.e., one that acts on its own) in the breathing process, one should not try to control it consciously once the proper breathing motion has been established.

Breathing from the diaphragm is natural breathing. It is instinctive for babies to breathe this way, and adults most often breathe from the diaphragm when asleep. However, the tendency to breathe from the upper chest without diaphragmatic descent is common from an early age. This may be cultural, as in the case of waistline-consciousness, or instinctive, as when the body calls for a rapid exchange of air during vigorous activity. Nevertheless, this inverted process becomes habitual and is detrimental to good breath management.

External intercostals are muscles that also help in the inhalation phase of the breathing cycle. These muscles are located between the ribs and slant diagonally downward from the backbone (see Figure 7–27). When these contract, they move the rib cage upward, allowing for expansion of the thoracic cavity and inhalation of air. Acting together, the diaphragm and the external intercostals serve as the two basic muscle sources for the inhalation phase of the breathing motion.

Internal intercostals are muscles that lie between the ribs and beneath the external intercostals. These muscles run from the backbone upward and outward in the opposite direction of the external intercostals (see Figure 7–27). The internal intercostals serve to pull the ribs inward and downward, contracting the thoracic cage and producing exhalation.

In the natural breathing cycle, exhalation occurs when the diaphragm and external intercostals relax, the internal intercostals contract, and the abdominal wall contracts from its extended position. Other muscles, including the "transverse thoracis" (connected to the lower portion of the sternum and to the second through sixth ribs) also help in depressing the ribs during exhalation.

There are other, less important muscles involved in the breathing process. Those involved in the inspiratory cycle are the "scaleni," the "serratus," and the "levatores costarum." Expiratory muscles include the "intercostals intimi," the "subcostals," and to some extent the muscles of the back. As the back muscles are primarily postural, they make breathing possible by providing a base for the muscles of respiration. Their direct application to the breathing process remains uncertain (Appelman, 1967).

BREATHING-MOTION EXERCISES

Goal: The student will develop the technique of correct breathing motion (the cycle of inhalation-exhalation) through exercises involving active use of the major breathing muscles.

It is quite common for students to invert the breathing motion for singing, using inward movement of the abdomen and lower ribs upon inhalation, and outward movement of the abdomen and lower ribs upon exhalation. This type of clavicular breathing or chest heaving is wrong, but is the norm for most students. Remember not to tell students to take a "big" breath, as this will invariably call into action a clavicular breath; instead, direct students to take a full or deep breath.

The exercises for breathing motion are designed to help students develop the correct breathing pattern for inhalation and exhalation, without regard to managing the breath. This crucial step must be started before any type of breath control or support can be taught. If a student takes the initial breath incorrectly, he or she will never be able to manage properly the breath for singing.

Correct breathing motion through the fast reflexive "hot dog" pant is the final objective of this set of exercises. Once they master it, students will breathe correctly at the subconscious or habitual level.

Level 1: Natural Breathing (Exercise 2)

Horizontal Breathing. Direct students to lie on their backs with legs drawn up toward the buttocks. Ask them to breathe naturally and quietly; watch for the rise and fall of the abdominal and lower-rib area (belly) of the torso. Direct the students to take a fuller breath than usual; note the greater extension of the abdominal area. Direct the students to place a book or their hands over the abdominal area, lifting the object upon inhalation and allowing it to drop upon exhalation. Set a rhythmic breathing motion by counting 1 for inhalation, and 2 for exhalation. The instructor should then begin a slow rhythmic count, observing students for correct or faulty movement.

Group students as partners, boys with boys and girls with girls. One student should kneel beside the other, observing the breathing motion for correct or faulty movement. Have those students kneeling and observing report any problems with the other students' breathing motion. Alternate students so that each gets to breathe with observation or help from the partner.

Direct the students to stand (be careful that they do not stand too quickly and become dizzy), maintaining the breathing motion. Place the fingertips over the abdominal area. Fingertips should move forward upon inhalation. Upon exhalation, direct the students to apply a gentle inward pressure on the abdominal wall with the fingertips. Blowing out through a small opening in the lips is often helpful in these initial stages at slowing the process, thus allowing for greater concentration. Do not be surprised if students return to inverted breathing when they stand. Horizontal breathing only establishes the concept; it does not guarantee that students will breath properly when they stand.

If it is not possible to practice horizontal breathing in a lying-down position, have the students bend at the waist, hands resting on the knee-caps. Direct the students to inhale and exhale, noting the movement of the waistline. (It is almost impossible to breathe incorrectly in this position, but do *not* tell them!) Direct the students to stand and maintain the proper breathing motion.

Begin checking individual students for proper breathing motion. Some may not be able to breathe correctly, while others will be able to do it with much concentration.

The Balloon. Another way in which to develop the concept of deep breathing is through the use of a balloon. Blow up a balloon, demonstrating to the students the roundness and expansion caused by the filling of air. Then inhale properly, noting the expansion of the midriff area of the torso. Compare this to the balloon. Squeeze off the balloon at the midpoint, allowing for only half the balloon to be usable. Inflating the balloon again, call attention to the fact that only the upper half of the balloon can be filled when the bottom is held closed. Indicate that a balloon only half full is not much good.

Demonstrate that a person can be only half full of air by taking a clavicular breath. Indicate that such a breath is not much good for singing or speaking, whereas a full or deep breath enables greater breath pressure, resulting in better singing. Just as the balloon has more bounce when it is filled with air, so voices have more bounce and carry farther when full of air. An underinflated ball never bounces very well, and an underinflated voice never sings well. Demonstrate taking a deep breath, noting that the expansion of the midriff area is comparable to the balloon when fully inflated. Again demonstrate a shallow upper-chest breath and before exhaling, inhale more by relaxing the abdominal area. Direct the students to note how deeply the air can be inhaled when the abdominal area is relaxed.

Direct elementary students to imagine that they are balloons. Each child should stand with arms raised in a circular fashion with fingers touching (imitating the roundness of a balloon). Tell the students to exhale slowly and shrivel bodily to the floor (bending at the knees) as the air is released. Now direct the students to fill the balloon by slowly sipping in air. Their bodies should rise (stand) and expand (arms extended into a forward circle) as the air is inhaled. Make the point that when the body is full of air its expands, but when air is exhaled, the body contracts, just like the balloon.

The Slow Sip. Once the concept of diaphragmatic breathing is established, deep breathing will be encouraged by using a slow sipping action, as through a straw. The slow or gentle sip is associated with an action (drinking through a straw) that calls for diaphragmatic contraction (descent) upon inhalation. Students rarely lift the chest when using a straw, because it is such a gentle action. The slow sip is an excellent technique for helping students to learn correct breathing motion. It can be further enhanced by using a visual cue for the sipping action during introductions to songs and exercises. The cue is a gesture in which the fingers of both hands begin by touching in front of the body, and draw apart (as in pulling taffy) to signify the deep-breathing action (Figure 7–28). This will visually encourage the students to take a low breath. Also, directing students to breathe deeply "into the hips" is another helpful way to encourage the low breath.

Level 2: Deep Breathing (Exercise 17)

Eagle Spread.   This exercise encourages the natural movement of the body to help develop a proper breathing motion. Direct students to stand and place their hands behind their heads with fingers interlocked. Elbows are extended outward to the sides. Exhale by bending over from the hips while keeping the elbows outward (using "sshh" on exhalation). Say, "Over and exhale" (Figure 7–29). The bending action will help move the air from the body. Now stand slowly and inhale through pursed lips while keeping the elbows back. Say, "Up and inhale." Elbows back will anchor the chest. This time, exhale while standing, elbows back, keeping the chest elevated and the abdominal muscles consciously contracting upward and inward. Say, "Up and exhale." Now inhale while standing with elbows drawn back. Say, "Up and inhale." Encourage students to relax the abdominal muscles for inhalation. Repeat the above sequence. Include this exercise as a part of a muscle-mover sequence in the postural warm-ups. Always begin the breathing motion cycle with exhalation, which is easier to coordinate than inhalation in the beginning stages. Once an incorrect inhalation is taken, the following exhalation also will be wrong.

The Gasp.   Using the same positions as for the "eagle spread," bend at the waist and exhale. Stand without inhaling; this will cause a tightening in the abdominal area. Hold this position for a few moments and then release (relax) the abdominal area with a gasp, as the air rushes into the lower lungs.

Deep Yawn.   Direct students to yawn deeply while maintaining the standing position of the eagle spread (sternum elevated), which will cause a contraction of the diaphragm and a rushing of air into the lower lungs. Repeat several times.

Level 3: Breath Suspension (Exercise 32)

There is a moment between inhalation and exhalation when the breath is in a state of suspension (i.e., not moving in or out). The throat (or vocal folds) should not be closed at this point; rather, the breath should be held by the contracted diaphragm, as in the peak of a yawn.

FIGURE 7–28. Slow-Sip Cue for Deep Breathing: (*a*) Fingers Touching in Front of Abdomen; (*b*) Slow Sip through Puckered Lips while Moving Hands Outward.

FIGURE 7–29. Eagle Spread for Deep Breathing: (*a*) Hands Interlocked behind Head.

FIGURE 7–29. Eagle Spread for Deep Breathing: (*b*) Bend Over from the Waist, Keeping Elbows Extended.

Inhalation.   Direct students to inhale by yawning. Hold the yawn, noting the moment of suspension that occurs between inhalation and exhalation.

Suspension.   Direct students to yawn again, this time lengthening the time between inhalation and exhalation. Caution against closing the throat (vocal folds).

Exhalation.   Direct students to exhale and listen for any glottal clicks, the presence of which would indicate that students were holding the breath with closed vocal folds. Some students will not be able to hold the breath without closing the vocal folds, and glottal clicks will be audible. Continued practice should remedy this. Students must learn that the breath can be held without closing the throat (glottis). In this, people differ from balloons, which only can be kept inflated by closure at the neck. People can be kept inflated without closure at the neck! Practice inhalation, suspension, and exhalation (without yawning), maintaining an even flow of air without glottal clicks.

Discuss the shape of the diaphragm (see Figure 7–26), its function, and how it works to draw air deeply into the lungs. A detailed explanation is not necessary, and what is said will be determined by the age of the students. With younger students, the idea that the diaphragm is like a pizza located in your middle is helpful. The movement of the diaphragm can be visually demonstrated by showing a plain piece of paper curved upward for exhalation and pulled flat upon inhalation. Do note the expansion of the abdominal and lower-rib area caused by the descent (contraction) of the diaphragm. Students should be able to identify the diaphragm as the major muscle of inhalation.

Level 4: Breath Rhythm (Exercise 47)

Locomotion.   This exercise will begin to develop a rhythm in the breathing motion. Direct the students to raise their arms at their sides with bent elbows and hands extended forward as fists in imitation of wheel drivers on the old steam locomotives. Tell them to inhale on the sound *woo* while extending their arms forward in the same direction the abdominal wall should be moving. Direct the students to exhale on the sound *ch* while pulling back their arms in the direction in which the abdominal wall should be moving (inward). Begin the movement slowly, like a train pulling out of a station. Increase the speed gradually, making sure the students stay with the tempo. Warning: Many students will become confused as the speed increases and will revert to inverted breathing. This exercise must be kept under control and not permitted to run away with itself. When done correctly, it will habituate students to the correct breathing motion.

Silent Rowing.   This is an alternative exercise for older students. Direct the students to imitate the rowing of a boat while seated. Arms and hands are placed as if holding oars. Exhale first by contracting the abdominal muscles and simultaneously pulling back on the oars. Inhale by relaxing the abdominal muscles and simultaneously thrusting the oars forward. As with the locomotion, guard against moving too quickly, or students may revert to inverted breathing.

Counting 1–2.   Direct students to inhale by counting 1 on the intake of breath and to exhale by counting 2. The counting is not phonated, but should sound like a forced whisper. Use the *t* of the 2 count for a marked exhalation. Monitor for a falling-away or relaxation of the abdominal muscles on the 1 count.

Level 5: Tired Dog Pant (Exercise 62)

The Tired Dog.   This exercise continues to build the rhythmic cycle for habitual breathing motion. It is a slow and measured panting. Direct the students to pant like a tired dog, through the mouth, to a slow count of 1 (inhale) and 2 (exhale). Breathing should be very quiet, moving only a small amount of air. Monitor breathing motion very carefully for correct movement. Monitor also for dizziness. Direct students to suspend the breath if dizziness occurs, waiting for the head to clear. The count and breathing cycle pace may be increased gradually. Monitor for any reversion to inverted breathing. Monitor also for quiet breathing. The exchange of air should not be audible.

Quiet Breathing.   Direct students to sit or stand quietly and to breathe normally (easily), while monitoring their own breathing. The natural breathing motion should be evident. Students should be made conscious of their own breathing pattern from time to time. If at this stage of development the correct breathing motion is not occurring, individual remediation with help from the instructor is necessary.

Level 6: Hot Dog Pant (Exercise 77)

The Hot Dog.   This is the final objective of the breathing-motion exercises—fast, reflexive panting. When they master it, students will be breathing automatically in the desired mode. Direct the students to increase the pace of the panting very slowly by gradually increasing the counting tempo. Do not rush the tempo. For many students, this is a difficult exercise because they cannot think fast enough to make it work. The goal is for this quick motion to become reflexive, with no conscious thought having to take place. Monitor individuals for inverted breathing. Increase the tempo of the hot dog panting to a fast and light speed. Students are now on their own (without counting). Caution students to move only a small amount of air. The students' ability to do this exercise will greatly determine the degree to which the habit of correct breathing motion is established. When this is accomplished, the breathing-motion cycle will be a reflex, a part of the subconscious pattern for breathing.

Evaluation.   Evaluation of correct breathing motion should be a formal activity at this stage of development. Evaluate students individually for the ability to pant in a slow measured sequence and in a fast reflexive one. Caution students not to move much air and to keep the panting as quiet as possible.

BREATH MANAGEMENT (SUPPORT AND CONTROL)

In quiet breathing, the forces of respiration are rather passive. Breathing for singing requires active forces that must be managed by the student if good singing is to result. The singer must learn to both support and control the process of forced exhalation. The inhalation process also must become more active as the descent of the diaphragm and the expansion of the ribs increase.

Breath support is the power behind the act of singing. Its origin is in the contraction of the abdominal musculature and in the muscles of the lower back. During inhalation the abdominal muscles must relax, allowing the lungs to be infused deeply with air. During exhalation these muscles contract upward and inward against the abdominal viscera and diaphragm, creating internal pressure (energized air column), which should be constant and balanced.

The feeling of expansion around the entire waistline is essential to proper inhalation and will happen only when the muscles of the abdomen and lower back are relaxed. This bulging of the waistline is countered by the already elevated sternum and expanded rib cage. Deep breathing should not result in a greatly distended abdominal region if the thorax is properly elevated prior to inhalation. This is part of assuming the correct posture for singing and gives meaning to the statement that "we expand to breathe; we do not breathe to expand."

The inability to relax the abdominal muscles for inhalation is often a problem in learning to take a deep breath. Tension in this area may limit the descent of the diaphragm, especially among those who are waistline-conscious.

The **abdominal muscles** are the major source of power in breath support, or energized exhalation. There are four muscles that are involved in the process of contracting and pressurizing the contents of the abdominal area, which then exert pressure upon the diaphragm. These muscles are the "rectus abdominis," the "transverse abdominis," the "external oblique," and the "internal oblique" (see Figure 7–27).

Each of the four abdominal muscles functions differently. The outermost layer, the **rectus abdominis,** is primarily a flexor; its fibers run vertically from the rib cage to the pelvic bone. To feel this muscle, lie on the floor, knees bent, feet flat, head raised. Now touch your upper abdomen. That hard layer is the rectus abdominis.

The next layer is the **external oblique,** a broad, thin muscle that originates at the borders of the lower eight ribs and runs obliquely forward and downward. To feel it, place your hands at your waist and bend to the side; you should be able to feel the external oblique tighten up. Running underneath the external oblique is the **internal oblique.** Its fibers start at the hip and run obliquely upward to meet the lower ribs. This muscle is too deep to be easily seen or felt, but its action is apparent when you "suck in" to button a too-tight pair of pants. It is important in the breath-support process.

The fibers of the innermost muscle, the **transverse abdominis,** run across the abdomen from side to side. Although it is also too deep to be easily seen or felt, it is probably the most important of the abdominal muscles in providing the necessary compression and contraction for good breath support. The other three muscles of the abdominal set interact with the transverse abdominis to aid in energizing the breath column.

Breath control is the act that permits the slow emission of the energized air column at the vocal-fold level. The major muscle of control is the diaphragm, which, when relaxed, slowly counteracts the internal pressure created by the contraction of the abdominal muscles. This type of "balanced resistance" between the abdominal muscles and the slowly relaxing diaphragm is helped by the external intercostals, which can continue to hold the ribs out as needed during exhalation. By maintaining a smooth application of the abdominal muscles up and against the diaphragm, a steady stream of pressurized breath will create a constant subglottal pressure against the vocal folds, resulting in a steadiness of pitch.

The amount of air, or "vital capacity," one inhales is not nearly as important as how the air column is supported and controlled in a steady and continuous manner. There is no evidence that lung capacity has a direct relation to singing achievement. It is not how much air one is able to breathe but how one manages (supports and controls) the exhaled breath that is important to good singing.

The process of control and support is aided by the internal intercostals, which can fine-tune breath emission by contracting the lower ribs inward when needed. At the onset of singing, it is recommended that the rib cage be held out to keep from overloading the voice with too much air. As the abdominal muscles contract upward and inward and the diaphragm slowly relaxes, the internal intercostals can contract the lower rib cage as needed. Caution must be taken that the outward hold of the rib cage is not confused with any type of holding out of the diaphragm.

The diaphragm always ascends (although slowly) for singing on exhaled breath. Any attempt to control or hold the diaphragm in a downward position for singing will result only in unwanted muscle tension. What is often believed to be the holding-down of the diaphragm during singing may actually be the flexing of the rectus abdominis. Research has demonstrated that the diaphragm must ascend on phonation and will ascend naturally if allowed to operate involuntarily.

Three general approaches to breath support are known among voice teachers. The first approach states that for proper support and control the singer should bear down or push out in the abdominal area upon exhalation. The second approach states just the opposite; singers should draw in vigorously the abdominal muscles for needed support. The third approach believes that a high and expanded rib cage should be maintained for singing, while the gentle pressure of the contracting abdominal muscles sets up an energized air column for breath management.

Richard Miller, a voice teacher, and Erkki Bianco, a physician, investigated the three known approaches to breath management in a research study presented at the Symposium on the Care and Training of the Professional Voice in 1985. The investigators asked trained singers to sustain single pitches while using each of the three approaches. The movement (relaxation speed and control) of the diaphragm of each subject was monitored through fluoroscopic (X-ray) pictures. The results of the study showed that for the bear-down and draw-in approaches, the diaphragm relaxed and ascended very quickly. For the approach with expanded rib cage and gentle abdominal contraction, the diaphragm was shown to have its slowest rate of relaxation-ascent control.

Based on Miller and Bianco's findings and the author's own experimentation with these various techniques, the approach to support used in the exercises to follow is the one with expanded rib cage and light abdominal contraction. Vigorous pushing or pulling of the abdominal muscles is not recommended. Such activity has been experienced by the author and others as resulting in unwanted physical tensions. The study by Miller and Bianco has demonstrated that such action does not provide for maximum control of the air column for singing. The rate of relaxation of the diaphragm can be controlled, not through the conscious manipulation of the diaphragm, but through an elevated sternum and expansive lower rib line, to which the border of the diaphragm is attached. When greater pressure is needed in the upper vocal range, the lower rib line may contract faster with ensuing relaxation of the diaphragm. When less breath pressure is needed in the lower range, the rib line maintains an outward position, contracting slower for a more gradual relaxation of the diaphragm. The sternum, however, should remain comfortably high. This is known in the international Italianate school as appoggio technique, about which Miller (1986) writes the following practical description:

In "appoggio" technique, the sternum must initially find a moderately high position; this position is then retained throughout the inspiration-expiration cycle. Shoulders are relaxed, but the sternum never slumps. Because the ribs are attached to the sternum, sternal posture in part determines diaphragmatic position. If the sternum lowers, the ribs cannot maintain an expanded position, and the diaphragm must ascend more rapidly. Both the epigastric and umbilical regions should be stabilized so that a feeling of internal-external muscular balance is present. This sensation directly influences the diaphragm [p. 24].

Teaching students to support and control the breath through abdominal-diaphragmatic-costal interaction is the major goal of breath-management training. However, for students habituated to chest breathing, it is best to ignore the rib-cage movement, or "hold," for a period of time until the abdominal-diaphragmatic management is working properly. Calling attention to rib movement may induce a return to chest heaving. Do emphasize an elevated sternum through proper posture before and throughout the act of singing. The lower ribs and intercostals will work together with the diaphragmatic, abdominal, and back muscles to coordinate a natural support-and-control process. Costal control (rib-cage management) can be taught for fine-tuning the breath system after the basics are mastered. It is a technique used by many fine contemporary singers, as noted by Jerome Hines in *Great Singers on Great Singing* (1982).

BREATH-MANAGEMENT
EXERCISES

Goal: The student will develop the technique of breath management through exercises involving the support (energized air column) and control (slow emission of air) of the exhaled air when applied to vocal production.

The following breath-management exercises do not involve phonation or vocalization and like the breathing-motion exercises, are not an end in themselves. The exercises emphasize the role of the abdominal muscles for support and the interaction of the abdominal, diaphragmatic, and costal muscles for control. The importance of breath-management exercises is in applying them to phonation and resonant tone production as the basic gross and fine motor skills are defined and become habitual. Initially, breath-management exercises should be practiced regularly until the student becomes habituated to them. Once these exercises are added to phonation and tone production, they may be deleted from the regular practice session, but should be returned to periodically for reevaluation.

Level 1: Abdominal Lift (Exercise 3)

The following exercise will help sensitize students to the role of the abdominal muscles in the support process and encourage the lifting-up thought for singing.

Isometric Exercise. This exercise is intended to break the habit of students' inhaling when lifting the upper chest with a corresponding drawing-in of the abdomen. Direct the students to contract the abdominal muscles up and in firmly without breathing (between breaths), while they hold in and flatten the belly. Now relax the abdominal muscles forward, and follow with another firm contraction. Repeat the motion without breathing, as in a belly dance. Note that the abdominal muscles can work independently of the breathing motion.

The Lift. Direct the students to contract the abdominal muscles and then exhale quickly. Release and relax the abdominal muscles and allow the air to fall into the lungs automatically. If done correctly, the release of the abdominal contraction will naturally encourage the air to fill the lungs. Some students may continue to inhale when they contract their abdominal muscles. Repeat the isometric exercise above.

The Cycle. Direct students to exhale with an abdominal lift and to inhale by relaxing the abdominal area forward. Repeat a number of times. Use the slow sip or yawn to encourage the correct inhalation phase. This is a gross motor exercise and should be started shortly after the first breathing-motion exercise is introduced.

It is best to begin the breath cycle by exhaling first, as this often will break the habit of improper inhalation movement. Lifting the abdominal muscles upward and inward upon exhalation not only prepares the student for the support process but also encourages the proper breathing motion. Be careful, for some students may lift the abdominal muscles inward, but not exhale! Others may lift them inward and exhale, but upon inhalation they will not release the abdominal contraction, taking breath only in the upper chest! Incorrect muscle habits are often difficult to break.

Level 2: Breath Stream (Exercise 18)

The following are initial exercises for teaching students to lift (support) the air stream up and out of the body from the diaphragm. The exercises also develop a basic idea of controlling the airstream.

The Foul Shot. This exercise imitates a basketball player making a shot from the foul line. Direct students to bounce an imaginary ball and prepare for the shot by holding the ball in position. Inhale while slightly relaxing the legs at the knees. Shoot the ball with an upward thrust of the torso and arm and an audible exhalation. This upward thrust and lifting of the shooting arm will encourage the air to be drawn from the diaphragm. Practice the exercise without flexing the knees, noting how the inner lift is lost. Include this exercise as a part of the muscle-mover routine.

Ball and Pipe. Obtain several ball-and-pipe toys from a commercial toy or variety store. This toy will float a ball at the end of the pipe when the air is blown through the stem. Direct students to keep the ball floating as long as possible on a steady stream of breath. Blowing too hard will cause the ball to be blown out of the bowl, while an even stream of air keeps the ball floating slightly above the bowl.

Pinwheels (based on an idea suggested by Betty Bertaux). Obtain several pinwheel toys from a commercial toy or variety store. This toy has a stick handle and a revolving star, or pinwheel, at the top (Figure 7–30). Demonstrate how a pinwheel spins when the breath is directed gently toward it in a steady stream. Direct students to experiment with the pinwheels to determine how the pinwheels operate. Blowing too hard will stop the pinwheel from turning. Help students find the correct balance and flow of air to keep the pinwheel turning. Question: Where must this steady flow of air come from? Answer: Low in the lungs around the waistline. Time students to see how long they can keep the pinwheel turning on one breath. Students may compete to see who can keep the pinwheel spinning the longest on one breath. Keep the pinwheels in a container where they can be obtained before class. Students who come early to rehearsal may practice at keeping the pinwheels spinning. You will be surprised at how quickly breath control begins to develop.

Level 3: Breath Articulation (Exercise 33)

The following exercises begin with gross motor exercises intended to further strengthen the abdominal muscular response for breath support. The support process is refined through a more even and gentler application of the abdominal musculature upon exhalation of the breath.

Mini-thrust. Direct students to exhale, inhale, and suspend. Exhale, alternating on nonvocal *p* and *f*, for six exaggerated slow puffs. Repeat several times. Watch for the rebound of the abdominal region, which should draw in some air following each thrust. Do not consciously inhale between thrusts, allowing the rebound to do the breathing.

Maxi-thrust. Direct students to exhale, inhale, and suspend. Open the mouth wide and exhale a strong aspirate nonvocal *huh*, exhaling with one swift contraction of the abdominal muscles. As a health precaution, direct students to place a hand about two inches in front of the mouth to divert the flow of breath and germs. Repeat several times. Exhalation should be quiet, with no excessive noise.

Mini-bump. Direct students to exhale, inhale, and suspend. Ex-

FIGURE 7–30. Pinwheels to Develop Breath Control.

hale through pursed lips with five shorts puffs of air. This is done on one breath for all five bumps. Hold up five fingers on one hand like candles and blow out each "candle" on each breath.

Maxi-bump. Direct students to inhale and suspend. Exhale with five short contractions of the abdominal muscles on aspirate nonvocal *huh-huh-huh-huh-huh.* This is done with one breath for all five bumps. To keep students bumping together, the instructor should signal each bump with the fingers and thumb of one hand. From an open hand position, turn down one finger or thumb in time with each bump.

Level 4: Breath Pulse (Exercise 48)

These exercises apply the breath in a continuous stream, as is done in singing. Monitor for correct pulsing of the abdominal area.

Extended Pulse. Direct students to exhale, inhale, and suspend. Exhale on a continuous pulsing of the breath in short connected puffs through pursed lips. Extend the pulsing as long as possible on one breath. These pulses are not as separated as for the mini-bump but should be identifiable (lightly heard) as separate pulses of the breath.

Echo Pulse. (Figure 7–31). Direct students to echo rhythm patterns as given by the instructor (one measure in common time) using the *ch* sound (as in *church*). Extend to two-measure patterns on one breath. Each *ch* should result in a mini-contraction of the abdominal area. Students also may be selected to lead this exercise.

Level 5: Breath Extension (Exercise 63)

These exercises develop and refine the exhalation process needed for breath control (slow emission of the energized air column).

Slow Leak. Direct students to inhale and then exhale on a soft *ss* sound, while the instructor counts 1, 2, 3, and so on. Encourage a soft, slow leaking of air. Most students will spill too much air at first. Generally increase the count from 10 to 30. Have the students begin in a standing position, being seated as they run out of air. Warning: This creates a sense of competition in which younger students vie to remain standing the longest and sometimes cheat (sneak a breath) to do so!

An alternative approach is to direct students to leak only when the instructor's forefinger and thumb are open. Stop the leak (suspend the air) when forefinger and thumb touch, and continue to leak when both are separated. Warning: Watch that students do not stop the air from flowing with the tongue against the teeth.

Lip Trill. Direct students to inhale and suspend. Wet the lips. Exhale, directing a small and steady column of air through the lips so that the lips vibrate in a moderately slow cycle. The lips must be relaxed in

Instructor   Students

1	2	3	4	
ch,	ch,	ch,	ch	echo
ch-ch,	ch-ch,	ch,	ch	echo
ch-ch,	ch,	ch-ch,	ch	echo
ch,	ch-ch,	ch-ch,	ch	echo
ch,	ch,	sssssshhhh,		echo
sssssshhhh,	ch,	ch		echo
ch,	ch-ch,	sssssshhhh,		echo

FIGURE 7–31.   Echo Pulse Patterns.

order for this exercise to be successful. Many students will tend to over-blow at first, losing too much air. For those students who have trouble getting their lips to vibrate or trill, direct them to imitate the sound of a car engine, as in a child's game. Such short bursts of sound through the lips often helps to relax the lips enough to sustain the lip trill. The lip trill can be combined with vocalises as a means of keeping the articulators relaxed during phonation.

The lip trill can cause near hysteria in a class setting! Students who cannot do it initially (and even those who can) often resort to laughing. It is impossible to do this exercise with the mouth open! The exercise is excellent for developing breath control, but should perhaps be practiced at home!

Level 6: Costal Control (Exercise 78)

Costal control makes possible the fine-tuning or control of the breath-management process. By maintaining a hold on rib contraction, it enables the abdominal support muscles to apply just the right amount of pressure without overloading and producing a breathy sound. At no time should the abdominal muscles be held out during the act of exhalation-support. To do so would be to defy the natural relaxation and ascent of the diaphragm upon exhalation. Lower-rib contraction may be needed when the length of a phrase demands this reserve air or when singing pitches in the middle or upper parts of the vocal range. This is an advanced technique and should only be used with students who are advanced in breath-management training. To emphasize it too soon may result in lack of contraction of the abdominal area upon exhalation, which is crucial to proper breath support.

Lower-rib Hold. Direct students to place their hands on the rib cage at the sides and base of ribs (but not on the waist). Inhale, suspend, and exhale with a swift abdominal thrust, but do not allow the ribs to contract. Use only the abdominal muscles upon exhalation. Exhale the remaining air (the reserve) by relaxing the rib cage. Repeat the above and note the expansiveness of the rib cage as air is exhaled from the abdominal contraction. Pant from the diaphragm-abdominal region only, not moving the rib cage. Inhale and maintain rib expansion while exhaling forcefully with a full thrust. Note the intrathoracic pressure and expansiveness of the rib cage. Repeat the slow-leak and lip-trill exercises without relaxing the rib cage. Direct students to sing and sustain a pitch in the lower adjustment (c^1 or c for changed voices). Place the hands on the lower ribs and maintain the "hold" of the lower rib line as long as possible. Sing as if the body is continuing to inhale rather than exhale.

Midrib Hold. The ribs cannot be held out indiscriminately for all pitches of the vocal range. In the singer's lower range, hold on the lower ribs should be the point of concentration. Pitches in the middle range should shift the hold to midrib position.

Direct students to sing and sustain a pitch in the upper middle vocal range (c^2, and c^1 for changed voices). Place the hands at the midrib position and maintain the hold at the midrib line as long as possible. Note that the lower rib line will begin contracting soon after the onset of pitch. This is normal for the extra support needed. However, continue to maintain an elevated sternum position.

Upper-rib Hold. Pitches in the upper vocal range should concentrate on hold across the upper chest-rib line. Holding the lower ribs out for upper-range pitches will negate the action needed by the cooperation of the abdominal muscles and the internal intercostal muscles for sufficient breath support.

Direct students to sing and sustain a pitch in the middle of the upper vocal range (e^2, and e^1 for changed voices). Place the backs of the hands against the upper ribs, under the armpits, and feel the stretch across the upper chest as pitches in the upper range are sung. The lower ribs and midribs will contract and coordinate with the abdominal lift for the extra support needed for upper-voice production. Sternum position remains high.

Practice singing pitches in the various parts of the range with the differing holds in this exercise. A feeling of expansiveness is generated at the rib line, not from the abdominal wall. This holding-out of the rib cage is transferred from the lower ribs to the upper ribs as the pitch ascends from the lower vocal range to the upper vocal range. It is especially important in the lower range not to overtax the breathing apparatus by allowing the lower ribs to contract. Expansion of the upper ribs (elevated sternum) on higher-range pitches takes the pressure off of the larynx and permits greater freedom in the support process.

STUDY AND DISCUSSION QUESTIONS

1. Why should elementary and secondary music teachers be concerned with teaching students to breathe properly?
2. What has breath research shown in regard to young singers, and at what age has breath instruction traditionally been started?
3. What is the goal of respiration training, and what constitutes the three basic areas of instruction?
4. What are the seven basic requirements for good singing posture? Why do so many students demonstrate poor posture for singing?
5. What are "muscle movers," and why are they an important part of the vocal exercise program?
6. Describe the movement of the torso for a correct breathing motion during inhalation and exhalation.
7. What is the major muscle of inhalation for singing? Describe its action for both inhalation and exhalation and its effect on the thoracic cavity, lungs, and air.
8. What is the movement of the abdominal wall during proper inhalation and exhalation for singing?
9. Should the diaphragm be consciously controlled during singing? Why or why not?
10. Describe the "inverted" breath common to young singers. Why do young people develop this style of breathing?
11. Describe the action of both the internal intercostals and external intercostals in breathing.
12. What are the two parts of breath management? How does each function to "manage" the breath?
13. State the four abdominal muscles, from outermost to innermost.
14. Where does the power or support for singing come from, and what is the major muscle of control?
15. What are the secondary muscles that help breath support and control?
16. Describe "balanced resistance" in breath management.
17. Which is more important—the amount of air or how it is managed?
18. Why should the outward hold of the lower rib line not be used when singing in the upper vocal range?

19. What are the zygomatic muscles, and how should they be used for singing?
20. What is the Alexander technique?

References

APFELSTADT, H. (1985). Choral music in motion: The use of movement in the choral rehearsal. *Choral Journal 25*, 37–39.

APPELMAN, R. D. (1967). *The science of vocal pedagogy: Theory and application.* Bloomington: Indiana University Press.

BARKER, S. (1978). *The revolutionary way to use your body for total energy.* New York: Bantam.

CAMPBELL, E. J. M. (1958). *The respiratory muscles and the mechanics of breathing.* Chicago: Year Book Medical Publishers.

DUARTE, F. (1981). The principles of the Alexander Technique applied to singing: The significance of the "preparatory set." *Journal of Research in Singing 5*(1), 3–21.

GEMBIZKAJA, E. (1962). Systematic development of the child's singing voice in Russia. *International Music Educator, 5,* 146–148.

GORDON, L. W. (1975). Body movement exercises in the choral training program. *The Choral Journal, 15*(7), 12–13.

GRAY, H. (1977). *Anatomy, descriptive and surgical.* T. P. Pick & R. Howden (Eds.). New York: Crown.

HINES, J. (1982). *Great singers on great singing.* Garden City, NY: Doubleday.

MCCOY, C. W. (1986). The effects of movement as a rehearsal technique on performance and attitude of high school choral ensemble members. (Doctoral dissertation, The University of Iowa). *Dissertation Abstracts International, 47/08A,* 2940.

MILLER, R. (1986). *The structure of singing: System and art in vocal technique.* New York: Schirmer Books.

MILLER, R., & BIANCO, E. (1985). Diaphragmatic action in three approaches to breath management in singing. In V. Lawrence (Ed.), *Transcripts of the fourteenth symposium: Care of the professional voice, vol. II, pedagogy* (pp. 357–360). New York: The Voice Foundation.

PHILLIPS, K. H. (1985a). Respiration for singing: Torso movement and related research. *Journal of Research in Singing, 9*(1), 1–10.

PHILLIPS, K. H. (1985b). The effects of group breath control training on selected vocal measures related to the singing ability of elementary students. *Journal of Research in Music Education, 33*(3), 179–191.

STRANSKY, J., & STONE, R. B. (1981). *Joy in the life of your body.* New York: Beaufort.

8

PHONATION ❧

Goal: The student will develop for speaking (as an aid to singing) the skill of habitual clear phonation, through the application of abdicostal respiration to laryngeal function.

A. Oren Gould (1968) conducted an extensive study on children's singing and found that attention to the speaking voice is a vital link in the development of children's singing voices. Poor speech habits often result in poor singing habits, and medical authorities are reporting numerous cases of vocal nodules in children as a result of improper use of the speaking voice.

While good speech habits were once emphasized in school classrooms, a lack of this emphasis today has all but destroyed this vital link to singing; little attention is given either to the quality or projection of the voice. The use of amplification has made the necessity of voice culture obsolete. Nevertheless, a clear, supported speaking voice is foundational to good singing, and students should be monitored constantly for the quality and projection of their speech. Students who have breathy or husky speaking voices most often have trouble producing a clear singing tone. Speaking too low (the macho image) is another common problem that will inhibit the development of the singing voice. Speech habits often become singing habits!

Preparing the Way

The cultivation of speech not only lays the foundation for good vocal production but also may eventually reduce the reluctance of some students to sing. Speaking is a common experience, while singing can be very intimidating. Children make all sorts of noises and sound imitations with their voices, and the inclusion of such exercises in this method is fundamental to the development of good speaking and singing. In classes where resistance to singing is great (e.g., in junior high and middle school general music courses), the instructor may wish to dwell upon the speech activities in this method until the students have a fundamental concept of a properly supported and placed speaking voice. Oral and interpretive readings, poetry, and dramatic scenes can all be used to help in the development of proper vocal production. Each student should understand that his or her voice is unique and tells a great deal about a person. In hiring, an employer often will form an opinion about a prospective employee by his or her speech. Someone who speaks with confidence, has good speech habits, and articulates clearly will make a better impression than someone who speaks in a weak or indistinct manner.

Direct students to listen to motion-picture actors and actresses, noting how actors use their voices to depict the various parts they are playing. The development of the speaking voice is very important in the acting profession, as well as in singing. Call upon the hidden desires of the students to be movie stars in motivating them to develop their speaking voices. You might also ask, "In what other professions is the speaking voice important?" (Answer: teaching, law, sales, etc.)

The inclusion of speech activities in the music class may appear to duplicate what is done in the speech class. This has not been the author's observation. It seems that the activities of speech classes center on the mechanics of speech writing (the demonstration speech, the informative speech, etc.), and little, if anything, is done to improve the actual speaking quality or projection of the voice. Sound amplification provides for most public speaking to be done via microphone, and at the elementary or secondary levels little emphasis seems to be placed on the development of good speech habits. The speech, rather than the speaker, too often receives the main emphasis. Thus, music teachers with the knowledge of proper voice production can fill this educational gap by developing the speaking voice on the way to developing the singing voice.

Phonation

The act of phonation centers in the human larynx, or organ of voice. This wondrously built part of the human anatomy sits on top of the trachea (windpipe), and serves not only as a source of sound vibration but also as a passageway for respiration. Its lining is extremely sensitive, as experienced by anyone who has ever ingested food or liquid into its chamber. The coughing spasms that ensue clear the area of foreign matter, sending it away from, and thereby protecting, the delicate area in which sound vibrations are produced—the vocal folds.

The human larynx can move up and down for various purposes. Clearing the throat or swallowing will cause the larynx to rise, while yawning will cause the larynx to lower. Care must be taken that the larynx not be permitted to rise during phonation or singing and that it not be depressed lower than an otherwise normal position. A high laryngeal position is common among pop and young singers, who by straining and poor breath management elevate the larynx unconsciously. A raised larynx can be injurious to the vocal folds and restricts the pharynx, thus diminishing vocal quality and quantity. A depressed larynx produces a throaty sound and tends to blur diction. The larynx should maintain its normal at-rest position for both speaking and singing.

The human vocal folds, which lie within the larynx, are small in size when compared to the rest of the body, yet are capable of producing a tremendous amount of sound. These "sound generators" are fascinating organs, but as yet are not understood completely as to property or action. However, it is known that the vocal folds, as they alternately close and open from breath pressure, generate energy in the form of complex sound waves. These sound waves travel through the air and are perceived as sounds with the quality of pitch.

Any given pitch represents the rate of vibration of the sound source, expressed as a number of cycles per second (cps) or hertz (Hz), each cycle being composed of a compression half (pressure released through folds) and a rarefaction half (pressure stopped by closed vocal folds). The vocal folds are capable of vibrating at very fast cycles (e.g., pitch a[1] equals 440 Hz) and of changing their shape quickly so as to make possible rapid pitch variation. In addition to the fundamental pitch (that which is perceived or heard), the vocal folds also produce a series of "overtones," or higher-frequency pitches that add resonance to the voice. (The concept of resonance is discussed in Chapter 9.) These overtones are the fundamental frequency multiplied by 2, 3, 4, 5, and so on, which produces a harmonic series of octave, fifth, fourth, major third, and so on. Overtones progressively decrease in energy as they rise. It is the fundamental that generates the most energy and is heard as the pitch.

Vocal Registers

As noted in Chapter 3, Manuel García, the nineteenth-century voice teacher and one of the first vocal scientists (as inventor of the laryngoscope), was the first to describe the basic actions of the vocal folds, noting that the folds vibrate on their thin inner edges (producing an upper voice) or across their full width (producing a lower voice). More recent research in this area (Reckford, quoted in Hines, 1982) has shown that these two registers can be used separately or in combination, producing a third, overlapping register. The approach to phonation presented here is based upon this three-register theory (upper, middle, and lower). While some voice teachers hold to the two-register approach, and some hold to every pitch being in its own register, scientific evidence points to the physical reality of three vocal registers. Appelman (1967), Klein (1972), and Vennard (1967) all endorsed the three-register concept. The present author refers to these three registers as the lower adjustment, the middle adjustment, and the upper adjustment.

The three registers of the voice are apparent even in the child's voice. The upper adjustment corresponds to the upper singsong, or head, voice. It is light, clear, and whistlelike in quality. The lower adjustment corresponds to the lower, or speaking, voice, which develops in strength and depth as children grow older. The middle voice is a combination of the upper and lower adjustments and is most readily apparent when children are playing vocal games involving the imitation of sirens or vocal glissandi.

It was once taught (and some vocal instructors maintain this notion) that children should never sing in the lower adjustment. Francis Howard (1895), a child-voice specialist at the turn of the twentieth century, was influential in propagating this belief. Howard believed that children should sing only in the upper adjustment, because the lower-adjustment tone in the child's voice was harsh and unmusical. He did admit, however, that proper lower-adjustment singing for children was possible, but very difficult to produce. Therefore, the lower adjustment was best ignored in the child's voice. Unfortunately, this practice led to rather weak, anemic singing in the middle voice (c^1 to c^2), where the tone must be kept light in order to keep the lower voice from emerging. The American Academy of Teachers of Singing took a firm stand against this approach (Roe, 1983, p. 66), but its practice held on for many years as a result of the English choirboy model.

One aspect of Howard's teaching that remains credible is the belief in systematic training of the child's voice. He, along with others of his day, knew the necessity of teaching children to sing. It is most probable that the vocal training that children received in the first decades of the twentieth century enabled them to sing the higher ranges of songs in the songbooks then published. The present trend to lower song ranges in established song series seems to indicate that children are not being taught to sing in the upper voice.

Most children speak in the lower adjustment and carry this production over into their singing. While a well-defined and natural lower speaking voice should be encouraged (but not artificially forced low), singing in a pure lower adjustment should not be encouraged above middle C, as the tone will be harsh. Primary children should be encouraged to sing only in a middle voice that combines both upper and lower adjustments (see Chapter 3). This will produce a robust sound. Caution against loud, boisterous singing, which would result in a pure lower (chest) sound that tends to be strident.

The pure lower adjustment can produce a beautiful tone in the intermediate child's and adolescent's voices when produced for pitches from middle C and lower. It also can add a beautiful color to the voice when used properly in combination with the upper adjustment between middle C and one octave above. Children who sing only in the upper adjustment between middle C and c^2 (English choirboy model) lose vocal quality and vitality as they sing in the range from g^1 down to middle C. Children who sing only in the lower adjustment (popular-song style) tend to belt and strain. Care must be taken that children at any age do not carry the pure lower voice above middle C, as this will produce a harsh, strident (pop) sound.

The cultivation of the lower voice, however, should not be omitted from voice study, as a properly produced lower adjustment sound (unforced) is basic to the speaking voice and proper phonation. It is the voice with which children are initially the most comfortable. Betty Atterbury (1984) recommends that young children be encouraged to explore this voice in their singing, as they are more likely to match pitch in the lower adjustment in a limited range. However, as soon as possible, children should be encouraged to find their upper voices and move to a more balanced type of singing by blending the upper and lower adjustments between c^1 and c^2. Using the two adjustments separately and in combination is the core of this method. It is for this reason that the phonation exercises in Part II employ the lower and upper voices separately and in combination. This same approach is carried into Part III, on resonant tone production.

Adolescents with changing and changed voices are encouraged to exercise both lower and upper adjustments separately and together. Boys do not lose the capacity to sing in the upper adjustment during the voice change. This has been documented by Frederick Swanson (1977) in his extensive research on the boy's changing voice. Boys may lose the ability to sing a full upper-adjustment range (c^2 to c^3), but they are able to continue to sing in the upper voice between c^1 and c^2 (or even e^2). Members of the Royal School of Church Music traditionally keep boys singing only in the upper voice throughout the voice change. Unfortunately, they do not develop the lower voice concurrently, which results in the infamous voice break when boys try to adjust to the new growth of their vocal folds. John Dawson (1902) warned against boys singing only in the upper voice during puberty. However, it is necessary to continue the exercise of the upper voice during and after puberty, for as Sally Herman (1988) has noted, it is the "key" to the successful coordination of the head voice in the adult male (changed voice).

Men do not sing in the pure upper voice typically (the exception being countertenors and today's rock singers), but combine the upper voice with the lower voice to produce the passagio, or head-voice range from middle C to one octave above. Phonation exercises in the pure upper adjustment help adolescent boys find and strengthen the singing range between middle C and c^2. Phonation exercises in the pure lower adjustment help them establish and strengthen their emerging lower speaking voices.

The distinction between what is called "pure upper voice" (adjustment) and what is termed "falsetto" should here again be reviewed. These terms (defined in Chapter 3) are not synonymous. Reid (1985) characterizes the falsetto voice as one that is thin in quality and incapable of crescendo. The lack of resonance in the falsetto voice keeps it from being considered a part of the "legitimate" voice, although men and women may sing in a falsetto voice and not know it. The falsetto voice lacks resonance (like the sound of a trumpet mouthpiece blown without a trumpet), a condition that seems to arise when the pitch produced by the vocal folds does not match the proper resonator in the vocal tract. Improper positioning of the larynx (too high) appears to be the cause of this condition (Klein and Schjeide, 1972). However, the pure upper voice is one that is full and vibrant; it is most often associated with the pitches from c^2 to c^3. This is commonly known as the upper soprano range, and changed male voices are capable of producing vibrant pitches at least at the lower end of this octave.

The singing voice in this method is approached through the registers of the speaking voice. While it is common to speak only in the lower adjustment (today even among women), the upper and middle adjustments are exercised and discovered through speechlike activities. A more modulated and focused speaking voice will aid in developing a properly produced singing voice and will promote vocal health in general.

LARYNGEAL PHYSIOLOGY

The teacher of singing should have at least a rudimentary knowledge of the basic sound producing actions of the larynx. The various cartilages, ligaments, and muscles of the larynx are numerous and complicated in their relationship to one another. Only those parts of the laryngeal mechanism that are essential to the understanding of proper sound production are given here.

The Cartilages

The **thyroid cartilage** is the largest cartilage of the larynx, which by its shape and size protects the other parts of the larynx from all but the most damaging blows (Figure 8–1). It comprises two plates, or laminae,

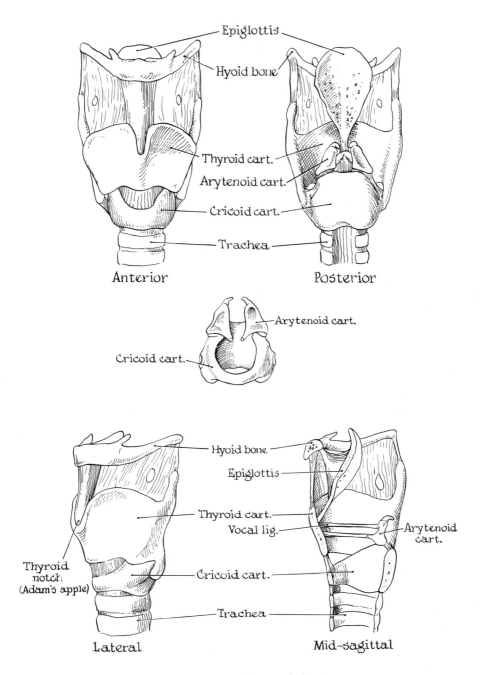

Epiglottis

Hyoid bone

Thyroid cart.

Arytenoid cart.

Cricoid cart.

Trachea

Anterior

Posterior

Arytenoid cart.

Cricoid cart.

Hyoid bone

Epiglottis

Thyroid cart.

Vocal lig.

Arytenoid cart.

Thyroid notch (Adam's apple)

Cricoid cart.

Trachea

Lateral

Mid-sagittal

FIGURE 8–1. Cartilages of the Larynx.

joined at the front to form the thyroid notch, or Adam's apple. The plates surround the larynx laterally, and each is joined to the cricoid cartilage by a downward projection known as the inferior cornu. This serves as a hinge permitting the thyroid and cricoid cartilages a certain degree of articulation while attached to one another.

The **cricoid cartilage** is surrounded anteriorly by the thyroid cartilage and forms a ring that sits on top of the trachea, to which it is attached. The cricoid cartilage is wider and taller posteriorly, giving the appearance of a signet ring.

The **arytenoid cartilages** are pyramidal in shape and are located posteriorly on top of the cricoid cartilage. These two cartilages can rotate and slide from side to side or forward and backward on the cricoid. To the base of the these cartilages are attached the posterior ends of the vocal folds.

The **epiglottis** is the cartilage that closes off the larynx during swallowing. Its shape resembles the tongue of a shoe, and it is attached at its lower end to the inside of the thyroid cartilage (just below the thyroid notch) and at its upper end by a ligament to the hyoid bone.

The Hyoid Bone

The **hyoid bone** is the only bone of the laryngeal structure and serves as the upper end of the larynx. It is attached to the thyroid cartilage by the thyrohyoid membrane (Figure 8–1) and to the superior cornu of the thyroid cartilage. The hyoid bone is unique in that it is not attached to another bone of the skeletal system. It, along with numerous muscles, serves as a positioning regulator of the larynx, allowing the larynx to move upward and downward to accommodate yawning, swallowing, clearing the throat, and the like.

The Intrinsic Muscles of the Larynx

The **cricothyroid muscles** (vertical and oblique) are attached to the anterior base of the cricoid cartilage and extend upward to the lower border of the thyroid cartilage. The cricothyroid muscles are primary pitch-control muscles, lengthening and tensing the vocal folds for higher pitches (Figure 8–2). When the cricothyroid muscles contract, the front of the cricoid cartilage rises and the rear portion tilts backward. As the arytenoid cartilages (to which the vocal folds are attached posteriorly) sit on top of the cricoid, they also move backward, causing the vocal folds to lengthen, become thinner, and increase in tension (Figure 8–3). This action causes pitch to rise.

The **thyroarytenoid muscles** lie within the vocal folds. They are attached (as part of the vocal folds) anteriorly at the base of the thyroid notch and posteriorly to the arytenoid cartilages. When they contract,

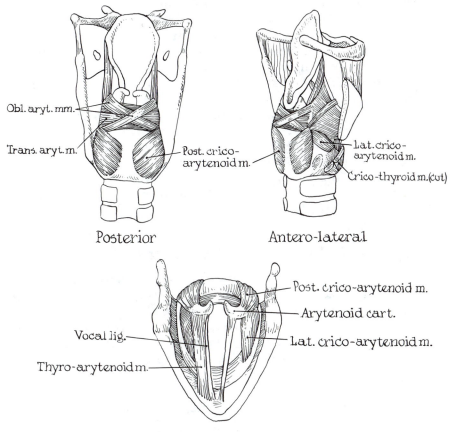

Obl. aryt. mm.

Trans. aryt. m.

Post. crico-arytenoid m.

Lat. crico-arytenoid m.

Crico-thyroid m.(cut)

Posterior

Antero-lateral

Post. crico-arytenoid m.

Arytenoid cart.

Lat. crico-arytenoid m.

Vocal lig.

Thyro-arytenoid m.

FIGURE 8–2. Intrinsic Muscles of the Larynx.

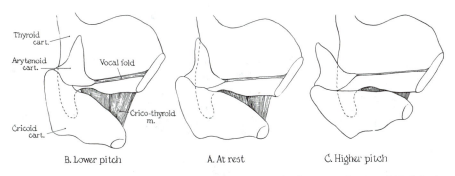

Thyroid cart.

Arytenoid cart.

Vocal fold

Crico-thyroid m.

Cricoid cart.

B. Lower pitch

A. At rest

C. Higher pitch

FIGURE 8–3. Movement of the Cricoid Cartilage and Vocal Folds in Response to Contraction of the Cricothyroid Muscles.

they cause the vocal folds to shorten and thicken, thus lowering pitch. This reverses the action of the cricothyroid muscles.

The **lateral cricoarytenoid muscles** are attached from the cricoid arch and extend laterally, attaching to the arytenoid cartilages. Contraction of these muscles helps bring the vocal folds together (adduction).

The **interarytenoid muscles** (transverse and oblique) attach to the arytenoid cartilages and, upon contraction, draw the vocal folds together (Figure 8–2). They are aided in this process by the cricothyroid muscle (lateral portion) and lateral cricoarytenoid muscles.

The **posterior cricoarytenoid muscles** are attached at the back of the cricoid cartilage and extend upward to the arytenoid cartilages. Contraction of these muscles moves the vocal folds apart (abduction) for normal respiration. In this position, the opening between the two vocal folds is called the "glottis."

The Extrinsic Muscles of the Larynx

Infrahyoid Muscles (strap muscles).   The **sternohyoid muscles** attach to the sternum and to the hyoid bone (Figure 8–4). Contraction of these muscles helps to lower the hyoid bone and loosens all the laryngeal tissue because it shortens the distance between the sternum and the hyoid bone.

The **sternothyroid muscles** attach to the sternum and to the thyroid cartilage. Contraction of these muscles helps to lower the thyroid cartilage of the larynx.

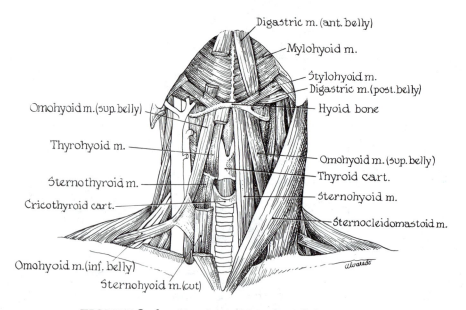

FIGURE 8–4.   Extrinsic Muscles of the Larynx.

The **omohyoid muscles** attach to the hyoid bone and to the shoulder blades. Contraction of these muscles helps to lower the hyoid bone and the larynx.

The **thyrohyoid muscles** attach to the thyroid cartilage and to the hyoid bone. Contraction of these muscles raises the thyroid cartilage and lowers the hyoid bone, as in swallowing.

Suprahyoid Muscles (above the larynx). The **digastric muscles** are situated in the sides of the lower jaw, attaching the jaw to the hyoid bone.

The **stylohyoid muscles** are situated in the sides of the neck, attaching to the styloid process and to the hyoid bone.

The **mylohyoid muscles** are triangular and form a muscular floor for the cavity of the mouth. They attach to the front line of the jaw (symphysis) and to the hyoid bone.

The **geniohyoid muscles** lie just above the mylohyoid muscles in the jaw and attach to the front line of the jaw and to the hyoid bone.

All of the above suprahyoid muscles raise the hyoid bone for swallowing and should not be employed for singing in this manner. When the hyoid bone is fixed by its depressors and those of the larynx, the suprahyoid muscles depress the lower jaw. Trying to swallow with the mouth open is difficult because the functions of the above muscles become confused!

The Open Throat

Children and adolescents must be taught to maintain an open throat for speaking and singing. The throat becomes constricted and tone quality suffers when the swallowing muscles are engaged for phonation as a means of compensating for inadequate breath management. A rigid or trembling tongue, tight jaw, and elevated larynx signal a constricted throat.

In addition to the swallowing muscles listed earlier, there are three large muscles that form the wall of the pharynx (throat). These are called the **upper,** or **superior, constrictor;** the **middle constrictor;** and the **lower,** or **inferior, constrictor** (Figure 8–5). Their function in swallowing is to make the throat as small as possible, squeezing the bolus (the food to be swallowed) into the esophagus (the tube that extends to the stomach). They should not be employed for singing, and beginners must consciously relax them (see Part IV [diction-training outline], Vocal-Tract Freedom, for specific exercises).

The Vocal Folds

The two vocal folds (or cords) are the source of vibrations for vocal sound (Figure 8–6). They are pyramidal in shape, quite small, and capa-

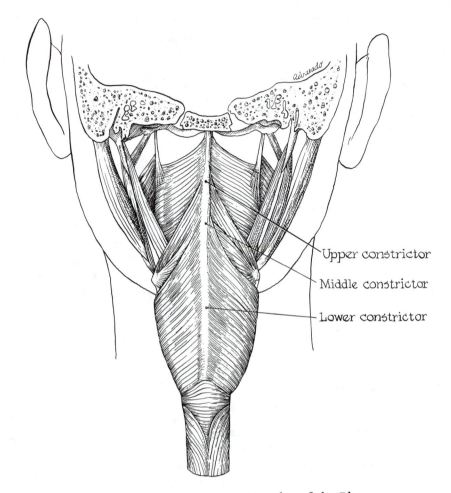

FIGURE 8–5.   Constrictor Muscles of the Pharynx.

ble of rapid changes of thickness, length, and tension. When the vocal folds are brought together for phonation, the pressure of the expired air forces the folds apart; almost immediately the mechanical properties of the folds and the air passing between the folds draws the folds together (the Bernoulli effect), while other mechanical properties and the non-uniform contact of the vocal folds produce a pressure differential that in turn forces the vocal folds apart again, creating oscillations. When the inner portions of the vocal folds vibrate, the upper voice is produced. As the folds shorten, the vibrations spread laterally to include more of the fold, and the pitch is lowered. When the full width of the vocal folds is set into vibration, the lower-adjustment, or chest, voice is produced.

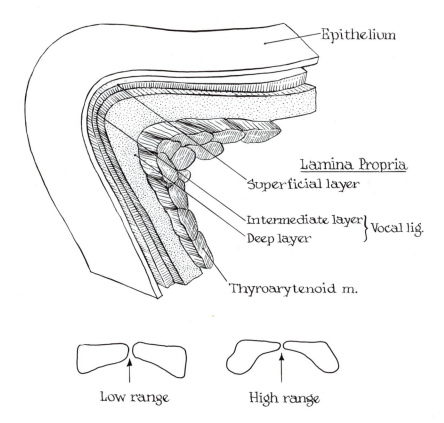

FIGURE 8–6. The Vocal Folds.

The opening between the vocal folds when they are at rest for quiet breathing is the glottis. Bringing the vocal folds together at the beginning of phonation is called "stroke of the glottis," while locking the folds together before producing a sound with a force of air is called "shock of the glottis." The latter is not a desirable technique, although it is characteristic of the German school of singing.

The **epithelium** is the outermost layer of the vocal folds. It is a very thin mucous membrane covering.

The **lamina propria** is below the epithelium and is divided into the superficial, intermediate, and deep layers. It is made up chiefly of elastic fibers. The intermediate-to-deep layer is also known as the "vocal ligament," where the strongest vibrations occur in the vibratory cycle of the vocal folds.

The **thyroarytenoid muscle** is the deepest layer of the vocal fold. It is often described as being in two parts: the **thyrovocalis,** or thinner portion, and the **thyromuscularis,** or thicker portion. The thyroarytenoid muscle is dense with nerve fibers. Tension of the thyroarytenoid muscle alone shortens the vocal folds and lowers pitch.

The **vocal ligament** is a band of elastic fibers (mostly the intermediate layer of the lamina propria) that runs the length of the inner portion of each vocal fold. This is the place within the vocal folds where the strongest vibrations occur.

The **ventricular bands,** or "false vocal folds," lie above the true vocal folds and attach to the inside of the thyroid cartilage anteriorly and the arytenoid cartilages posteriorly. These folds contain only a few muscle fibers and should not contract during phonation. Their purpose is to protect the true folds from foreign matter (phlegm) and to close for heavy lifting or exertion.

PHONATION TRAINING

The outline of phonation training contains three major divisions: lower adjustment, upper adjustment, and adjustment coordination. Each division comprises six sequential exercises, for a total of eighteen exercises in phonation training. This outline is given for teacher-training purposes only and is not intended as the total sequence for group instruction. These phonation exercises are built upon training in respiration and serve as a basis for the development of singing tone in Part III.

PART II. PHONATION-TRAINING OUTLINE

Lower Adjustment

1. Animal Farm
2. Voice Placement
3. Energized Voice
4. Lower Wheelie
5. Accented Pulse
6. Choric Speech

Upper Adjustment

1. Animal Farm
2. Marcato Thrust

3. Staccato Bump
4. Upper Wheelie
5. Sustained Howl
6. Soundscape

Adjustment Coordination

1. Animal Farm
2. Woofers and Tweeters
3. Voice Inflectors
4. Spiral Wheelie
5. Sustained Bleat
6. Vocal Glissando

LOWER ADJUSTMENT

Goal: The student will develop the technique of lower-adjustment voice production through exercises involving vocal clarity, placement, and projection.

Some students speak with a harsh, guttural quality of the voice. Others speak with a puny, whispery quality. Many do not have a well-defined lower-adjustment voice. Care must be taken not to force the lower voice but to develop it with care. Young children often develop vocal nodules or polyps because of vocal abuse mostly associated with playground activities. The vocal abuse caused by cheerleading is well known. The well-produced lower adjustment has a center to its pitch, resonates in the mask, is free of breathiness (excluding adolescent voices), and can be heard distinctly in the normal classroom without forcing or shouting. The following exercises are used to help students discover and develop their proper speaking voices as a means of developing their proper singing voices.

Level 1: Animal Farm (Exercise 4)

Vocal Imitations (elementary grades only). Direct students to explore the sounds of animals with lower-adjustment voices. With elementary children it can be made into a game. "Who can make the sound of an animal with a low voice?" (Dog, "Woof"; tiger, "Roarrrr"; bear, "Grrrrrr"; cow, "Mooooo"; etc.) Follow this with sequence exercises 5 and 6 (Animal Farm in upper and middle voices).

The Cow. Direct students to imitate the sound of a cow, and listen for a clean, easy buzzing sound that rises in pitch as it is sustained. Check students individually; many will at first produce a rather indistinct, whispery sound. They will improve when given a good vocal model by others and the instructor. Be sure that your model is not pitched too low, as students will artificially lower their voices and produce an unacceptable vocal quality. Begin the imitation in the midrange of the speaking (lower) adjustment, sliding to the upper end of the lower adjustment. There will be a slight falling-off of pitch at the end of the imitation as the support relaxes; this is to be expected and reflects reality.

Adolescents need not play the game, but should imitate the sound of the cow by mooing with firm application of the support (abdominal lift) muscles. Repeated group imitation will avail little; check students individually. Listen for the clean glottal closure with vocal buzz (without breathiness) and ease of production. Stress the necessity of a well-modulated sound that is vibrant and energized by the breath. It can be explained to adolescents that the speaking voice is produced by the full vibration of the vocal folds (lower adjustment).

Big Dog.   Direct students to "woof" like a big dog. Do not use *arf*, as this sound is throaty. Woofing, when done correctly, activates the abdominal-lift and the support musculature. As for the cow, do not permit phonation that is too low. Listen for clear phonation and a well-supported sound. Limit group response, and monitor frequently for individual production.

Level 2: Voice Placement (Exercise 19)

Children and adolescents often speak too low, which reflects a cultural bias for a macho or sexy sound. In extreme cases, the vocal folds may relax so much that they "bow," creating severe vocal problems such as nodules. There is a natural pitch level for each voice that is conducive to vocal health. The voice-placement exercise will help students to find this natural pitch level for speaking.

Voice quality also is affected by tonal focus. Students need to be taught to project the voice from the "mask," a physiological area that includes the bridge and sides of the nose down to, and around, the lips (Figure 8–7). This point of focus may be thought of as the broad end of a megaphone, which begins at the narrow, laryngeal level and passes through the pharyngeal and oral resonators or vocal tract. Forward placement in the mask avoids a throaty sound and gives a ringing, resonant quality to the voice. The nationally acclaimed speech therapist Morton Cooper, in his book *Change Your Voice, Change Your Life*, notes:

> By producing sound through the mask (as opposed to the lower throat or the nose alone), the voice opens up, becomes flexible, and is filled with expression and warmth. It has carrying power and range. Speaking through

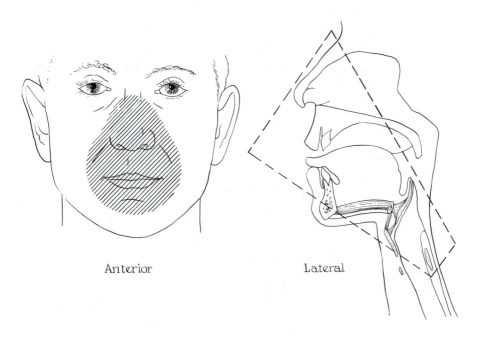

Anterior   Lateral

FIGURE 8–7.   Focus in the Mask.

the mask gives the voice oral-nasal resonance, which creates tone focus, which, in turn, gives the sound aesthetic appeal. It is correct tone focus that gives properly used voices a hypnotic effect [1984, p. 15].

Cooper also notes that "breath support for speech should be centered at the level of the diaphragm. . . . Upper-chest breathing . . . is incorrect and detrimental because of the tension it creates around the throat area" (p. 20).

Focus in the Mask. Direct the students to make the sound *hmmmmmm* with the mouth shut and the teeth clenched. Note the vibrations in the nose exclusively. Now repeat the sound with the teeth apart as far as possible without parting the lips. Note the vibrations are deep in the throat, which will produce too dark a sound. Repeat the *hmmmmmm* with the lips still together but teeth slightly parted. Note that the vibrations cause the lips to tingle and that they center in the oral-nasal area (across the hard palate), but also somewhat in the lower pharynx (throat). This balance of resonance (two-thirds oral-nasal and one-third lower pharyngeal) is the desired resonance for the mask, or tonal, focus of the voice. Make the *hmmmmmm* again with the articulators in this latter position and open to a spoken *ah* sound. Direct students to maintain the feeling of the *ah* on the lips as the sound is projected forward across the hard palate. Listen to, and monitor, individual production of this sound.

Natural Speaking Pitch.   Keeping the lips touching but teeth slightly parted, make the sound *umm-hmmmm* (as in "OK") using a rising inflection of the voice. Repeat several times. The pitch of the inflection should be the natural or correct speaking pitch. This must be a natural response, and not contrived. Students must not try to match the model of the instructor. Younger students will have difficulty hearing their own voices in a group setting. Go quickly through the class and have each student do the exercise individually or have students put their fingers in their ears.

Repeat the *umm-hmmmmm* and each time follow it with a vowel sound (e.g., *umm-hmmmm-ah*, *umm-hmmmm-oh*, *umm-hmmmm-ay*, etc.). Stress the need to speak the vowel on the upper-pitch level of the *hmmmm*. Monitor students individually for natural pitch production and resonance in the mask.

Abdominal Pulse.   Another means of checking for natural pitch production is to pulse the abdominal region manually while sustaining a *hmmmmmmm*. Direct students to place the tips of the first two fingers on the abdominal region just below the sternum (Figure 8–8). While sustaining the *hmmmmm* sound in the lower adjustment, rapidly press and release the abdominal musculature to create a pulsing sound. This additional support will help free the voice to find its natural speaking pitch. Repeat the pressing action while changing from the *hmmm* to the vowel *o*. As students progress in lower-adjustment development, this exercise will prove excellent for awakening the lower voice at the beginning of class.

Student voice placement cannot be corrected easily in a group setting. Once students who may have voice-placement problems are identified, the exercise should be used with those students individually. The instructor must determine aurally the best sound for each voice.

Level 3: Energized Voice (Exercise 34)

The following exercises are all overt means by which to "energize" the speaking voice through application of the energized air column (abdominal support) to phonation.

The Giant.   Imitate the sound of the "Jack and the Beanstalk" giant's voice in the lower adjustment, using "Fee, fi, fo, fum, I smell the blood of an Englishman!" Exaggerate the *f* at the beginning of each syllable so as to encourage the contraction of the abdominal muscles for good support. Randomly test individuals for a clearly projected sound. Little can be determined in these exercises via group participation.

The Sea Captain.   Say *yo-ho* with a mini-thrust on the *YO* and a full thrust on the *ho*. Use much exaggeration on the aspirate *h*. Say *land-ho* with an even application of abdominal support. Encourage hesitant students to project the voice across the room by cupping the hands around the mouth like a megaphone while calling.

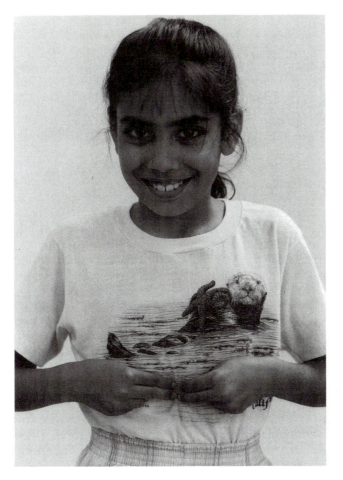

FIGURE 8–8.   Position for Abdominal Pulsing.

The Belly Laugh.   Using a variety of ascending and descending pitches in the lower voice, model five staccato voice pulses on *ha*. Keep the pulsing light, as in a laugh. Randomly test individuals for the ability to project each light pulse of the laugh.

Level 4: Lower Wheelie (Exercise 49)

Lower Wheelie.   This exercise will encourage a further refinement of abdominal support as it is applied to phonation. The pulsing action required of the abdominal musculature creates a flexibility in the support process that more nearly reflects what is taking place (in a gross manner) in the application of breath to voice.

Direct students to imitate the sound of an auto engine with a dead battery "turning over." Use a rolling pulse on *yo-o-o-o-oh* in the lower adjustment on one breath, with short contractions of abdominal support. Encourage students to speak slowly in the midvoice range. Listen for the even pulsing action in the voice.

Abdominal Pulse. Direct students to apply the abdominal pulse with their fingers on the abdominal area as a way of checking for proper support. Alternate this manual pulse with rolling the pulse naturally.

When a student fails to respond to his own abdominal pulsing, the instructor may need to help in the following manner: Direct the student to make a fist and place it in the abdominal area below the sternum. The instructor places his hand over the student's fist and exerts a mild pressure, moving the fist in and out of the student's abdominal area while the student intones a sustained *yo* in the lower adjustment. Caution the student not to resist the pulsing action. This exercise will often help a student find the correct feeling of support and glottal closure when the student is relaxed and cooperative. If a student fights the abdominal pulsing action by the hardening of the abdominal musculature, the exercise will not work. The abdomen is to remain relaxed in a Jello-like state. The abdominal-pulse exercise should be used regularly with vocalises as a means of establishing the support contact.

Level 5: Accented Pulse (Exercise 64)

This is another exercise that is used to strengthen the lower adjustment. High school boys especially like this one! Direct students to pulse the lower adjustment on seven repeated patterns of the sound *yah-ah-ah* with an accent (abdominal mini-thrust) on the first pulse of each series. Sustain a final accented pulse on *ah*. This is the same as the lower wheelie, only slower and more pronounced. Keep the sound light and rolling on one breath. Listen for the clear closure of the vocal folds.

Level 6: Choric Speech (Exercise 79)

This exercise in lower-adjustment production is the final goal of the speech activities in this method. Students are to demonstrate speaking voices that are well modulated, clear, and projected. The speech activities below are recommended for evaluation and development of students' speaking voices.

Speech Choir. There are a number of volumes of choral readings available in libraries. Choral reading has become a lost art and should be revived, if only as an excellent intermediary step toward improving the singing voice. There are a number of choral-speaking octavos available from choral music publishers, and poetry is another excellent source for speech-choir activity. The following choral octavos are a small sample for the reader to explore: *Gotta Be Spring* (B. Ludlow, Shawnee Press A1214, Delaware Water Gap, PA, 2 pts.), *Have You Heard?* (B. Ludlow, Shawnee Press A1215, 2 pts.), *The Dance* (J. Gilbert, Shawnee Press A-1691, 4 pts.), and *Used Car Lot* (B. Dobbins, Shawnee Press A-1675, 4 pts.).

Song Texts. Direct students to speak the texts of the song repertoire using well-supported and -modulated lower-adjustment speaking voices. Go down the line and have each student read successively one line of text. Encourage interpretive reading, not flat speaking.

Vocal Rap. "Rapping" (speaking rhyme with a rhythmic backing) is popular among students. Have the students compose their own raps to be spoken in class with good vocal projection. Use a percussive ostinato as a background for the rapping. The following is a model with which to begin (the slash marks indicate bar lines):

IT'S HOT! (in 4)

Kenneth Phillips

It's / hot, it's hot, it's / so darn hot, and I /
can't think it's cooler 'cause I / know it's really not! As I /
lie here baking in the sun I / pause to wonder why—Am I /
really getting nice and tan or / might I up and die? It's/
hot, it's hot, it's / so darn hot, and it / isn't any cooler even
though I sweat a lot! With my / body really burning and my /
eyes tired of the glare, I / wonder if it's worth it all and /
should I really care? For the / vanity within me says I'll /
surely look real good, but the / common sense within me says I'm /
burning just like wood! It's / hot, it's hot, it's / so darn hot!

UPPER ADJUSTMENT

Goal: The student will develop the technique of upper-adjustment voice production as a means of finding and strengthening the upper adjustment for singing, through exercises involving clarity, placement, and projection.

Producing a pure upper-adjustment vocal sound is the key to establishing the upper singing range in the voice. This is not a falsetto voice, which is a nonresonated sound (high laryngeal position), but rather, a full upper-adjustment sound capable of crescendo. It is produced with only the inner edges of the vocal folds vibrating. The instructor must be capable of producing this sound, in order to provide a clear model for student imitation. Most women will have no trouble producing the pure upper-adjustment sound, as their vocal folds change little from childhood to adulthood. Men, however, may have trouble finding this voice, as men more commonly tend toward a falsetto or a passagio in the upper register.

Boys will imitate more easily the model of a male instructor using the upper adjustment than that of a female instructor. For female instructors the task is more difficult, as the upper voice is used most often by women and does not sound "masculine" to boys. In this case, the female instructor should try to recruit a male student who seems able and willing to find this voice in a private lesson. Once found, the male student can serve as the model for other male students. Another technique is to ask an adult male who can model the upper-adjustment sound to visit the class. Boys who resist the exercise of the upper adjustment should be reminded of its use by many male pop singers.

As indicated previously, boys do not lose the ability to sing in the upper adjustment when the voice is changing or after the change. Care must be taken, however, that the larynx remain at rest, and not be allowed to elevate when singing in the upper adjustment. The typical "necktie tenor" (jaw jutting up and out) is the result of laryngeal elevation and strain. This hyperfunctioning of the larynx results in a weak, falsetto sound and is detrimental to good singing. When the larynx remains down (at rest), the adolescent male can produce a full and ringing upper-adjustment sound in what was previously his middle adjustment, middle C to one octave above. Singing in the soprano octave (c^2 to c^3) in the upper adjustment is mostly lost to the adolescent male and is not cultivated in music for the male voice.

The adolescent male with a changing voice is a challenge to vocal-music teachers. The pitches above middle C tend to become strained as the male vocal folds lengthen and thicken. The male with a changing voice must learn to sing these pitches with a new distribution of vocal-fold vibrations. The incremental sharing of vocal adjustments (upper and lower) becomes more of a problem for the young man than for the boy with an unchanged voice, as the added length and thickness of the folds makes this coordination of adjustments more difficult.

In classical voice training, the adult baritone and tenor develop a passagio adjustment for the pitches in the vocal range above middle C. This head voice is most difficult to develop in adolescent male singers, because the vocal folds are adjusting to the physical changes of puberty. Therefore, it is recommended that adolescent males be taught to sing the upper part of the male range (e^1 to c^2) in the pure upper-adjustment voice. This eliminates the strain so commonly found in the upper vocal range of adolescent males. Once these young men learn how to pass into the upper adjustment with ease, the upper range becomes easy to sing and the sound blends beautifully within a choral ensemble. Then, as these young men mature, they can be taught the requirements of the passagio, or covered, voice, which requires a well-developed upper-adjustment foundation. It is important to remember that males do not lose the ability to sing in the upper adjustment once the voice changes. Keeping the upper adjustment alive and strong is the basis for developing the male passagio and the upper range of children's and women's voices. In this method, the upper adjustment is first established and strengthened through phonation exercises related to the speaking voice, which lead to its use in the singing voice.

Level 1: Animal Farm (Exercise 5)

Vocal Imitations.   Elementary children may again play a game of imitating birds or animals with upper-adjustment voices:

(*a*) cuckoo: *koo-koo*   (*c*) puppy: *mm-mm* (whimper)

(*b*) owl: *whoo-whoo*   (*d*) cat: *meow*

Intermediate students often have trouble finding their upper voices, but animal imitations afford a good way to do so. The whimper of the puppy is especially helpful with difficult cases. Keep the lips lightly touching for the whimper.

Mickey Mouse.   A technique for finding the upper voice with adolescents is to have them imitate the voice of the cartoon character Mickey Mouse. When Mickey says, "Hello, folks," it is in a strong upper-adjustment voice! Students can readily match a good model from the instructor.

High Hooty Land.   Primary children enjoy having conversations in High Hooty Land, a fictional place in which people speak only in their upper voices. This can be much fun and encourages upper-adjustment vocal development. Designate a portion of the class period when all children must speak only in their upper voices.

Level 2: Marcato Thrust (Exercise 20)

Hooking Up.   The purpose of this exercise is to hook up the breath stream with the upper voice. Direct students to produce a well-thrusted *hooo* in the upper adjustment (after the instructor's model). Let the pitch descend or glide downward after the attack. Repeat, bending slightly at the waist on each *hooo*. Monitor for a swift abdominal contraction. Use plenty of aspirate *h*. Listen for a whistlelike quality. It should not be a falsetto voice.

The Foul Shot.   This vocal-exploration exercise should be combined with the foul shot (exercise 18) for best results. Add the lifted *hoooo* on the breath as the students shoot for the basket. The pitch of the *hoooo* imitates the lift of the ball as it arches forward and then down through the hoop. Direct students to note how the voice is lifted from the center of the body with an abdominal lift.

Abdominal Pulse. Some students will have trouble finding the freedom to lift this upper-adjustment sound. Direct them to sustain the upper adjustment *hoooo* while manually pulsing the abdomen (slightly below the end of the sternum) with the first two fingers of each hand (exercise 19). This should cause the vocal sound to pulse actively, indicating that the source of the sound is from the "motor," or abdominal support musculature. Check students individually for this pulsing action. Remind them not to push out with the abdominal muscles, but to lift these muscles gently for phonation.

Level 3: Staccato Bump (Exercise 35)

Koo-koo Bumps. The purpose of this exercise is to apply the breath in light staccato bumps (exercise 34) to the upper voice. Direct students to bump a light *koo* five times in the upper adjustment. Repeat several times. Monitor for the mini-contractions of the abdominal musculature on each bump. Use a strong *k*. All bumps are from one breath. Listen for the whistlelike quality of the voice. Direct students to bend slightly at the waist on each bump like a woodpecker. This will encourage correct support action of the abdominal musculature.

Ha-ha Bumps. Direct the students to bump a light *ha* five times in the upper adjustment. Repeat several times. Monitor for the mini-contractions of the abdominal musculature on each bump. Use a well-aspirated *h*. All bumps are on one breath. Listen for a light but ringing quality in the upper adjustment.

Light Laugh. Direct students to laugh lightly in the upper adjustment using the *ha* sound. This may be modeled as an upper-adjustment laugh that rises and falls in pitch. Each time model a tonal variety, which the students should then echo and imitate. Warning: Students can get carried away with this artificial laughing and may not support with enough air. Insist on proper breath management! Use a light action of the breath impulse (light aspirate) instead of the heavier aspirate of the Ha-ha Bumps.

Level 4: Upper Wheelie (Exercise 50)

Upper Wheelie. This exercise will help develop the flexible application of the support process to the upper voice. Direct students to produce an upper adjustment wheelie using *yoo-oo-oo-oo-oo* and a rolling pulse of the abdominal musculature (five pulses). This exercise sounds like the engine of a car with a weak battery turning over, but in the upper voice. It need not be explained, but merely imitated. When correctly demonstrated by the instructor, most students will have no difficulty imitating the desired sound. However, those with improper support or improper laryngeal functioning may not be able to sustain this sound. They will need continual remediation in finding the upper voice by using the previous exercises in this section.

Abdominal Pulse. The manual pulse may be used as a remedial technique in finding the flexible pulsing action of the abdominal muscles. Direct students to pulse the abdominal area manually each time for each of the five pulses of the wheelie.

Level 5: Sustained Howl (Exercise 65)

This exercise is a check for breath support and upper-voice coordination. Those students who are not developing abdominal support will not be able to sustain the howl and will need individual remediation for breathing technique.

Direct students to produce an upper-adjustment howl like that of a coyote, using *rroo-oo-oo-oo* on one breath. (Do not lift the chin as coyotes do!) This exercise is done with the rolling pulse, which, again, is best imitated by the students after the instructor's model. Do not prolong group participation, but listen to students individually. Note those students who cannot produce a healthy pulsing sound in the upper adjustment. Use the abdominal pulse and other breathing exercises to encourage proper coordination. It is almost impossible to do this exercise without the proper coordination and makes this technique most discriminating.

Level 6: Soundscape (Exercise 80)

Vocal Exploration. Exploring the voice (upper, middle, and lower) through sound imitations is fun and a creative way to vocal strength and flexibility. Encourage students to write programs of vocal sounds for events in their lives (e.g., a circus, a trip to an airport, ball games, or road races). All types of sounds may be used, including even nonsense words or syllables. Begin by discussing the various sounds of the environment. Direct students to imitate the sounds of the wind, various animals, transportation vehicles, and the like. Encourage them to explore and catalog the wide variety of sounds that can be made with the human voice.

Summer Storm. The following program of a summer storm may serve as an example to be assigned (vocal parts) and conducted by the instructor:

Vocal parts: wind (air through pursed lips), rain (clicking of tongue), lightning (sharp guttural sound), thunder (vocal *brooooooom*), birds (light chirping).

Program:

1. silence
2. the wind beginning to blow, gradually becoming stronger
3. raindrops beginning to fall lightly, and then a deluge
4. lightning followed by thunder
5. a raging torrent with more thunder and lightning
6. storm beginning to lessen
7. storm ending
8. birds singing and chirping

Charting and Conducting. These soundscapes may be charted or written out in a graphic form as a way of understanding the purpose of a composer's musical score. Students should be directed to assign the vocal parts and serve as conductors for these class events. Standard gestures for cueing, cutoffs, crescendo, and descrescendo will be needed.

ADJUSTMENT COORDINATION

Goal: The student will develop the technique of vocal-adjustment coordination through exercises involving vocal clarity, placement, balance, and projection.

The adjustment from middle C to the octave above (c^1 to c^2) is the most difficult to coordinate in all voices. In women's voices, this is the register in which a break between the lower and upper adjustments often occurs at approximately the pitch a^1. In men's voices, this is the passagio, or upper octave, ending in the tenor high C. In both cases, the objective is to smooth over the break between the lower and upper adjustments, creating a smooth passage between the two registers. This is less important for the early-adolescent male, whose changing vocal folds make this transition difficult to negotiate.

The unchanged child's voice (male and female) is like the woman's voice in that a perceptible register break usually appears somewhere in the middle-voice octave, c^1 to c^2. Because of the great flexibility in the child's voice, it is often possible for the child to carry the lower adjustment far into the range where the middle voice or even upper voice adjustment should be used. This must not be permitted. Children who learn to sing with a lower adjustment forced too high sing with a strident quality that often results in damage to the young voice.

The following exercises are intended to identify and bridge the gap between the upper and lower adjustments of the speaking voice as a basis for the singing voice. They are especially good for the early-adolescent male who needs to learn to move between the lower and upper adjustments with ease. However, exercises 51 (spiral wheelie) and 81 (vocal glissando) should not be used with adolescent males in the voice change, because bridging the gap between the upper and lower voices is done more as a "shift," rather than a "blend," of registers at this stage of development (see Chapter 4).

Level 1: Animal Farm (Exercise 6)

The Donkey. Ask the students if they know of any animal who has both upper and lower voices. The donkey is the answer. Direct students to imitate the voice of the donkey using *hee-haw* from upper to lower adjustments. Be sure that the break between the two voices of the *hee-haw* is clear. Students should be able to make the shift easily.

Identifying the break between the two adjustments is extremely important before bridging the gap can take place. Students must be able to distinguish between the upper and lower adjustments. This is especially important for adolescent males with changing voices.

The Horse. The horse is an animal that uses a combination of upper and lower adjustments. Direct students to imitate the voice of the horse using a *hyeeee* sound in the middle adjustment. Call attention to this middle voice. This imitation calls for strong support from the abdominal musculature if it is to be done correctly. Check students individually, and encourage a strong whinneying through abdominal support. Do not practice the horse with adolescent males whose voices may crack on this exercise.

Level 2: Woofers and Tweeters (Exercise 21)

These exercises further help students explore the difference in vocal production between the lower and upper adjustments. They are fun activities, but should not be prolonged as group exercises.

Little Dog. Direct students to imitate the sound of a little dog barking using *yip, yip.* Keep the sound light and in the upper voice. The initial *y* of the imitation is good for activating the support musculature.

Dog Fight. Direct pairs of students to imitate the sounds of dogs barking in a dog fight. Use *woof* for the larger dogs and *yip* for the smaller dogs. Monitor for swift contractions of the support musculature, and lower voice (*woof*) and upper voice (*yip*) production. Be sure to use *woof* and not *arf*, as *woof* calls into action the support of the abdominal muscles; *arf* is too guttural. Monitor individual students for a fully supported sound, not one that originates from the throat.

Tweeters. Direct students to imitate the sounds of various birds.

Listen for the clear differentiation among vocal adjustments. The instructor must provide a good vocal model for each of these imitations:

1. talking parrot (lower voice): "Polly want a cracker!"
2. crow (middle voice): "ca-ca"
3. cuckoo (upper voice): "koo-koo, koo-koo"

Level 3: Voice Inflectors (Exercise 36)

Each of the following imitations directs the student to elevate the voice from the lower adjustment (speaking voice) to a midvoice range (combination of upper and lower adjustments). All of the inflections require firm abdominal support.

Ah-choo. Direct students to imitate a sneeze with a rising inflection from "ah" to "choo." Monitor abdominal support and a voice that is out of the throat and into the mask. Check students individually.

Aha! Direct students to say *aha* with a rising inflection on the *ha* and plenty of marcato thrust. Monitor abdominal support and a voice that lifts and projects. Check students individually.

Sky Diver (elementary only). Direct students to make an airplane out of a closed fist, extending the thumb and little finger for wings. Start the engine by winding a make-believe propeller with the index finger of the free hand. Try to start the engine (with too little air) twice, buzzing the lips in the lower adjustment. Fuel the airplane with plenty of air (a deep breath) and start the engine again. Success! As the plane takes off, switch over to upper-adjustment humming as the plane gains height, elevating the airplane-fist. On a cue from the instructor, pop a sky diver from the airplane (the hand becomes cupped like a parachute) and float to earth with a descending vocal glide from upper to lower adjustment! This exercise is fun, especially for primary children. It will bring the upper adjustment down into the lower adjustment, thus bridging the gap between adjustments.

Monitor individuals on the different voice-inflector exercises to determine the application of breath support to vocal inflection. Group practice masks the individual voice.

Level 4: Spiral Wheelie (Exercise 51)

Spiral Wheelie. The spiral wheelie is excellent for vocal stimulation of all the vocal registers when time permits little else in the way of phonatory practice. Direct students to produce a wheelie spiraling from the upper adjustment to the lower adjustment without a register break. Use the rolling pulse, beginning with *yoo-oo-oo* in the upper adjustment, changing to *yoo* (as in *book* or *your*) in the middle voice, and changing to *yoh* (as in *go*) in the lower adjustment. Hand cues may be used (circling index finger) to aid in the placement progress from upper to lower adjustments: above the head for upper, eye level for middle, and below the chin for lower.

Abdominal Pulse. The manual-pulse exercise may be needed for students to check the action of the abdominal muscles as they support the voice.

Level 5: Sustained Bleat (Exercise 66)

This exercise is a check for glottal closure. Students who cannot do it have yet to coordinate the breath-support process with firm (not pressed) closing of the vocal folds upon phonation. For those students, remediation with this exercise will help to bring about coordination between breath and glottal closure.

Direct students to imitate the sound of a bleating sheep with *ba-a-a-a*, using a firm contraction of the abdominal musculature while emitting short, light grips of the vocal folds. Do not prolong group practice, but listen for individual performance. Students who cannot execute this exercise (i.e., make one long breathy sound instead of a string of little bleats) should be encouraged through proper vocal modeling by other students or the instructor. They need to learn to firm the vocal folds with breath energy, and often this will happen through repeated modeling and practice.

Level 6: Vocal Glissando (Exercise 81)

Descending Glide. This is a most demanding vocal exercise, requiring the student to glide from the upper adjustment down and through the middle adjustment to the lower adjustment without an audible voice break. Direct students to glide from the upper adjustment to the lower adjustment on one vowel [u]. Stress a smooth glissando without a register break. Apply the sustained support of the abdominal musculature throughout the glissando.

The lower adjustment must be drawn into the upper adjustment as the glissando descends. This will result in a middle voice that is robust. If only the upper voice is used throughout the glissando, the middle voice will become weaker as the line descends and there will be no lower voice.

Ascending Glide. Direct students to slide on the vowel [u] from the lower to upper voice, which is more difficult than descending. Students will have more trouble lightening the voice on the ascending glide than creating a heavier sound on the descending glide. The lower adjustment must be eliminated from the middle voice as the glissando ascends. This is a difficult technique and requires good breath support.

The goal is distinctive lower and upper voices that are joined together in the middle to produce one vocal line.

Midvoice Glide. Direct students to slide on the vowel [u] up and down in the middle voice over the break. Keep the production light, and listen for the mix of voices. As always, the instructor must provide a good vocal model.

STUDY AND DISCUSSION
QUESTIONS

1. What is the link in the development of the young singing voice? How may this help to develop confidence in singing?
2. Describe the action of the larynx for both pop and trained singers. What is the result of a depressed larynx? What position should the larynx maintain for speaking and singing?
3. Practically speaking, how many vocal registers are there? To what does each of the vocal adjustments correspond?
4. Describe the correct use of the lower adjustment for children's singing for pitches below c^1 and between c^1 and c^2.
5. What adjustment does the English choirboy model use from c^1 to c^2, and what often are the results of such registration?
6. Do boys lose the ability to sing in the upper adjustment during and after the voice change? Relate this to the infamous "voice break" among male adolescents.
7. What is the key to the production of the adult male head voice?
8. Describe the difference between the pure upper-adjustment tone and the falsetto tone. In what part of the vocal range should the pure upper adjustment be used in children's singing?
9. Describe the major cartilages of the larynx and how each functions.
10. What is another name for the thyroid notch? What anatomical purpose does it fulfill?
11. What is the hyoid bone, and how does it function?
12. Describe the two sets of muscles of the larynx that regulate pitch and how each functions.
13. Describe the three sets of muscles of the larynx that open and close the vocal folds and how each functions.
14. Describe the three sets of muscles that help to lower the larynx and the one set that raises the thyroid cartilage.
15. Describe the various actions of the vocal folds in producing pitch in the various adjustments. What is the name given to the opening between the vocal folds when they are open?

16. Describe the various layers of the vocal folds and what is contained in each layer.
17. What are the ventricular bands? How do they function in singing?
18. What is the difference between "stroke" and "shock" of the glottis?
19. What is the function of the epiglottis?
20. Describe the action of the cricoid cartilage when pitch ascends.

References

APPLEMAN, R. D. (1967). *The science of vocal pedagogy: Theory and application.* Bloomington: Indiana University Press.

ATTERBURY, B. W. (1984). Are you really teaching children how to sing? *Music Educators Journal, 70*(8), 43–45.

COOPER, M. C. (1984). *Change your voice, change your life.* New York: Macmillan.

DAWSON, J. J. (1902). *The voice of the boy.* New York: E. L. Kellog.

GOULD, A. O. (1968). Developing specialized programs for singing in the elementary school. Washington, DC: Research in Education. ERIC Reproduction Service No. ED 025530 24 TE 499967

HERMAN, S. (1988). *Building a pyramid of musicianship.* San Diego: Curtis Music Press.

HOWARD, F. E. (1923). *The child-voice in singing* (rev. ed.). New York: H. W. Gray. (Original work published in 1895.)

KLEIN, J. J., & SCHJEIDE, O. A. (1972). Singing technique: How to avoid vocal trouble. Anaheim, CA: National Music Publishers.

HINES, J. J. (1982). *Great singers on great singing.* Garden City, NY: Doubleday.

REID, C. (1985). The intensity factor in vocal registration. *Journal of Research in Singing, 9*(1), 43–60.

ROE, P. (1983). *Choral music education* (2nd ed.). Englewood Cliffs, NJ: Prentice-Hall.

SWANSON, F. J. (1977). *The male voice ages eight to eighteen.* Cedar Rapids, IA: Ingram.

VENNARD, W. (1967). *Singing: The mechanism and the technic.* New York: Carl Fischer.

9

RESONANT TONE PRODUCTION 🍃

Goal: The student will develop the skill of clear, resonant, and accurate singing, through the application of abdicostal respiration and laryngeal phonation to resonant tone production.

A beautiful voice is one that is rich in resonance. Such a voice can be characterized as having uniformity of vowels, depth and fullness of tone, and projection, or "ring." While such terms are highly subjective, these qualities are recognized by vocal authorities (Alderson, 1979; Appleman, 1967; Klein and Schjeide, 1972; Miller, 1986; Vennard, 1967) as being characteristic of the resonant voice.

Resonance may be defined as "constructive interference" of sound waves within the vocal tract. As energy is generated from the vocal folds, a complex sound wave is produced. This wave travels through the pharynx (throat) and out of the oral cavity (mouth), resulting in a loss of energy. A portion of the wave, however, is reflected at the lips back into the vocal tract, where it is acted upon and rearranged according to the shape of the vocal tract for the sound (vowel) being phonated. It is this interference of waves within the vocal tract that transforms a rather indistinguishable sound at the laryngeal level into a resonant tone. Thus, the vocal tract has acoustic properties apart from the pitch and harmonics produced by the vocal folds. Without this property of resonance, all voices would tend to sound alike and variation of vowel color would be impossible.

Formants

The term *formant* (F) is used to identify the resonance frequencies of the vocal tract. Formant frequency is not to be confused with fundamental frequency (f), which is the pitch as heard (e.g., standard pitch of a^1 = 440 Hz). While it is possible to generate a pure tone (sinusoidal wave) with no harmonic frequencies, such sounds do not exist in the human voice. Every sound of the human voice is a combination of fundamental frequency and formant frequency.

Music teachers should already have a basic understanding of the laws of acoustics and the overtone series as it relates to musical instruments. In general, the overtone or harmonic series of any instrument is a fixed set of frequencies above the fundamental (the fundamental multiplied by 2, 3, 4, etc.), which, when dampened or strengthened by the shape and size of the instrument, determines the quality (timbre) and resonance of that instrument.

Formant frequencies of the voice are similar to overtones, except that formants are not fixed. Formants are thought of more accurately as frequency regions or bands of frequencies. These regions can be changed (lowered or raised) according to the configuration of the vocal tract. It is this change in shape of the vocal tract that distinguishes the human voice from every other instrument; the vocal tract is capable of countless changes that result in a variety of vowel sounds, consonants, and resonances that we call language. Whereas instruments produce fundamental pitches and a fixed set of overtones (octave, fifth, fourth, major third, etc.), voices produce fundamental pitches and accompanying formant regions that can be varied by changes in the articulators (tongue, jaw, lips, etc.).

Vowel Production

Vowels form the basis of resonant tone production. The various vowels of languages are determined by distinct patterns of formant frequencies. In any vocal tract, there are possible an infinite number of formant regions. Individual vowels may have from five to thirty formants, although the first four (lowest) formants are the most important to vowel identity and quality. The lower two formants (F_1 and F_2) provide most of the identity of the vowel, enabling the hearer to distinguish one vowel from another. The upper two (F_3 and F_4) are more quality-determinant formants, as are the other higher formants, enabling the hearer to distinguish one voice from another. Voice scientists remain uncertain as to the role formants play in helping to distinguish the gender or age of a speaker.

The average male vocal tract (a uniform vocal tract, or perfect cylinder, closed at the glottis and open at the lips) is 17.5 centimeters long.

Such a voice producing the schwa, the sound *uh* (symbolized ə), will produce formant frequencies at 500 Hz, 1,500 Hz, 2,500 Hz, and 3,500 Hz (Figure 9–1). These formants are not fixed and may vary within given regions (the perimeter of the bell curve in Figure 9–1) and still maintain vowel identity. The shorter vocal tracts of women and children will shift all formant frequencies 17 percent and 25 percent higher, respectively. Longer vowel tracts, as in the deep bass voice, will shift all formants lower.

Each vowel is determined by its own arrangement of formant frequencies. The changing shape of the vocal tract determines the shifting of formants as one vowel changes to another. The length of the vocal tract (larynx and lip position); the positions of the jaw, tongue, and soft palate; and the expansion or contraction of the pharynx are responsible for these changes.

When the jaw is more constricted in the front (small mouth opening), it lowers F_1 and raises F_2. Comparing the schwa to the vowel [i], F_1 shifts down to 250 Hz, and F_2 shifts up to 2,300 Hz (Figure 9–2). For the vowel [ɑ], F_1 rises to 700 Hz, while F_2 falls to 1,100 Hz (Figure 9–3). The

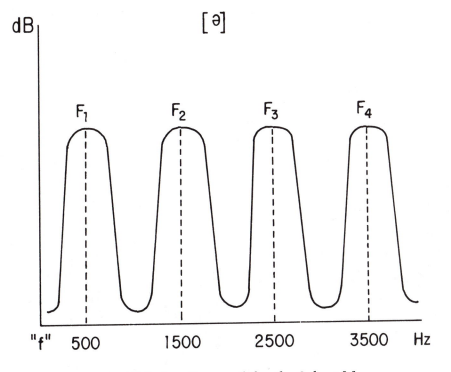

FIGURE 9–1. Formants for the Schwa [ə].

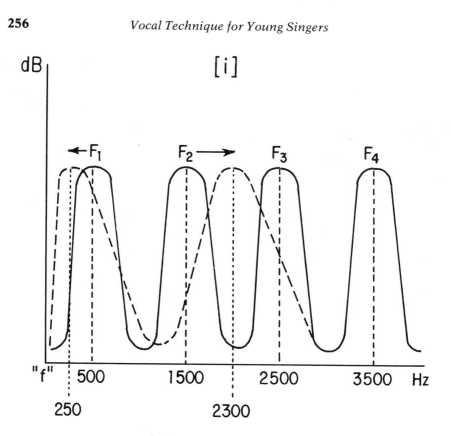

FIGURE 9–2. Formants for the Vowel [i].

back constriction with the mouth more open for this vowel causes F^1 to rise and F_2 to lower. The formant frequencies (shown as broad regions) of F_1 and F_2 are given in Figure 9–4 for the basic long and short vowels (average male voice).

The Resonators

Although the pharynx and mouth are the major resonators of the voice, they are not the only resonators of the voice. The chest cavity, larynx, nasal cavity, and sinuses do play some part in the resonance of vocal sound. The degree to which they contribute is unclear to vocal scientists; most authorities state that the contribution of these cavities is minimal when compared to that of the pharynx and oral cavity.

The "pharynx" is the cavity above the larynx that extends upward behind the mouth and nose (Figure 9–5). It is comprised of three parts: the "laryngopharynx," the area below the level of the tongue; the "oropharynx," the area behind the oral cavity and tongue; and the "nasopharynx," the area above the soft palate behind the nasal cavity.

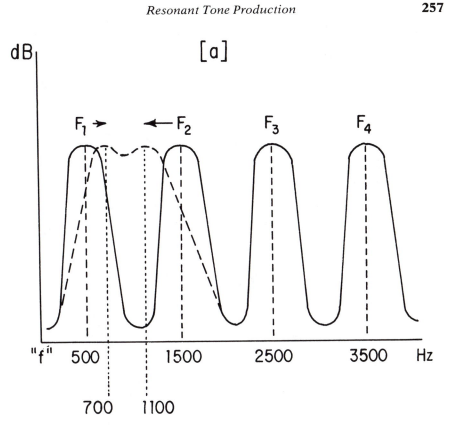

FIGURE 9–3. Formants for the Vowel [ɑ].

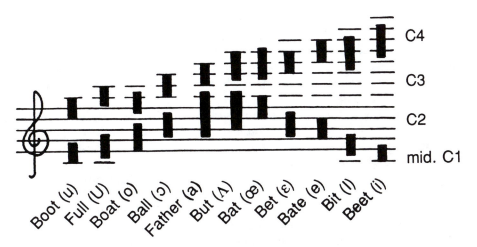

FIGURE 9–4. Formant Regions for Long and Short Vowels.

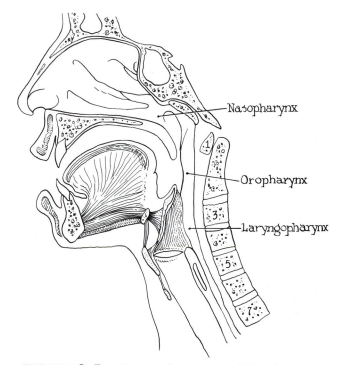

FIGURE 9–5.   Resonating Areas of the Pharynx.

The nasopharynx can be closed off from the rest of the pharynx by the arching of the soft palate. How much the nasopharynx adds to the resonance of vowels is uncertain. Some vocal authorities recommend using a lowered soft palate, especially for upper-adjustment pitches. The reasoning is that a raised soft palate closes the nasopharynx, thus limiting resonance in this area. Others teach that the soft palate must be "raised and arched" to maximize pharyngeal space and resonance.

Scotto di Carlo and Autesserre (1987) have shown in their research of trained singers that the velopharyngeal port (opening into the nasopharynx) is not actually closed for singing, but rather the "arching" of the soft palate, to which singers commonly refer, is a transversal tension of the velum, resulting in the feeling of a raised soft palate. The authors recommend that the soft palate be lowered for singing so that the entire pharynx remains open. However, Troup and associates take exception to this earlier finding and note that "velum closure in singing depends on many factors: the instructor, the language, the singer and the style of singing" (1989, p. 35). The authors report case studies of singers using xeroradiographic analysis and note the wide range of results as to velum closure at differing pitch levels. Even with the use of sophisticated equipment, two sets of researchers have found conflicting results.

The feeling of a stiffled yawn (lips lightly touching) is recommended by some vocal authorities to help raise or arch the soft palate during singing. As the soft palate is an involuntary mechanism, it is best not to call attention to it (especially with children), allowing it to take its natural placement when the pharynx is relaxed. However, the present method does attempt to open and expand the pharynx through indirect techniques (e.g., inner smile and cool spot), which are helpful in learning to sing with an open and relaxed throat.

Both the laryngopharynx and the oropharynx can be constricted and made smaller by the action of the tongue moving too far back, and the tensing of the pharyngeal swallowing muscles. An open throat is conducive to good singing. The pharynx must be open and relaxed, without undue constriction from the swallowing muscles, which are a major source of interference in singing.

The Tongue

The tongue gives shape to both the oral cavity and the pharynx. Carried too far back, it causes a constriction of the pharynx and a loss of resonating space. The tip of the tongue should rest on the fleshy ridge at the base of the lower front teeth. The back of the tongue should be kept forward and arched high enough to keep it out of the throat. The vowels [u], [i], and [e] have the highest positions for the back of the tongue. The vowels [o] and [ɑ] progressively lower the tongue to the base of the mouth. Care should be taken to keep the tongue higher than usual for these broader vowels in order to keep the tongue forward. The tongue should not be grooved or flattened for any vowel! Doing so will place it too far back into the pharynx, diminishing resonance.

The muscles of the tongue that often tense and interfere with phonation and resonant tone production are the "genioglossus," the "hyoglossus," the styloglossus," and the "palatoglossus" (Figure 9–6). All of these muscles are used in the swallowing process and in varying ways help to constrict the pharynx. The tongue must remain relaxed for singing. Any rigidity will necessarily cause a constriction of the vocal tract and reduce vocal resonance. A rigid or trembling tongue signals that the swallowing muscles are being used to compensate for poor breath support and control.

Maximize Resonance

The difference between pop singing and trained singing is most readily evidenced in their attitudes toward pharyngeal resonance. Trained singers are taught to use the pharynx to its greatest advantage, producing a tone that is rich in resonance and one that will carry without amplification, but pop singers, who generally use sound amplification, do

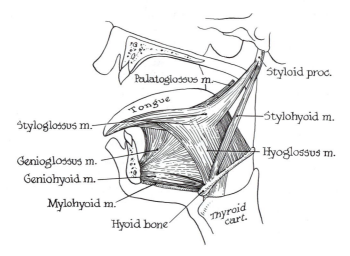

FIGURE 9–6. Muscles of the Swallowing Process.

not find it necessary to develop much depth to the voice. In fact, many pop singers have rather weak voices when heard without amplification. The popular singer, often because of lack of training, uses a style of singing that emphasizes the mouth as the major vocal resonator. This choice is not a conscious one, but rather happens unconsciously through imitation of other singers and poor singing habits. Because so many popular singers lack proper breath support, vocal strain is common. This strain results in a raised larynx, which because of its elevated position in the throat, negates the natural qualities of much of the pharyngeal areas. The less pharyngeal area available as a vocal resonator, the weaker the formants and the weaker the vocal sound.

The trained voice uses the pharynx to its fullest advantage. While there are those trained singers (even opera stars!) in whom strain and elevation of the larynx can be detected, the overwhelming majority of professional singers note the importance of the relaxed, lowered larynx (Hines, 1982), which should not be confused with a "depressed" larynx, which is artificially lowered by some singers to produce a darker, more mature sound. This type of throat singing is to be avoided. A relaxed larynx that remains in its normal, at-rest position throughout the singing range is to be cultivated. It allows for maximum pharyngeal resonance and maximum development of resonant vocal tone. Singing with the larynx elevated activates the swallowing process, which in turn causes throat constriction. For an open throat, the larynx must remain relaxed in its normal position. This condition is greatly aided by proper support of the breath and consistent breath pressure.

The Singer's Formant

Professional voices, such as those of opera singers, must be able to project above an orchestral accompaniment. These singers (especially males) often develop an extra formant that increases the power of the voice. This has been described by Sundberg (1977) as the "singer's formant," or an extra formant produced in the average male vocal tract at a frequency of approximately 2,800 Hz. The origin of this additional formant is theorized to be at the laryngeal level, when the larynx is down (at rest) and the opening of the larynx (laryngeal orifice) into the pharynx is at a ratio of 1:6. When these conditions are present, this formant resonates in the pyriform sinuses (Figure 9–7). It is believed that the larynx must remain in a relatively low position for the larynx to act in such a way as to produce a formant capable of adding brilliance and tremendous carrying power to the voice. Although relatively new, this explanation of how the professional singer achieves optimum projection has gained much acceptance in voice science.

Developing Resonance

Two characteristics of the resonant voice are depth (richness) and projection (brightness). These qualities can be developed through proper tuning of the vowel formants. The singer must learn to tune the vocal

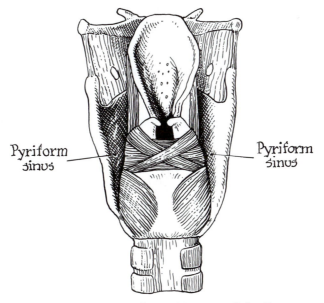

FIGURE 9–7. Pyriform Sinuses of the Larynx.

tract (adjust the articulators) to the frequency region of the lowest formant of any given vowel. The closer the fundamental pitch interacts with the formant frequency of any vowel, the clearer and more resonant the vowel and its pitch will sound.

Sung vowels, even in children's voices, should be richer than spoken vowels if the length of the vocal tract is maximized. For a richer sound with more depth, formants must be lowered. This is accomplished by the lengthening of the vocal tract, either through lip extension (flare) or rounding and/or keeping the larynx at rest. The overly dark, hooty voice is the result of a larynx that has been lowered too much or depressed. The larynx that remains in the at-rest position throughout the vocal range enhances the richness of tone. When this is coupled with an extended oral cavity (flared lips), varying degrees of depth may be achieved by the singer. Rounded lips, as for the vowel [u], while also darkening the sound, tend to discourage the second objective of a resonant voice—projection, or ring.

A trained voice is one that projects easily; its strength is enhanced by its brightness or ring. For a brighter sound with more ring, formants must be raised. This is accomplished by lip spreading or greater jaw opening. It also may be accomplished in the upper soprano range (c^2–c^3) through a slight smile. However, when used throughout the vocal range, this technique tends to counter depth and richness, resulting in an overly bright sound. Generally, the trained singer wants to maximize resonance by extending the vocal tract (with lip flare and at-rest larynx) and lowering the jaw (opening the mouth). Children and adolescents commonly sing with too little mouth opening and must be encouraged to relax the jaw more for all vowels. This method speaks of singing uniformly with "tall," or vertical vowels, rather than with "smiling," or horizontal, vowels. Encouraging students to flare the lips for vowel production helps to produce a warmer, more beautiful sound.

Projection or strength of voice is increased when the fundamental pitch frequency closely interacts with the formant frequency. The closer pitch frequency is to formant frequency, the greater the amplitude of the voice. The goal in increasing strength and projection of the voice is to match as closely as possible the fundamental pitch frequency to the first formant frequency for maximum enhancement of sound. When this is done, the output of sound can be changed as much as 30 dB without increased pressure or effort. In Figure 9–8, the first formant is lower and stronger than the fundamental pitch. More jaw opening from the singer raises the first formant until it more closely intersects with the fundamental, increasing the amplitude or strength of the voice.

The instructor must listen and watch for vowel tuning if resonance and in-tune singing are to be advanced. Experimenting with different vocal-tract positions for different vowels will be helpful in eliciting the best, most resonant sound. When vocal-tract positions (e.g., mouth

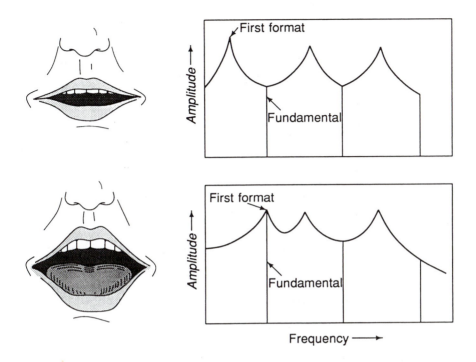

FIGURE 9–8. Greater Jaw Opening Yields Greater Interaction between Pitch Frequency (f) and Formant Frequency (F).

opening) differ widely among singers in a group, resonance is weakened because vowel formants are not closely matched. This also may affect intonation. The resulting formant frequencies can become "out of phase," and "beat" against one another, producing a pitch that sounds out of tune. The vowel is the basis of all vocal sound and must be developed systematically if superior vocal resonance is to result.

The development of resonant voices is one of the greatest challenges for the vocal-music instructor. Unlike the breathing musculature, which can be somewhat visually monitored, the vocal tract is difficult to see. An open and relaxed throat, free of constriction by the swallowing muscles, can be developed indirectly through exercises in vocal tract conditioning (Part IV, section A). Shaping of the vocal tract according to the principles presented in this method (especially as to laryngeal positioning and vertical vowels) will greatly aid in the development of vocal resonance. In the end, however, it is the ear of the music instructor that must be relied upon to determine the correct sound for each voice. Without an aural image of correct vocal tone for students at various levels of maturity, the instructor is greatly handicapped. This problem is compounded by the fact that acceptable or beautiful singing tone is a subjective cultural phenomenon. Listening to recordings of choirs and voices of outstanding reputation is one way in which to develop an aural awareness of proper resonant tone production for students at various ages.

The vocal tracts of children and adolescents are not as long as those of adults and therefore not as capable of producing as rich and resonant a vocal sound. This does not mean that young voices must necessarily be weak and lifeless. On the contrary, young voices produce a quality that is unique to their age, one that is characterized by a bright, buoyant, ringing sound. As children mature, the vocal tract lengthens, permitting more depth of resonance through increased lower formants. Constant monitoring of laryngeal position is needed to ensure that the full length of the vocal tract is involved in producing as rich a tone as possible, even among younger children. Care also must be taken that the larynx not be artificially lowered in trying to manufacture a more mature sound in an otherwise immature body.

Instrumentation in Voice Analysis

The computer age has made it possible to analyze the voice according to scientific measures. Ralph Appelman (1967), professor emeritus of voice and former director of the Institute of Vocal Research at Indiana University (Bloomington), is the inventor of the Vowelometer. This instrument plots the optimum resonance for vowels at fixed points on a television monitor. When a vowel is sung into a microphone, a luminescent dot of light appears on the screen. The closer the dot of light appears to the fixed position of the vowel, the greater the resonance. This instrument is costly and relies upon subjective opinion as to what constitutes the optimum resonance for each voice model programmed into the computer.

The real-time Vowel Spectrum Analyzer is another instrument for studying the complexity of waveforms. It is used for analyzing formants as they change over time. Figure 9–9 represents the tracting of the personal pronoun *I*, as spoken into the microphone of the spectrum analyzer. This word is a diphthong composed of [ɑ] and [i]. The first two formants of the [ɑ] vowel are very close together, as seen at the front of the tracing. Note the separation of these formants to different positions as the vowel migrates to [i] over time. The first formant decreases to a lower frequency, while the second formant increases to a higher frequency, changing the pattern in the sound waves and making the detection of [ɑ] from [i] possible. This also is a costly piece of equipment, making it impractical for use in the music class.

Other computer advances include the Visipitch, an instrument used in the analysis of pitch accuracy. It enables the researcher to quantify the accuracy of sung pitch to a given standard of pitch using a computer program. Ingo Titze, a speech scientist at The University of Iowa, has developed a computer-program model for the study of the vibratory patterns of the vocal folds. Such a model makes possible detailed analyses that are impossible to do on live human subjects. Future study of the human voice through computer technology will undoubtedly lead to more sophisticated means of vocal development.

Vowel Modification

It is difficult to sing pure vowels throughout the vocal range, especially on pitches above f^2 in adult female voices and f^1 in adult male voices. This is an acoustical problem that happens when the frequency of the sung fundamental is higher than the first formant frequency of any vowel. When this occurs, the vowel that is sung migrates—that is, is "modified" and heard as another vowel. Sopranos and tenors know that the higher they sing, the more the jaw must open if vowel integrity is to be maintained; greater jaw opening results in raising the vowel formant (F_1) to the area of the fundamental pitch frequency. At pitches above f^2, it becomes most difficult to raise the formant frequencies to the pitches sung. At this point in the scale, the singer must modify and shape all vowels to either [ɑ] or [ə].

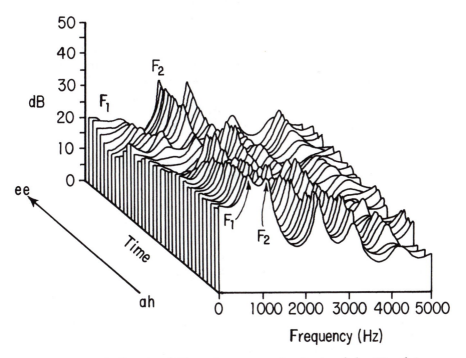

FIGURE 9–9. Real-Time Spectrum Analysis of the Word *I*.

When the fundamental pitch frequency is lower than the first formant of any vowel, the vowel integrity will be maintained. Most pitches in the adult male vocal range are below the first formant of all vowels. As pitch rises above f[1], however, the formants of some vowels fall below the fundamental frequency, necessitating vowel modification similar to that of the female voice. Fortunately, the formant frequencies of children's voices are so much higher than those of adults' voices that vowel modification is not a problem. However, the vocal instructor must be aware of this phenomenon when dealing with young adult voices at the high school level.

Vocal Vibrato

Vocal vibrato is heard as a slight undulation of pitch at between five and six cycles per second. While voice scientists have established a number of theories as to the source of vocal vibrato (McLane, 1985), good breath management and a relaxed throat seem to be essential to its emergence. In Western culture, vibrato is considered a mark of a beautiful singing voice.

Are children and adolescents capable of producing vibrato? Yes— the voices of children and adolescents will develop a natural vibrato through proper vocal production. While this is a controversial subject among child-voice specialists, there are those who believe that young students will produce a natural vibrato when vocal technique is developed correctly. Vibrato is not taught to the students, but rather is the outcome of vocal training that frees the voice, allowing it to pulse naturally.

When vibrato becomes excessively fast, it is called a "tremolo." A "wobble" arises from a change of amplitude accompanied by a slowing of the vibrato cycle. These are undesirable qualities in a voice. While vibrato enhances vocal tone quality and gives it a certain luster, the tremolo and wobble interfere with the tone and corrupt its beauty.

The source of the tremolo and wobble seems to be either a weakened abdominal musculature (lack of support) or tension in the laryngeal-pharyngeal areas. The latter is usually the result of the former. Poor breath management is the source of many vocal problems!

The tremolo and wobble are vocal problems most often associated with older adult singers who have developed poor muscle tone in the abdominal region. Women who have stretched the abdominal musculature in childbirth often have difficulty regaining the firm abdominal support needed for proper breath management. The result of this weakening of the abdominal musculature is heard as interference in natural vibrato. Children and adolescents are not susceptible to this problem, as their abdominal musculature has not been weakened by stretching or age.

Resonant Tone-Production Training

The outline of resonant tone production here is given for teacher-training purposes only and is not intended as the total sequence for group instruction. Beginning exercises in respiration and phonation precede the following exercises.

PART III. RESONANT TONE-PRODUCTION OUTLINE

Vocal Resonance

1. Sustained Humming,
2. Staccato Koo-koo
3. The Attack
4. Rolling Pulse
5. Intonation
6. Warm-up Tunes

Uniform Vowel Colors

1. The Model Vowel
2. Solfège Patterns
3. Vertical Vowels
4. Legato Movement
5. Short Vowels
6. Diphthongs

Vocal Coordination

1. Pitch Exploration
2. Upper to Lower
3. Octave Lift
4. Lighten Up
5. Midvoice Balancing
6. Ho-ho Choruses

VOCAL RESONANCE

Goal: The student will develop the technique of vocal resonance through exercises involving freedom, focus, and projection of the voice.

Exercises for increasing vocal resonance are now added to respiration and phonation exercises. These vocal warm-ups help to prepare the voice for more demanding singing. Such exercises must be more than mindless vocalises; a program of voice development requires vocal objectives for each exercise that go beyond vocal stimulation. Merely warming up the voice may be enough when time is limited and performance polishing is the objective. Without definite vocal objectives, however, a warm-up period will rarely help students become better singers. The purpose of vocal development is to strengthen the voice and to keep it healthy.

Level 1: Sustained Humming (Exercise 7)

Perhaps one of the best voice stimulators is sustained humming. Performed correctly, humming prepares the voice for more vigorous singing and helps to create a sense of tonal focus in the mask. It also develops a sense of "inner hearing" of one's own voice, which is noticeably lacking in many primary children who fail to match pitch. Most important, this vocalise encourages the support of the voice with the breath through active pulsing of the abdominal musculature. This hookup between breath and voice is vital in teaching students to sing "on the breath."

Whole-note Hum.   Direct students to exhale, inhale through the slow sip, and sustain vocal humming (*Mm*) four counts to one pitch, as shown in Example 9.1. Changed voices will sing one octave lower. Breath should be taken on each eighth rest, but caution must be taken that students do not inhale too much air, because doing so can tax the respiratory system and make breath management more difficult.

Correct humming requires that the lips be placed lightly together while the jaw is relaxed and teeth slightly parted. The tongue should be forward with the tip lightly touching the base of the lower front teeth.

"AP" = Abdominal Pulse
"NP" = No Pulse

EXAMPLE 9.1.   Vocalise: Sustained Humming.

Direct students to sing an *ah* first and then close the lips lightly, but not the teeth. They should feel a light buzz on the lips. Once they know how to hum correctly, they need not start by singing the *ah*.

Alternate measures are to be sung using an "abdominal pulse" movement (noted by "AP" above each measure). Place the first two fingers of each hand on the abdominal area just below the sternum (see Figure 8–8). Refer to this as the "soft spot" where the breathing motor pulses the air into the voice. Gently pulse this area in and out with the fingers; it should move easily. If the students have their fingers too low on the abdominal wall, the rectus abdominus muscle may tend to flex and harden outward; this is to be avoided.

Once the pulsing action is established, begin the humming exercise by gently pulsing the first measure. The voice should respond with a slight pulsing sound, and the student will hear how the action of the abdominal muscles is reflected in the action of the voice. Repeat the same pitch in the second measure with no abdominal pulse (noted by "NP" above the measure), and direct the students to feed the voice with the breath from the soft spot of the abdomen. Do not try to make the voice pulse as actively as before, but do encourage the lifting-up thought (exercise 3) while humming without the manual pulsing. The third measure moves up a whole step in pitch and repeats the manual pulse, followed by the fourth measure with no pulse, and so on.

Humming Movement. Variations in the basic humming exercise are given in Example 9.2. Alternate measures with and without the abdominal pulse movement. Breathe on the quarter rest in the first two exercises. The last exercise of the set requires that four measures be sung on one breath.

EXAMPLE 9.2. Vocalise: Humming Movement.

Level 2: Staccato Koo-Koo (Exercise 22)

The "staccato koo-koo" (Example 9.3) connects the breath in light pulses using the *k* to build breath support actively under the voice. It is one of the best exercises for teaching students to sing in a well-supported upper adjustment, and it also trains the ear in the intervals of the descending minor third and minor second. Most important, it encourages the movement of the upper voice down into the middle adjustment, where it combines with the lower voice for a robust sound. This vocalise may be sung as written for all voices.

Koo-Koo-Koo-Koo   Koo - oo,   Koo -Koo-Koo-Koo   Koo - oo, etc.

EXAMPLE 9.3.   Vocalise: Staccato Koo-Koo.

Direct students to separate lightly each pitch marked "staccato" and to slur the half notes, keeping the half step high! At first the piano made be used to reinforce pitch, but gradually the students should learn to keep the vocalise in tune without the aid of an instrument.

Prepare this vocalise by directing the students to phonate a series of four *k*'s without singing. Encourage mini-contractions of the abdominal muscles on each *k*. When this is done correctly, the abdominal muscles will relax slightly after each contraction, allowing the breath to fall back into the lungs. Direct the students to watch this bouncing action of their abdominal musculature. An additional help for elementary students is to bend slightly at the waist on beats 1 and 3 of the staccato sequence. This will aid in activating the contraction of the abdominal musculature on each phonated *k*.

Once the support action is established, sing the vocalise as written, modulating down a perfect fourth by half steps. Sing lightly at a mezzo piano level with moderate tempo. All voices (male and female) may begin this exercise on pitch c^2 in the upper adjustment; changed voices may begin an octave lower. Listen for the emergence of the lower adjustment as the pitch descends. Take caution to prevent the lower adjustment from becoming heavy. This will happen when the dynamic level becomes too loud. Keep the singing light, but not so light as to exclude totally the lower adjustment from producing a robust, resonant singing quality in the middle voice. The two adjustments (upper and lower) should be equally balanced at or around the pitch f$^{\#1}$.

Level 3: The Attack (Exercise 37)

This vocalise (Example 9.4) teaches students to apply the breath easily but with firm support at the onset of pitch production. Using a healthy aspirate attack will encourage application of the breath to the voice. The final objective of the vocalise is to use an imaginary aspirate attack without an audible exhalation of breath. This stroke-of-the-glottis technique (vocal folds coming together at the inception of pitch) is not to be confused with the shock-of-the-glottis technique (vocal folds closing before the attack) and is generally undesirable for singing. (One acceptable use is for articulating a glottal attack lightly when a word begins with a vowel and distinct separation is desired from the preceding word.)

EXAMPLE 9.4.   Vocalise: Vocal Attack.

Direct students to begin each pitch with a light thrust of the abdominal musculature. Breathe between pitches on the quarter rests. Use a light aspirate *h* for maximization of the breath to tone. A changed voice should sing this vocalise one octave lower than written. A changing voice may sing as written in a pure upper-adjustment voice.

Sing the vocalise at a mezzo forte level and at a very slow tempo. Be careful not to force the voice. Use a jaw prop (see Chapter 10, exercise 25) to help vertical vowel position and to increase pharyngeal resonance. Repeat without the jaw prop. Modulate the exercise downward by half steps a perfect fifth. As students increase in their ability to sing in the upper adjustment, begin the exercise gradually higher, up to and including pitch c^2 (or c^1 for changed voices).

When a secure attack is evident, direct the students to sing the exercise without the aspirate *h* and using all primary vowels. Direct students to maintain a mental image of the *h* without actually using it. The vocal folds are to come together at the onset of each pitch.

Level 4: Rolling Pulse (Exercise 52)

The rolling-pulse (Example 9.5) exercise further refines the pulsing action of the abdominal musculature as it is applied to the voice. It activates the support process while keeping the abdominal muscles from becoming tense or rigid for singing. This flexibility of the breath support encourages the voice to float on the breath without being driven by the breath. Singing with a "balanced resistance" between the support and phonation mechanisms is the ultimate goal of this exercise.

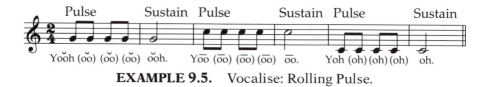

EXAMPLE 9.5.   Vocalise: Rolling Pulse.

Preparation for this vocalise begins by directing students to sustain a lower-adjustment pitch on *yoh*, rolling or pulsing (lower-wheelie exercise 49, in Chapter 7) four times before sustaining the final vowel in an upward vocal inflection. Exaggerate the abdominal pulsing so as to produce a noticeable pulse in the voice. Repeat this action with the upper wheelie (exercise 50) and the spiral wheelie (exercise 51).

Midvoice Pulse.   Apply the rolling or pulsing action to the voice as shown in the middle adjustment. The first measure is pulsed while the second measure is sustained without the pulse. Use the *yooh* sound as in the word *your*. Encourage the lifting-up thought on the second measure and monitor for a free sound. Begin on pitch g^1 (an octave lower for changed voices), singing the two measures on one breath. Use a jaw prop to increase pharyngeal resonance and the abdominal press to increase the pulsing action for those students who need remedial help.

Upper-voice Pulse.   Repeat the pulsing action in the upper adjustment on pitch c^2, or c^1 for changed voices. Use *yoo* as the upper adjustment vowel. Use a jaw prop to increase pharyngeal resonance and the abdominal pulse for these students who have trouble making the pulsing action work.

Lower-voice Pulse.   Repeat the pulsing action in the lower adjustment on pitch c^1 (an octave lower for changed voices). Use *yoh* as the lower-adjustment vowel. Use a jaw prop to increase pharyngeal resonance and the abdominal pulse as a remedial technique. When doing this part of the exercise with young adolescents, gradually lower the pitch by half steps to G below middle C. Take care that the females do not push into the lower adjustment (chest register) with a strident sound. Keep the tone light, and maintain forward placement.

Listen for an emerging vibrato on the sustained pitch following the pulsing action in each of the three adjustments. As the abdominal musculature begins to coordinate with the voice, natural vibrato will appear. Students should be told that this is a natural phenomenon that will occur when their voices are being produced correctly, and not something that is manufactured. It can be compared to the well-tuned engine of a car that idles smoothly. An even vibrato is a sign of a well-functioning voice.

Level 5: Intonation (Exercise 67)

Intonation exercises help to tune the ear for better pitch accuracy and part independence. Students need to learn to sing intervals by ear as well as by sight. A good sense of relative pitch can be developed through early training with pitch-discrimination exercises.

Tuning Pitch. It is possible to develop a sense of perfect pitch as well as relative pitch. Students will often begin to sing a song in the same key in which they learned it. This type of tonal memory should be encouraged by asking students frequently to sing or hum a tuning pitch before the pitch is given by an instrument. Many vocalises in this method begin in the key of C and often on the pitch g^1. This pitch (or another of the instructor's choosing) can be referred to as the "tuning pitch" in relation to which all other pitches are located. Some teachers have gone so far as to buy each student a tuning fork, which can be referred to frequently throughout the day. The important point is that the instructor ask the students for the initial pitch, and not always give the pitch to the students from an instrument.

When beginning a song, even before the accompaniment starts, direct younger students to hum the first pitch of the song (after the tuning pitch has been found) in unison. Direct students to listen to the group as a whole and for the unison blend of all voices. Also, have them sing silently (inwardly) before singing out loud. Inner hearing should be constantly exercised with young singers.

Moving by Half Steps. Direct all voices to sing *loo* on g^1 for elementary students or c^1 for adolescents. On repeated cues from the instructor, women or treble I move up by half steps, while men or treble II move down by half steps. Move up or down a major third until the interval of a minor sixth is reached. Call attention to the intervallic progression: unison, major second, major third, tritone, and minor sixth. With changed voices, the exercise can progress to the octave (f to f^1). This is a difficult intonation exercise and requires much concentration.

Tuning Intervals. Direct students to sing ascending and descending minor second intervals as shown in Example 9.6. (Changed voices will sing an octave lower.) Sing the pattern softly and slowly, breathing at the breath marks. Concentrate on making the ascending movement mentally bigger than the descending movement. Repeat the rhythm and movement of this vocalise with successively larger intervals: M2, m3, M3, and so on. When students can learn to sing major and minor seconds in tune from any pitch, they will be on their way to solving a majority of the intonational problems that occur in singing.

Steps. A resource for helping young singers identify intervals by sight, sound, and the way they "feel" in their voices is an interval study

doo-doo-etc.

EXAMPLE 9.6. Vocalise: Tuning Intervals.

entitled *Steps*, by Darlene Lawrence (Gentry Publications, 1988). This unique teaching tool contains eight songs, each emphasizing different intervals. The songs have interesting texts, are fun to sing, and can produce some profitable discussion about intervals. An accompaniment edition is available (JG0700), and a separate singer's edition (JG02071). A cassette accompaniment track also is available separately (JGTC2090). This is a musical means to learning intervals!

Level 6: Warm-up Tunes (Exercise 82)

Folk and Traditional Songs. As a change from vocalises, easy folk and traditional songs can be used as warm-ups. The songs chosen should be of the type that are easily sung and of limited vocal range. An excellent source is *Where in the World: Folksong Warm-Ups from Many Lands,* by Helen Kemp (Augsburg Fortress Press, 11-8910).

Rounds and Canons. Rounds and canons are very appropriate for use as warm-ups when the instructor wishes to vary the vocalise routine. "O Music," by Lowell Mason, is an easy canon (Example 9.7) that can be learned by all students. An arrangement by Doreen Rao with piano accompaniment is available from Boosey & Hawkes (OCTB6352).

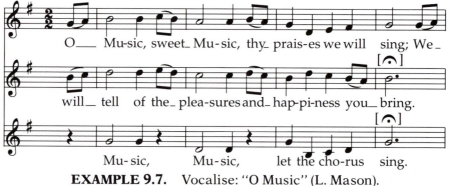

EXAMPLE 9.7. Vocalise: "O Music" (L. Mason).

Nonsense Songs. Songs that use nonsense syllables also make good warm-up tunes. "Kum-ma-la-ma" (Example 9.8) is a call-and-response-type song. The instructor sings each line, which is then repeated by the singers. The routine can be varied by choosing one of the students to be the leader in this fun song.

Gregorian Chant. The traditional melodies of Gregorian chant are among the most beautiful and simple of the vocal literature. Sung with ease and purity of vowel, they serve well as a vocal warm-up, especially for adolescents. "Hodie Christus natus est" (Example 9.9) is a chant that can be sung by both elementary and secondary students. It was used by Benjamin Britten in the opening of his *Ceremony of Carols,*

EXAMPLE 9.8.   Vocalise: "Kum-ma-la-ma" (Traditional).

and the Robert Shaw recording (RCA Victor LSC-2759) serves as a good model for the proper singing style of this chant.

There are four breath or pause marks used in chant. The "quarter pause" is a vertical line that extends through the top two lines of the staff; it indicates a subtle pause on the note before the vertical line, but no breath. The "half pause" is a vertical line in the center of the staff touching the middle three lines; it also indicates a pause, and an optional breath. The "full pause" is a traditional full bar line and indicates the end of a phrase and a breath. The "double bar" indicates the end of the chant.

Chironomy is the term given to the conducting of chant. It is a circular, rolling gesture of the hand that corresponds to the rise and fall of the melodic line. Chant is nonmetric and does not use regular bar lines or traditional conducting gestures. The music flows with the basic word rhythm and is sung in a declamatory, contemplative style. For further information on the correct singing of Gregorian chant, consult Hugle (1928) and *Liber usualis* (1934).

Hymns and Chorales.   Traditional hymns and chorales are excellent sources of warm-up materials. Part-singing, diction, and expres-

EXAMPLE 9.9.   Vocalise: "Hodie Christus natus est" (Gregorian Chant).

sive elements can be helped greatly by the singing of hymns and chorales, and much of the repertoire is in the public domain.

UNIFORM VOWEL COLORS

Goal: The student will develop the technique of uniform vowel colors for resonant singing, through exercises involving shaping of the vocal tract, increasing resonance, and legato movement.

Vowels form the basis of beautiful choral tone. Much time must be given to the study of proper vowel production if an individual or a group of singers is to achieve musical distinction. Vowel formants must be tuned so as to achieve the most resonant sound and in-tune singing. Poor speech habits become poor singing habits. Students need to understand that there is a singing diction that is separate from speaking diction. When words are sung, the vowels are often elongated and given different stress than for speech. Therefore, students will sing the language as they speak it unless trained differently. Singing diction requires that much attention be paid to the proper pronunciation of words in order that a beautiful tone be produced.

There are five primary vowels in the English language: *a, e, i, o, u.* Only the *e* is a "pure" vowel—that is, has only one sound. The other pri-

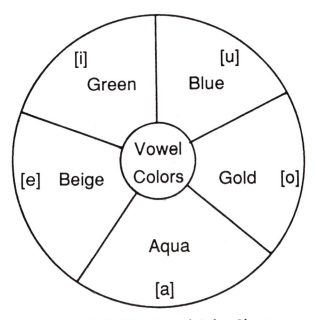

FIGURE 9–10. Vowel Color Chart.

mary vowels are combinations of two vowel sounds and are not especially conducive to vocalization. Therefore, most of the vocalises in this method use the Italian enunciation of these vowels, all of which are pure sounds: *a* (*ah*) [ɑ]; *e* (*eh*) [e]; *i* (*ee*) [i]; *o* (*oh*) [o]; and *u* (*oo*) [u]. The brackets contain the International Phonetic Alphabet (IPA) symbols that are used to represent these five primary sounds. A listing of these symbols is given in Chapter 10.

Each primary vowel "color" is to be taught with reference to a color of the spectrum. The instructor should make a color wheel of the various colors used in this part of the method (Figure 9–10). By associating a particular vowel sound with a certain color of the spectrum, students will learn a model by which to make both visual and aural comparisons of all future vowels of that class. When the proper production of a certain vowel is then questioned by the teacher, reference may be made to the color of the vowel, recalling for the students the proper model of the desired sound.

Students tend to sing all vowels with a rather small and narrow mouth opening. Resonance suffers from this type of production. Encourage tall, vertical production for all vowels. The old "two fingers in the mouth" technique, while not an especially effective means for developing habitual jaw drop for singing (the exercises under "Vocal-Tract Freedom" in Chapter 10 are given for this purpose), does give the students the initial idea of how much the mouth can open for singing diction. Horizontal or vertical hand signals from the instructor may be used to remind students of the difference between narrow (horizontal) and tall (vertical) vowel production. A thick rubber band pulled horizontally or vertically is another visual that can be used to demonstrate the incorrect (narrow) or correct (tall) mouth-jaw position for singing vowels (Figure 9–11).

Uniformity of vowels is a major objective of resonant tone production. Students naturally chew vowels, making much variation in the mouth-jaw position when changing from vowel to vowel (as in speech). Singing diction requires a more uniform, open mouth-jaw position for all vowels. The narrow vowels [u], [e], and [i], will not have as great a mouth-jaw opening as the broad vowels [ɑ] and [o], but more depth of opening is required of the narrow vowels if a uniform vocal sound is to be achieved. This method uses the vowel sequence [u], [o], [ɑ], [e], [i], as jaw opening becomes progressively more from the [u] to the [o] to the [ɑ] and progressively less from the [ɑ] to the [e] to the [i] (Figure 9–12). This variation, however, should be rather slight and hardly noticeable when gliding from one vowel to the next.

Vowels in this method are taught with a vertical, flared position to the lips—that is, with lips extended slightly forward (Figure 9–13). When the jaw is relaxed, the swallowing muscles are not as likely to trigger the elevation of the larynx. With the lips flared slightly forward there is less chance of a mouthy, thin sound because the vowel formants are lowered. The flared position of the vowels also counters the spread position that is so common for the narrow vowels.

Level 1: The Model Vowel [u] (Exercise 8)

Oo as in Blue. The [u] vowel traditionally has been used in the training of children's voices as the model for all other vowel production. The *oo* sound most naturally resonates in the pharynx when the larynx is permitted to remain in its natural, at-rest position. As pharyngeal resonance is most desirable, the *oo* sound serves well as a basis for establishing this quality in the singing tone.

In producing the *oo* vowel, care must be taken that the lips not be pressed into a very small mouth opening. This tends to darken the sound too much and counters the relaxation of the jaw. One finger's width between the teeth is recommended for proper [u] vowel production. Figure 9–14 shows the incorrect and correct mouth-jaw-lip position for the *oo* sound. Note that the lips are naturally extended in the correct position, and the jaw more relaxed than in the pressed position.

Direct students' attention to the blue of the color wheel. Explain that in the word *blue* is the vowel sound *oo*, one of the five primary vowel colors with which we sing. Now demonstrate the proper production of the word *blue* by speaking it with the lips extending slightly

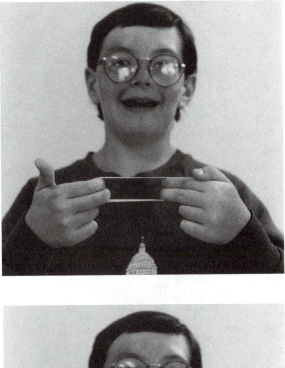

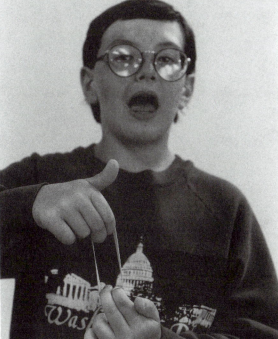

FIGURE 9–11. Rubber-Band Cues for Vowel Formation: (*a*) Incorrect Horizontal Vowel Formation; (*b*) Correct Vertical Vowel Formation.

FIGURE 9–12. Jaw-Lip Position for Vertical Vowel: (*a*) for the Vowel [u]; (*b*) for the Vowel [o]; (*c*) for the Vowel [ɑ].

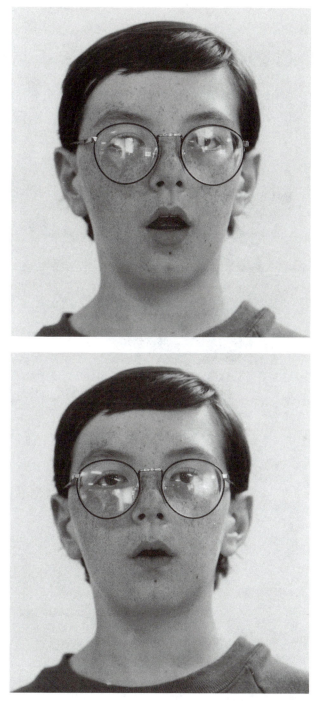

FIGURE 9–12. Jaw-Lip Position for Vertical Vowel: (*d*) for the Vowel [e]; (*e*) for the Vowel [i].

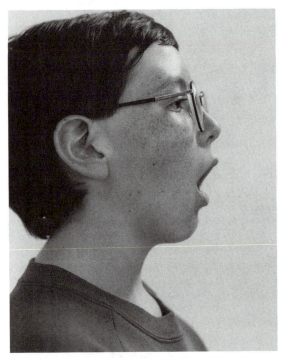

FIGURE 9–13. Vertical-Flared Vowel Position for the Vowel [ɑ].

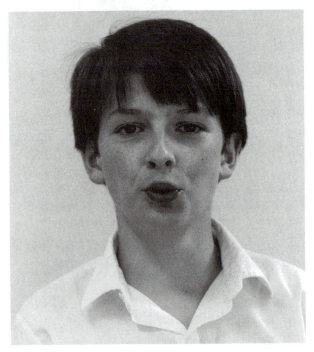

FIGURE 9–14. Incorrect Lip-Jaw Position for the Vowel [u].

forward and jaw relaxed. Direct the students to imitate your model. Many students will say *blue* with pressed lips and little jaw depth. Have them say *blah-blah-blah-blah-blah* (lots of giggles), noting how far the jaw drops on *blah*. Repeat by saying *blue-blue-blue-blue-blue* with as much jaw drop for *blue* as for *blah*. This will help to relax the jaw. Now place one finger width (first finger) between the teeth and say *oo* together. Repeat by withdrawing the finger while saying *oo*. Inform the students that this finger's width is the amount of opening required to properly sing the *oo* sound. Return to this procedure many times in checking students for the correct amount of mouth opening for the [u] vowel. Check individuals at random on their pronunciation of *blue*. Listen for clear glottal closure, or buzz, and look for the relaxed jaw and slightly extended lips.

Singing Oo.   Direct students to sustain a hum on pitch g^1 for unchanged, changing, and female voices, and small g for changed male voices. Lips should be lightly together, with teeth parted. On cue from the instructor (closed fist to open hand), students should open the hum to the vowel *oo* and sustain until directed to stop (Figure 9–15). Model this exercise and the desired tone quality. Keep the sound light, especially in children's voices, in which the tendency may be to sing everything in the lower adjustment. Check individual students at random, noting those with pitch problems or those who appear to sing in the wrong adjustment.

Lower the pitch to middle C (small c for changed voices) and repeat the hum to the *oo*, and listen to determine who can and cannot sing in the pure lower adjustment. Direct students to place one finger in an ear so as to better hear their own voices. Check students individually, especially those who appear not to be matching pitch. Primary students will often match pitch better when they sing individually than in a group.

Say *blue* in the upper-adjustment voice and direct the students to imitate this light upper sound. Raise the pitch to c^2 (middle C for changed voices) and repeat the hum to the *oo* sound. Listen again to determine who can and cannot sing in tune in the proper adjustment. Continue to emphasize the extended lips and relaxed jaw. Apply the abdominal pulse to this vocalise to check for the breath connection and lifting-up movement for singing.

This exercise is intended for guided practice in the vocal production of the model vowel in the various vocal adjustments (except for changed male voices, who only sing in this exercise in the lower adjustment). Remind the students of the three adjustments in which they are singing this vocalise. They should begin to identify the terms *upper voice, middle voice,* and *lower voice* with a sound and a feeling for each. Some students may be unable to produce a desirable tone quality in one or more adjustments. This is to be expected. Continue to model the *blue* vowel and use this exercise to inventory student achievement and progress.

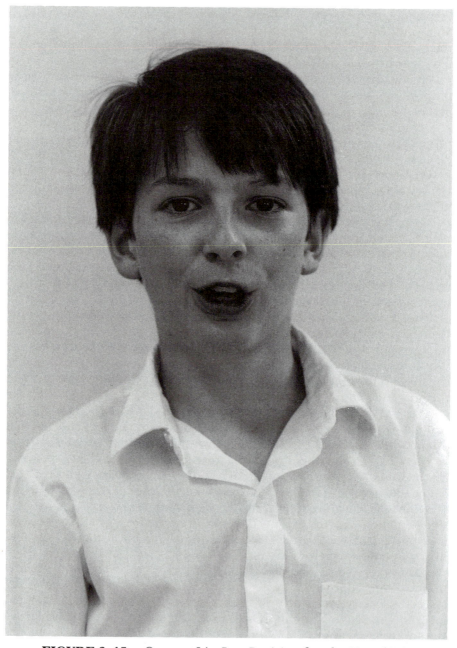

FIGURE 9–15.   Correct Lip-Jaw Position for the Vowel [u].

Level 2: Solfège Patterns (Exercise 23)

Solfège syllables include four of the five primary vowel sounds: [o], [e], [i], and [ɑ]. Since [u] was introduced in Level 1, the use of the traditional solfège syllables now expands the students' vowel vocabulary to the basic five sounds for vocalization: [u], [o], [ɑ], [e], and [i].

Latin Phonemes. Inform the students that they are going to learn a very old musical "language" as a help in learning to sing. This language has seven syllables: do, re, mi, fa, sol, la, ti, with do repeated at the end. Because these syllables are from a foreign language (Latin), they must be sung pure, as in Latin. (Everyone likes to have his or her name pronounced correctly, and therefore, the names of these syllables also should be spoken correctly.)

Model each of the syllables, being sure not to use English diphthongs. Have the students imitate the vocal model for each of the solfège syllables: do [o], re [e], mi [i], fa [ɑ], sol [o], la [ɑ], ti [i], do [o]. Now repeat the model vowel [u] before each of the other four primary sounds, directing students to keep the slightly extended lips from the [u] for each of the other vowels. When moving from the [u] vowel to the [i] vowel, the width of one finger between the teeth should be maintained. Direct students to say [u] to [i] with one finger's width between the teeth, with the tongue lightly touching the fingertip. Practice this a number of times, as students tend to close the mouth the most for the [i] sound and pull the tongue too far back into the mouth. Alternate the practice of [u] to [i] with and without one finger between the teeth.

Direct students to speak [u] to [o] and [u] to [e] as before. Note that the jaw will drop a bit more for the [o] and [e] sounds, but the lips should remain slightly extended. Now model and practice saying the solfège syllables.

The [ɑ] vowel is the most open of vowel sounds, with the approximate width of two fingers between the teeth. Model and practice moving from the [u] vowel to the [ɑ] vowel, noting the greater jaw depth needed for the [ɑ] sound. Check the [ɑ] production by placing the first two fingers between the teeth, and maintain this depth while speaking the vowel and removing the fingers. Now model and practice saying all of the solfège syllables. Check the individual syllables for proper lip extension and depth of jaw.

Tonal Patterns. Once the students are able to speak the solfège syllables correctly, they are ready to begin singing the syllables. Sing sustained pitches, modeling each sound correctly, and then have the students replicate the model. This may be followed by two- or three-note tonal patterns sung to the group and to individuals, with the students again replicating the model. Always monitor for pure vowels sung in the vertical position. Employ the Curwen-Kodály hand signals (Figure 9–16) as a means of visualizing tonal patterns. Changed voices will sing one octave lower.

Do

Ti

La

Sol

Fa

Mi

Re

Do

FIGURE 9–16. Curwen-Kodály Hand Signs for Solfège.

Level 3: Vertical Vowels (Exercise 38)

The following exercises are a continuation of the vowel-formation techniques that were begun in Levels 1 and 2. Through these vocalises the student is encouraged to form the habit of singing pure vowels with a relaxed jaw and slightly extended lips. This type of production provides both depth and ring for a vibrant tone quality.

Vowel Focus. A strong *vvv* sensation with upper teeth against the lower lips will help to direct the sensation of forward tone placement while maintaining a deep-set (pharyngeal) vowel. Direct students to say *voo-voh-vah-veh-vee* with an exaggerated buzz of the upper teeth against the lower lip and a forward feeling of the following vowel sound ("on the lips"). The lift of the upper lip on the *v* prior to the vowel is helpful in establishing the lip-flare movement.

Direct students to sing the vocalise in Example 9.10, gradually changing from the buzzing *vvvv* to the model vowel *oo*. Encourage the flared lips and repeat the vocalise a half step higher each time, changing the vowel. Changed voices will sing this vocalise an octave lower. Listen for a ringing sensation of the tone in the mask.

Vvvvvvvvvvvvvvvvoo - - - - - - -

EXAMPLE 9.10.   Vocalise: Vowel Focus on *v.*

VOWEL PURITY

1. Oh as in gold [o]. Direct students' attention to the gold color of the color-wheel. Explain that in the color gold is the vowel *oh,* the second of the primary vowels with which we sing. (Note: The word *gold* has very little of the vanishing *oo* sound as heard in such words as *go* and *no.* Develop the pure *oh* without the vanishing *oo* sound.)

Say the word *gold* with much pharyngeal resonance and flared lips in the lower adjustment. Direct students to imitate you. Model the *oo* vowel once again as a point of reference. Speak in a resonant lower adjustment with flared lips. Move from the *oo* to the *oh* while maintaining the same flared lips and pharyngeal ring. The jaw will drop a bit more for the *oh* vowel. Direct students to imitate the instructor's vocal model. If necessary, use a jaw prop to secure the correct pharyngeal placement and focus for the *oh* vowel.

2. Ah as in aqua [ɑ]. Direct students' attention to the aqua color of the color wheel. Explain that in the word *aqua* the first *a* is the vowel sound *ah* (third primary vowel as in *father*) while the second *a* is the neutral sound *uh.* It is the initial vowel in which we are interested as singers, as the neutral vowel *uh* is rather colorless and should be avoided as much as possible. Say the word *aqua* with much pharyngeal resonance and flared lips in the lower adjustment. Sustain the first *a*. Direct students to imitate you.

Model the *oo* vowel once again as a point of reference. Speak in a resonant lower adjustment with flared lips. Move from the *oo* to the *ah* while maintaining the same flared lips and pharyngeal ring. The jaw will drop more for the *ah* vowel (the width of two fingers). Direct students to imitate your vocal model.

3. Oo-oh-ah [u]-[o]-[ɑ]. Model the vowel sequence *oo-oh-ah* in the lower-adjustment speaking voice with much resonance and ring in the mask. Use a jaw prop to maintain pharyngeal ring. Direct students to imitate the vowel sequence *oo-oh-ah* with a little more jaw depth on each successive vowel. Sing the vocalise in Example 9.11 maintaining depth (flare) and ring (jaw opening) on all vowels.

4. Ay as in beige [e]. Direct students' attention to the beige color of the color wheel. Explain that in the word *beige* is the vowel sound *ay*, the fourth of the primary vowel colors with which we sing. (Note: The word *beige* has the compound sounds of *ay* and *ee* as a part of the diphthong *ei*. Minimize the vanishing *ee* vowel, and treat the *ay* vowel almost as *eh*. The word should be pronounced *behge*.)

Direct the class to watch your lips as you pronounce the word *beige*.

EXAMPLE 9.11.   Vocalise: Vowel Uniformity on [u]-[o]-[ɑ].

Speak the word with flared lips and more jaw drop than usual. Direct students to imitate you. As the *ay* sound tends to call for less jaw drop, practice speaking *ah* to *ay* with no jaw movement. Tell the students that there are to be no "pancake" (flat or shallow) vowels. *Ay* and *ee* tend to be too shallow (spread like a pancake) and require more jaw drop than normally.

5. Ee as in green [i]. Direct students' attention to the green color of the color wheel. Explain that in the word *green* is the vowel sound *ee*, the last of the five primary vowel colors with which we sing. (Note: The vowel sound *ee* is the most closed of all and will require special attention to keep from spreading and being shallow.) Direct the class to watch your lips as you pronounce the word *green*. Speak the word *green* with flared lips and more jaw drop than usual. Direct students to imitate you. Demonstrate speaking the vowel sequence *ah-ay-ee* with little or no jaw movement. Direct students to imitate you.

6. Oo-ay-ee [u]-[e]-[i]. Model the vowel sequence *oo-ay-ee* in the lower-adjustment speaking voice with much pharyngeal ring and mask placement. Sing the vocalise in Example 9.12 as written (changed male voices sing one octave below). Use a jaw prop, and repeat without the jaw prop, noting any vowel chewing. The jaw will relax slightly more for the [e] vowel and return to the [u] position for the [i] vowel (one finger's width).

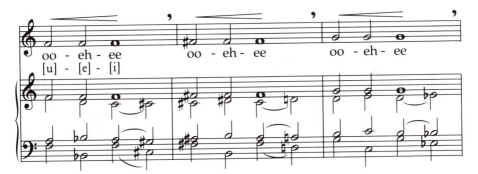

EXAMPLE 9.12. Vocalise: Vowel Uniformity on [u]-[e]-[i].

Level 4: Legato Movement (Exercise 53)

A smooth legato line is a requirement of fine singing. Students are encouraged to flow from vowel to vowel while maintaining uniformity of production.

Unison Movement.   Direct students to sing the vocalise in Example 9.13 using the five primary vowels as shown (changed male voices sing one octave below). Sing on one breath and glide from vowel to vowel with as little jaw movement as possible. Modulate up and down a minor third. Use a jaw prop to increase pharyngeal resonance, and keep the tongue forward in the mouth. Work for legato articulation.

oo___ oh____ ah___ eh____ ee__etc.
[u] - [o] - [ɑ] - [e] - [i]

EXAMPLE 9.13.   Vocalise: Unison Legato Movement on Long Vowels.

Four-part Movement.   The four-part vocalise in Example 9.14 is excellent for adolescent voices. It is quickly learned and can be sung a variety of ways: loud; soft; soft to loud; loud to soft; four bumps, or pulses, to the half note (to encourage application of breath to voice); and hummed. Maintain the legato movement from vowel to vowel.

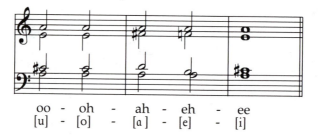

oo - oh - ah - eh - ee
[u] - [o] - [ɑ] - [e] - [i]

EXAMPLE 9.14.   Vocalise: Four-part Legato Movement on Long Vowels.

Level 5: Short Vowels (Exercise 68)

Seven Short Vowels.   There are seven short-vowel colors with which the students must learn to sing. While there are numerous variations of short-vowel sounds, the seven given here are the most common ones.

Short vowels are by nature shallow vowels. Short vowels need more jaw depth than usually given. Emphasize the need for more jaw drop and vertical positioning by writing a V under those words in the text that need more depth. Practice singing sustained pitches on the words given for each of the short-vowel sounds.

1. *e*   = red   [ɛ]   wed, tell, bed, said, head

2. *i*   = pink   [I]   him, tint, din, lift, since, pity

3. *a*   = black   [æ]   cat, lamp, can, have, magic, lamb

4. *u*   (stressed)   = buff   [ʌ]   sun, much, the, some, touch, love

5. *u*   (unstressed) = aqua   [ə]   Christmas, shepherds, angel, riot

6. *oo*   [ʊ]   put, full, crooked, brook, foot

7. *ur*   = purple   [ɜ]   err, burn, her, bird, world, word

The schwa vowel [ə] is particularly colorless in singing diction. It occurs in unstressed syllables and in many common words such as *the, of, from,* and *a.* It sounds affected to change the schwa to [ɑ], as in *Christmahs,* and this should be avoided. However, the schwa must be given more depth of jaw opening if it is to have more vertical room to resonate. All short vowels must be sung as vertical vowels if they are to have uniform depth and color.

Unison Movement.   Direct students to sing the vocalise in Example 9.15 using the five short vowels as shown (changed male voices sing one octave below). Sing on one breath and glide from vowel to vowel with as little jaw movement as possible. Modulate up and down a minor third. Use a jaw prop to increase pharyngeal resonance, and keep the tongue forward in the mouth. Work for legato articulation.

[ʊ]   [I]   [ɛ]   [æ]   [ʌ]

EXAMPLE 9.15.   Vocalise: Unison Legato Movement on Short Vowels.

Four-part Movement.   Repeat the vocalise in Example 9.13 using the five short vowels [ʊ], [I], [ɛ], [æ], [ʌ]. Carry the lip extension on the first vowel [ʊ] through the following vowels, and maintain the vertical positioning on all short-vowel colors.

Level 6: Diphthong Production (Exercise 83)

Six Diphthongs.   There are six basic vowel combinations (diphthongs) with which the students must learn to sing:

1. *i*   = *ah* + *ee*, as in *white*   [ɑi]
2. *ay*   = *eh* + *ee*, as in *gray*   [ei]
3. *o*   = *oh* + *oo*, as in *rose*   [ou]
4. *ow/ou* = *ah* + *oo*, as in *brown*   [ɑu]
5. *oy/oi* = *aw* + *ee*, as in *turquoise* [ɔi]
6. *ew/u* = *ee* + *oo*, as in *fuchsia*   [iu]

Madeleine Marshall (1946) notes that the second vowel sound in words such as *night, day,* and *boy* is [I] and not [i] (p. 167). Christy (1974), however, shows the second vowel to be long [i], and this is the sound preferred by the present author.

The first five vowel combinations are correctly produced by sustaining the initial vowel sound, adding the vanishing vowel color very quickly at the termination of the syllable. With the sixth vowel combination, the initial vowel (*ee*) is executed quickly, passing immediately to the second vowel (*oo*), which is sustained.

Correlate each vowel combination with the color given. Speak each color on a 4 count, sustaining the initial vowel (except number 6) to the end of the count, quickly adding the vanishing sound on the cutoff (the last half of beat 4).

Singing Diphthongs.   Direct students to sing the phrases in Example 9.16 (an octave lower for changed voices). Sustain the initial vowel (except number 6) as a dotted quarter note tied to a sixteenth note, adding the vanishing vowel on the final sixteenth. For number 6, move quickly through the [i] sound to sustain the [u] vowel. Notice that the word *tunes* is pronounced with the liquid [iu] combination, and not with [u] alone.

VOCAL COORDINATION

Goal: The student will develop the technique of vocal-register coordination, through various exercises involving pitch exploration and accuracy, register definition and coordination, increased resonance, and flexibility.

The middle register of the voice (middle C to one octave above) is

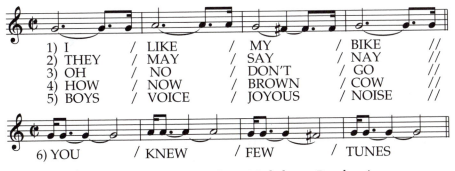

EXAMPLE 9.16. Vocalise: Diphthong Production.

the most difficult to coordinate correctly, and yet, it is the register in which most children's singing takes place. In children's unchanged voices, this register is like a mature woman's voice and often exhibits the same quality of voice break around the pitch a^1. In boys' changed voices, this register is the top, or tenor, register, and is known in the bel canto tradition as the passagio. In both cases, the register between middle C and one octave above is handled identically: the lower and upper adjustments must share the responsibility of pitch production. However, the passagio adjustment in the changed male voice is difficult to teach and learn, and is addressed separately in Chapter 4.

The following exercises for vocal coordination begin with pitch exploration for the purpose of discovering the various registers of the singing voice. "Upper to lower" brings the upper voice down into the lower, which is the best way of coordinating the voice. The "octave lift" applies the breath in a vital support thrust to the upper adjustment octave, and "lighten up" teaches the singer to make the transition from lower to upper adjustment. "Midvoice balance" trains the singer to listen for the balance between upper and lower adjustments, and the "ho-ho choruses" are a fun way to synthesize the vocal coordination process. Males with changed and changing voices are expected to exercise the upper adjustment as a means of strengthening and maintaining this part of the singing voice. Males do not lose the ability to sing in the upper adjustment as their voices change. While the range of the upper adjustment does become more limited, it is possible for the adolescent male to sing in the pure upper adjustment from c^1 to c^2, as discussed in Chapter 4.

Level 1: Pitch Exploration (Exercise 9)

Pitch Modeling (Example 9.17). Sing and model isolated pitches on *loo*, with the group echoing. Model in the three vocal registers: lower (chest), middle (combined) and upper (head). Check students individually for correct pitch matching, lip extension, and jaw depth (one

loo - loo-loo loo ___   loo-loo loo-loo loo ___   loo loo-loo-loo loo ___
(Tutti on each repeat)

EXAMPLE 9.17.   Vocalise: Pitch Modeling in Three Registers.

finger's width). Students should be able to feel and recognize when they are singing in the upper, middle, and lower voices.

Echo Patterns (Example 9.18).   Expand the pitch modeling into echo (rhythm) patterns. Work on tonal memory and inner hearing by directing the students to sing the patterns mentally before singing out loud. Gradually expand the period of silence before the echo. Permit no humming or other sounds during the silence. Students should be taught to listen with the inner ear. Gradually expand the patterns to include more complicated rhythms and intervals. Patterns also may be presented first at the piano, with students echoing on a neutral syllable.

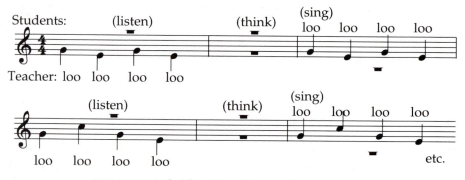

EXAMPLE 9.18.   Vocalise: Echo Patterns.

Remedial Techniques (inaccurate singers).   The following techniques may be used with students who have trouble matching pitch:

1. Provide many opportunities for young children to sing alone after a model.

2. Use tonal patterns rather than single pitches in pitch-matching exercises.

3. Review the animal-farm exercises. Find the desired register through animal-vocal imitation.

4. Remind students to use the upper voice. Some children forget about this voice until it becomes habitual.

5. Remind students to listen on the outside, listen on the inside (inner hearing), sing the pitch, and determine whether the pitch is correct.

6. Use the abdominal pulse (manual pulsing of the abdominal area) on sustained pitches. This will help to generate inter-thoracic pressure. Precede inhalation with the sip of air.

7. Match the student's pitch level, and move from there to various other pitches.

8. Have each student cover one ear while singing. This will aid the hearing of one's own voice.

9. Use visual aids and hand gestures to depict the level of the desired pitch.

10. Provide for feedback, first from the student (describing the "sensation") and then from you (positive reinforcement).

Level 2: Upper to Lower (Exercise 24)

The best way to develop the blending of vocal registers initially is from the top down. Singing downward in the upper adjustment will naturally bring in a mixture of the lower adjustment as the pitch descends. Working from the bottom up is a more advanced technique.

Upper to Lower 1 (Example 9.19). Direct students to sing descending triads (sol-mi-do), beginning in the pure upper adjustment. Lower by half steps. Listen for the emerging middle voice as the lower adjustment mixes with the upper voice. Keep the balance correct, and do not permit the lower adjustment to dominate before the pitch $f^{\#1}$.

(h)oo _____   (h)oo _____   (h)oo _____   (h)oo _____

EXAMPLE 9.19.   Vocalise: Upper to Lower 1.

Keep the *oo* [u] vowel open and relaxed. All voices may sing at the pitch level given. Do not sing the exercise any lower than middle C. Changed male voices may sing one octave lower, beginning also in head voice.

Upper to Lower 2 (Example 9.20). Direct students to sing descending scale pattern (sol-fa-mi-re-do) on a staccato *koo* [u]. Lower by half steps. As before, listen for the emerging middle voice as the lower adjustment mixes with the upper voice. Boys' changing voices will remain more in the pure upper adjustment and should not be encouraged to mix the voices too soon. Do not sing the exercise lower than middle C (one octave lower for changed male voices).

koo - koo - koo - koo - koo - koo.   koo - koo - koo - koo

EXAMPLE 9.20.   Vocalise: Upper to Lower 2.

Level 3: Octave Lift (Exercise 39)

Direct all students to sing the octave lift given in Example 9.21. Sing lightly! Emphasize much use of the aspirate in the upper adjustment. Changed and changing voices will shift into the upper adjustment, as should the other voices. If the unchanged and female voices do not shift, have them imitate the changed (changing) male sound.

la   hoo   la__,   la   hoo   la__etc.

EXAMPLE 9.21.   Vocalise: Octave Lift.

Raise the vocalise a minor third by half steps. As more experience is gained in singing in the upper adjustment, repeat the octave lift, hold the octave, and then gradually descend by step. Keep the lightness of the upper adjustment in the descent, but note also the gradual increase of the lower adjustment from pitch $f^{\#1}$ and lower.

Level 4: Lighten Up (Exercise 54)

Students must be directed to lighten up when singing from lower to higher pitches, especially in the octave from c^1 to c^2. Direct students to sing this simple arpeggio vocalise over the perfect fifth, as in Example 9.22. Transpose upward a major third by half steps. Sung in the octave written, it is excellent for developing the upper adjustment in the adolescent junior high boy's voice. These boys should sing it pure, without the blending of registers. Unchanged and female voices will begin in the middle voice on the lower-adjustment side. Be careful to have students lighten into the upper mix as they sing above $f^{\#1}$. The danger will be to carry too much of the lower voice up into the head-voice register.

hip,   hip,   hip,   hip,   hip!

EXAMPLE 9.22.   Vocalise: Lighten Up.

Level 5: Midvoice Balance (Exercise 69)

The purpose of these exercises is to blend further the register break between the upper and lower adjustments. Students can be taught to listen for the balance that should develop between these voices.

Half and Half (Example 9.23). Direct students to sing a descending five-tone pattern (sol-fa-mi-re-do) on *loo*, attempting to keep as much upper adjustment as possible in the lower tones. Begin on pitch d².

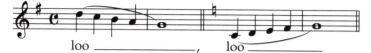

loo _____, loo _____

EXAMPLE 9.23. Vocalise: Half and Half.

Direct students to sing an ascending five-tone pattern (do-re-mi-fa-sol) on *loo*, carrying the lower adjustment to the top tone. This exercise should not be done with boys whose voices are changing, as they should be taught to keep this middle register in the pure upper form until the voice fully settles. It will be easy for most unchanged voices, as children are accustomed to carrying the lower adjustment up too high. Explain to the students that the ideal sound for the middle voice on f#¹ is somewhere between the lower adjustment and upper adjustment (approximately 50 percent of each).

Now sing the descending line again, attempting to gain more lower adjustment on the descent (i.e., maintaining support), but not totally going over to the pure lower adjustment. Likewise, repeat the ascending line and attempt to lighten or add more upper adjustment on the ascent.

Experiment by singing the f#¹ with different combinations of lower and upper adjustments. The instructor's voice will be the best guide in doing this. Tell students to envision pure lower and pure upper adjustments as two hands with fingertips touching; one hand represents the lower adjustment, and the other hand represents the upper adjustment. Singing from pure lower to pure upper (and vice versa) creates a break in the voice, which is not good. However, by bringing the two adjustments together (interlace the fingers of both hands) a bridge can be built between the two adjustments, making a smooth transition between voices possible.

Smooth Connection (Example 9.24). Direct students to sing the vocalise as given, working to create one continuous vocal line by correctly balancing the lower and upper adjustments in the middle voice. A catch breath may be taken between phrases. Transpose upward a minor third by half steps. Changed voices sing an octave lower. Vary the vowels so as to use all five pure vowel sounds.

EXAMPLE 9.24. Vocalise: Smooth Connection (from C. E. Johnson, *The Training of Boys' Voices*, Oliver Ditson Co., 1906).

Level 6: Ho-Ho Choruses (Exercise 84)

"Ho-ho choruses" are fun songs that activate the support process (using the aspirate) while exercising all of the vocal adjustments.

"Laughing Canon," by Cherubini (Example 9.25). This laughing canon must be sung with good staccato articulation on the "Ha!" The

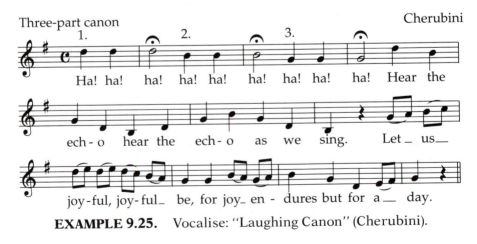

EXAMPLE 9.25. Vocalise: "Laughing Canon" (Cherubini).

EXAMPLE 9.26. Vocalise: "Ho-Ho Chorus" from *Dido and Aeneas* (Purcell).

EXAMPLE 9.26. Vocalise: "Ho-Ho Chorus" (*Continued*)

marcato holds in the first three measures serve only as breath marks, until the end. The canon ends with each voice holding at the fermata.

"Ho-Ho Chorus" from **Dido and Aeneas,** *by Purcell (Example 9.26).* This is an excellent "breath stimulizer" for high school students. It is an instant warm-up when time permits nothing more.

STUDY AND DISCUSSION QUESTIONS

1. Discuss the three basic characteristics of the resonant voice.
2. Define *resonance.* How is resonance achieved in the voice?
3. Discuss the concept of vowel formants and how changes in formant frequencies are achieved. What are the results of such changes?
4. F_1 and F_2 give what characteristic to a vowel? F_3 and F_4 give what characteristic to a vowel?
5. How do the formant frequencies of children's and women's voices differ from those of men's voices?
6. A small jaw opening as [i] does what to F_1 and F_2, respectively? A more open jaw [ɑ] does what to F_1 and F_2, respectively?
7. Identify the major resonators of the voice and any respective divisions.
8. Discuss the "arched soft palate" technique, its contribution to resonance, and how it should be handled when teaching children.
9. Discuss the concept of the open throat. What muscles are the major source of throat constriction? How can these be relaxed?
10. How should the tongue muscle be placed for singing? Discuss the problem of the grooved tongue.
11. What are the four muscles of the tongue that can interfere with the singing process? Why do these muscles interfere?
12. What is the difference between pop and trained singers as regards laryngeal position and vocal resonance? What causes this difference?
13. What is the characteristic sound of a depressed larynx? Why should this sound be avoided?
14. A relaxed larynx means the larynx is in what position? Why is this position beneficial to proper singing?
15. For a richer sound with more depth, how may formants be lowered? For a brighter sound with more projection, how may formants be raised?
16. What happens when the fundamental frequency (f) interacts closely with formant frequency (F)?

17. Describe the "singer's formant." What is theorized to be the origin of the singer's formant?

18. Explain the concept of vowel modification. For what voice parts is it a more common problem? When is vowel modification not a problem?

19. Discuss the phenomenon of the vocal vibrato. Are child and adolescent voices capable of producing a vibrato? How should it be taught?

20. Explain the difference between the vocal problems of tremolo and wobble. Why are vocal tremolo and wobble not common problems among children and adolescents?

References

ALDERSON, R. (1979). *Complete handbook of singing*. West Nyack, NY: Parker.

APPELMAN, R. D. (1967). *The science of vocal pedagogy: Theory and application*. Bloomington: Indiana University Press.

APPELMAN, R. D. (1986). Visual verification of auditory perception of the linguistic signal within an open servo-system and its relationship to vowel placement and textual intelligibility in singing. *The NATS Bulletin, 9*(10), 5–12, 41–42.

BENADE, A. H. (1976). *Fundamentals of music acoustics*. New York: Oxford University Press.

CHRISTY, V. A. (1974). *Foundations in singing*. Dubuque, IA: Wm. C. Brown.

HINES, J. (1982). *Great singers on great singing*. Garden City, NY: Doubleday.

HUGLE, P. G. (1928). *Catechism of Gregorian chant*. Glen Rock, NJ: J. Fischer.

KLEIN, J. J., & SCHJEIDE, O. A. (1972). *Singing technique: How to avoid vocal trouble*. Anaheim, CA: National Music Publishers.

LAWRENCE, D. (1988). *Steps, an interval study for young voices*. Alexandria, IN: Antara Music Group (Gentry Publications).

Liber Usualis (1934). Edition No. 801. Tournai: Desclée et Cie.

MARSHALL, M. (1946). *The singer's manual of English diction*. New York: Schirmer Books.

MCLANE, M. (1985). Artistic vibrato and tremolo: A survey of the literature (Pt. 1). *Journal of Research in Singing, 8*(2), 21–43.

MILLER, R. (1986). *The structure of singing: System and art in vocal technique*. New York: Schirmer Books.

SCOTTO DI CARLO, N., & AUTESSERRE, D. (1987). Movements of the velum in singing. *Journal of Research in Singing and Applied Vocal Pedagogy, 11*(1), 3–13.

SUNDBERG, J. (1977). The acoustics of the singing voice. *Scientific American, 236*, H. W. Freeman and Co., 82–91.

SUNDBERG, J. (1982). Perceptions of singing. In D. Deutsch (Ed.), *The psychology of music*. New York: Academic Press.

TITZE, I. R. (1981). *Principles of voice production*. Unpublished manuscript, The University of Iowa, Iowa City.

TROUP, G. J., WELCH, C., VOLO, M., TRONCONI, A., FERRERO, F., & FARTETANI, E. (1989). On velum opening in singing. *Journal of Research and Applied Vocal Pedagogy, 13*(1), 35–39.

VENNARD, W. (1967). *Singing, the mechanism and the technique*. New York: Carl Fischer.

10

DICTION ✑

Goal: The student will develop the skill of accurate and intelligible singing diction, through exercises relating respiration, phonation, and resonant tone production to vocal-tract conditioning, word pronunciation, and consonant group drill.

Drill is the manner in which a language is spoken. The study of diction is important for students, as word intelligibility is a primary requirement for effective communication, and beautiful tone quality is based on properly resonated vowels. A habit of correct diction also saves time in rehearsals and greatly assists in-tune singing. All too often, however, diction is studied only as needed after problems arise; this approach rarely produces lasting results. It is difficult for students to change habits of sloppy diction when such habits are practiced regularly in speech and song. Therefore, the present method makes the study of diction a formal exercise, encouraging the student to develop a "singer's diction."

The study of diction involves the areas of pronunciation (the manner in which a word is spoken), enunciation (the manner in which a vowel or syllable is spoken), and articulation (the manner in which a consonant is spoken). Correct vowel enunciation requires uniformity of vowel and diphthong production; deep-set quality (pharyngeal resonance), which gives depth and warmth to the voice; and high, forward placement (i.e., in the mask), which gives projection and ring. Distinct consonant articulation requires flexibility of the articulators (tongue, teeth, jaw, etc.), exaggeration of consonants (*s* and *sh* excepted), and rapid consonant production (except for tuned continuants). Taken together, vowels carry the resonant tone of the voice, while consonants make sense of the language. Consonants must not be permitted to destroy a uniform vocal line, but lack of proper articulation results in poor singing.

International Phonetic Alphabet

The study of diction is made easier if students understand the symbols of the International Phonetic Alphabet (IPA). Madeleine Marshall notes, "In the sentence 'Many a baby has a tall father,' there are six pronunciations of the letter *a*. Therefore we cannot speak of the 'sound of *a*' because no one would know which sound we had in mind" (1953, p. 123). The IPA designates one symbol for each vocal sound, regardless of the spelling. It is a universal system and so is used in the study of foreign languages.

There are thirteen basic vowel colors and six diphthongs that the student must learn to sing. The IPA symbols for these vowels and diphthongs are as follows:

IPA Symbol	**Color Word**
Long Vowels	
[u]	blue
[o]	gold
[ɑ]	*a*qua
[ɔ]	mauve
[e]	beige
[i]	green
Short Vowels	
[ɛ]	red
[I]	pink
[æ]	black
[ʊ]	orchid
[ɜ]	purple
Neutral Vowels	
[ʌ]	buff (stressed)
[ə]	aqu*a* (unstressed)
Diphthongs	
[ɑi]	white
[ei]	gray
[ou]	rose
[ɑu]	brown
[ɔi]	turquoise
[iu]	fuchsia

The IPA symbols for consonants are for the most part, identical to the letters used in spelling: *b, d, f, g, h, k, l, m, n, p, r, s, t, v, w, z.* The following nine symbols are unique:

[ŋ]	si*ng*
[θ]	*th*in
[ð]	*th*ine
[hw]	*wh*en
[j]	*y*ou
[ʃ]	*sh*e
[tʃ]	*ch*oose
[ʒ]	vi*si*on
[dʒ]	*G*eorge (soft *g*); *j*oy

The Articulators

There are eight articulators (Figure 10–1) that are responsible for the pronunciation of language (1) jaw, (2) tongue (lingual), (3) teeth (dental), (4) lips (labial), (5) soft palate (velar), (6) hard palate (palatal), (7) upper gum line (alveolar ridge), and (8) glottis (space between the open vocal folds). The student must learn to use these articulators efficiently if proper "singing diction" is to become a habit.

Classifications

Vowels are classified according to the amount of jaw opening used in enunciation. There are two classes: open vowels [ɑ], [o], and [ɔ], and closed vowels [e], and [i], and [u]. The closed vowels are particularly troublesome to singers, as they tend to be spread and thin in production. All vowels need to be exercised for vertical mouth placement.

Vowels are also classified according to natural darkness or brightness. The "dark" long vowels are [u], [o], and [ɔ]. The "bright" long vowels are [i], [e]. amd [ɑ]. All vowels need to be exercised for a balance between darkness and brightness.

There are two classification systems for consonants, according to physical origin and according to similarity of sound. The physical-origin classification is as follows:

1. bilabial:	*p, b, m*	(upper and lower lips)
2. labiodental:	*f, v*	(lower lip and upper teeth)
3. linguodental:	*th*	(tip of tongue and back surface of upper front teeth)

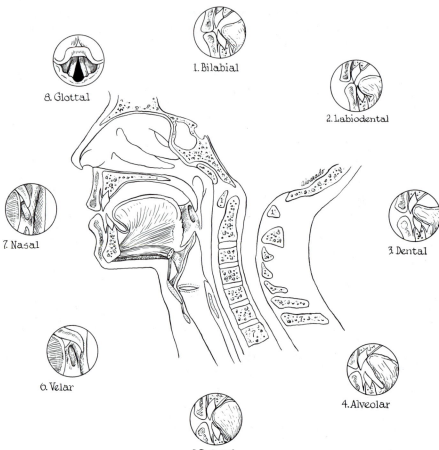

8. Glottal

1. Bilabial

2. Labiodental

7. Nasal

3. Dental

6. Velar

4. Alveolar

5. Palatal

Figure 10–1. The Vocal Articulators.

4. linguo-alveolar:	*t, d, n, l*	(tip of tongue and upper gum line)
	s, soft *c, z*	(sides of tongue against upper back teeth and gum)
5. glottal:	*h, wh*	(space between the vocal folds)
6. linguopalatal:	*ch, j,* soft *g*	(tip of tongue against hard palate)
	r	(as a voiced continuant or trilled)
	sh, zh	(side of tongue against upper back teeth and gum line, and front sides of tongue against hard palate)

7. velar:	*k*, hard *c*	(back of tongue and soft palate)
	hard *g*,	
	ng, q	
	x (ks)	(back of tongue and soft pal-
		ate to tip of tongue and jaw)

The second classification of consonants, according to similarity of sound, is perhaps the better for the musician to know. Because of the similar nature, these are used as group drill in the last part of the diction study in this method. This second classification system has three subdivisions: voiced (which carry a vocal buzz), tuned (which carry pitch), and voiceless (which do not carry pitch). Within these classifications, some consonants are considered to be "plosives," as they are caused by an explosive sound when the articulators come together and interrupt the flow of breath. The opposite of the plosives are the "continuants," in which the articulators briefly sustain the consonant on pitch. A third type comprises the "sibilants," in which the consonants are produced by a stream of air passing between the teeth or between teeth and lips. Lastly, the "aspirates" are silently produced by a stream of air at the glottis. It is not necessary for students to know these classifications. However, students should be drilled in the consonants of the various classes so as to become aware of the various manners of production. Stress the exaggeration and rapid execution of consonants that is needed for word intelligibility.

The "sound" classifications of consonants are as follows:

1. voiceless plosives: *p, t, k, ch*

2. voiced plosives: *b, d, g, j*

3. voiceless sibilants: *f, s, th, sh*

4. tuned continuants: *m* and *n* (sustained), *l* and *r* (not sustained)

5. voiced continuants: *v, z, th, zh*

6. aspirates: *h, wh* (voiced)

Diction for Singing

While unanimity generally exists among voice and choral teachers as to the necessity of vowel purity, uniformity, and the like, there are two schools of thought concerning consonant articulation. These have been identified by Fisher (1986) as sung-speech diction and rhythmic diction (p. 13). Fisher notes the following from vocal authorities Dorothy Uris and Harry Robert Wilson:

> Proponents of "sung-speech diction" suggest that since in spoken language the listener discerns messages from the speaker in acoustical blends of

vowels and consonants, technically termed "smear," it follows that singers should produce such blends to make the text understandable [Uris, quoted in Fisher, p. 13].

Supporters of "sung-speech diction" state further that this practice preserves the continuity of sound production and the legato phrasing that are vital to effective vocal musical performance [Wilson, quoted in Fisher, p. 13].

Concerning "rhythmic diction," Fisher notes,

"Rhythmic diction" practitioners argue that without an underlying rhythmic application of speech sounds in choral music, vowel purity, vowel uniformity, understanding of the text, musical continuity, and even legato may be seriously impoverished. By performing every sound in every syllable within a metered rhythmic structure of music, diction as text and diction as a musical medium are maximized [p. 13].

Music teachers, especially choral directors, should be aware of the rather recent debate between those who advocate sung-speech diction and those who advocate rhythmic diction. When Fred Waring and his glee club made choral singing a popular idiom a generation ago, sung-speech diction became the model that Waring used to promote his style of singing. Waring published a monograph entitled *Tone Syllables* (1951), which presented his approach to singing diction. He states, "The visual impression of space between printed words may be a handicap to the singer. In speech and singing there should be no such space; the end of each word or syllable is joined to the beginning of the following word or syllable" (p. 2). Shawnee Press, Waring's publishing company, published all of his group's music with a special type of phonetics under the text, indicating the joining of words and syllables. This type of "melted" (Waring's term) pronunciation became very popular and has been used ever since by many choral directors and voice teachers.

The choral and singing arts in America have become very sophisticated since Waring's time. This is in large part because of two organizations: the American Choral Directors Association (ACDA) and the National Association of Teachers of Singing (NATS). Striving for excellence in artistic integrity, these organizations represent teachers who are constantly improving upon the past and charting new directions for the future of vocal music, one of which is rhythmic diction.

One leader in the choral field, Robert Shaw (who first worked for Fred Waring as glee club director), has become known for his authentic and masterful interpretation of "classic" choral literature. Shaw was one of the first to break from the sung-speech diction of Waring in order to find a new clarity of rhythmic precision in singing. He recognized, as now have others, that the melting process of one word to another tends to blur the rhythmic nature of music, especially that of the baroque and classical periods. Rhythmic diction separates "every sound in every syllable within a metered rhythmic structure' (Fischer, 1986, p. 13). The result of this type of diction is singing that is "alive," "vital," and "buoyant."

Don Neuen, director of choral activities at the Eastman School of Music, and Sally Herman, junior high choral specialist and author of *Building a Pyramid of Musicianship* (1988), are two leading proponents of rhythmic diction. In her "rules of diction," Herman states, "Do not elide final consonants of one word into the beginning of the next word. . . . If double consonants fall together between words, pronounce them both" (Herman, 1988, p. 105). This type of pronunciation is directly opposite to that advocated by the sung-speech approach to diction.

A phrase from Handel's chorus "And the Glory of the Lord" from *Messiah* will serve to illustrate the difference between the two techniques being discussed. The phrase "and all flesh shall see it together," as pronounced with sung-speech diction would be sung as follows:

an-dall __ fle—shall __ see __ i—together

The words *and all* become *an dall*, the double consonants between words become single, and each syllable or word is connected to the next one. Sung with rhythmic diction the phrase would be sung:

and(uh) | all flesh ( ) shall see | it (uh) together

(The vertical stroke before *all* and *it* indicates a light glottal stroke, and the ( ) sign between *flesh* and *shall* indicates a slight separation). The rhythmic precision that this latter type of execution brings to this music (especially that of the baroque and classical eras) breathes new life and clarity into the vocal score. Fisher has conducted research into the perception of sung-speech versus rhythmic diction and concluded that "phonological studies, psychoacoustical research, and listener preferences appear to support the 'rhythmic diction' approach over that of the 'sung-speech' approach" (1986, p. 18).

Rhythmic diction is not appropriate for all styles of singing. It should not be used for music of a more ethnic or folk nature. Neither is it applicable for most pop music styles. Sung-speech diction is most appropriate for these genres. However, both types of diction should be known and practiced by students as required by the style of the music.

The present author finds one danger in the rhythmic-diction technique. When double consonants appear between words ("not to") and both are pronounced, there is a tendency to create a false rhythm if the *uh* of the first *t* becomes audible. In the *Messiah* example, if *it to* is sung *it*(uh) to, the rhythm may become a dotted eighth and sixteenth on *it*(uh) instead of a single quarter note. This must be guarded against, and it may be preferable to use only one *t* if this becomes a problem.

Singing in Foreign Languages

Singing in foreign languages should be encouraged for students of all ages. Not only does singing in a foreign language maintain the integrity of the original music, it also broadens the student's knowledge of the world of music in general. Today, when it is possible to be in another country in a matter of hours, students should have a world perspective, and singing in foreign languages can help to achieve that.

The instructor must provide a good vocal model when pronouncing foreign languages. The IPA is a valuable aid when using foreign-language diction texts for determining proper pronunciations. The Music Educators National Conference (MENC) has published the *Pronunciation Guide for Choral Literature* (May and Tolin, 1987), which contains phonetic pronunciations for French, German, Hebrew, Italian, Latin, and Spanish.

Make sure that students have a good translation of a foreign-language text being sung and that they have the general idea or sentiment being expressed. The audience also should have a translation provided for them in the concert program. If this is not possible, the director should tell the audience verbally what the text is expressing.

Pronunciation Problems

The following pronunciation problems (many of them freely adapted from those listed by Madeleine Marshall, 1956) are not given as specific exercises for student drill. These are common problems that must be handled by the instructor when the need arises. However, a general review of these pronunciation problems with older adolescents may save rehearsal time when encountering these specific examples. The instructor should know of these pitfalls in order to guard against improper handling of these pronunciation problems.

"Scooping" or "sliding" on initial consonants into vowels can be prevented by singing or thinking the consonant on the same pitch as the following vowel.

T is sometimes a silent letter as in *often, soften, Christmas,* and *chestnut.* However, the *t* must be sounded in *oft, soft, softer,* and *softly.*

In general, do not connect final consonants of one word into the beginning of the next word, for two reasons. First, the meaning of the text may be changed, as when "The wondrous cross I'd bear" becomes "The wondrous cross-eyed bear" or when "Let us pray" becomes "Lettuce spray"! Second, the clarity of the rhythm is blurred, especially in baroque and classical music (exception: pop ballads and ethnic styles in general).

Words with two inner identical consonants should be treated as though they were only one; for example, *butter* is sung *bu-ter*.

The correct stress of syllables is essential for good diction. When words have two syllables, it is important that they are not given equal stress; the second syllable is nearly always light.

Unlike *m* or *n*, initial *l* and *r* should not be prolonged or start ahead of the beat.

The consonant *w* is produced as the vowel *oo* as in *won* and *wow*. However, words beginning with *wh* begin with the aspirate as in *hwhen*.

When final *t* is followed by a word beginning with *t*, the following considerations determine whether one *t* or both should be heard: (1) the slowness or rapidity of the tempo, (2) the formality or informality of the composition, and (3) the importance of each of the two words.

When final *t* is followed by a word beginning with *s*, it is helpful to sing the *t* as the start of the second word using *ts*, as in *secret sorrow*.

Do not substitute the sound of one consonant for another, as in *budder* for *butter*.

Do not omit the *g* in final *ng* combinations, as in *singin*.

When *v* occurs between two vowels on the same pitch, start the *v* early, using part of the time value of the vowel that comes before it, as in *divv-ine* and *thyvv-oice*.

When *v* is followed by a consonant, start the *v* early, on the pitch of the vowel before it. In the words *love me*, sing the *v* on the pitch of the vowel *o*.

When a word ending in *v* is followed by a word beginning with a *v* or *f*, connect the two words as if they were one longer word, as in *love-for ever*.

When *heaven* is written *heav'n*, add a tiny second syllable (*ven*) at the very end of the note.

In speaking, the final syllables *dle* (*riddle*) and *den* (*sudden*) are pronounced with no vowel sound between *d* and *l* or between *d* and *n*. But in singing, there must be a vowel sound between the two consonants because a syllable cannot be sung without a vowel.

In speaking, *p* followed by *t* (*rapture*) is often imploded; that is, the *p* is stopped, but not exploded. In singing, this implosion is undesirable.

There are two articulations of *th*: voiced (as in *thine*) and voiceless (as in *thirty*). The voiceless *th* rarely presents a problem, except when a word ending in voiceless *th* in the singular becomes plural. In this case, the voiceless *th* becomes voiced, as in *path* (voiceless *th*) to *paths* (voiced *th*). Care must be taken to sing through the consonants when the *th* is voiced (as in *there*).

The word *with*, ending in a voiceless *th*, should be sung as a voiced *th* to increase word clarity and legato. However, when *with* is followed by a word beginning with a *th*, omit the *th* in *with* altogether (e.g., *wi[th] these* and *wi[th] thanks).*

The following common words are articulated with a liquid *u* sound: *dew, new, prelude, tune, Tuesday, student, gratitude, multitude.* Refer to Madeleine Marshall's rule for "Daniel sitteth" (1956, p. 139) when there is a question of using the pure [u] or liquid [iu] in words spelled with either *u* or *ew*.

Sing *thee* when the word *the* appears before a vowel (*thee apple*) or a silent *h* (*thee heirloom*). Sing *thuh* when the word *the* appears before a consonant (*thuh man*).

Madeleine Marshall states that the word *angel* is pronounced *an-juhl* with the unstressed schwa. Among singers it is more commonly pronounced *an-jel* with the short vowel [ɛ]. In any case, it should not be pronounced *an-jewels.*

Hallelujah (Hebrew) and *alleluia* (Latin) are pronounced so that the first and last syllables are identical [ɑ]. The last syllable should never be sounded as [ə], and the first syllable should never be sung as [æ]. *Hallelujah* is a contraction of three Hebrew words that mean "Praise (you) the Lord!"

Joy is pronounced as the diphthong [ɔI]. Note that the second vowel is [I], and not [i]. Be certain to sustain the first vowel [ɔ] as long as possible.

The second syllable of *Christmas* is pronounced with the unstressed schwa vowel, and not as [ɑ] or [I]. Be certain to drop the jaw more than usual to color the [ə] sound.

The first syllable of *divine* is pronounced with the short [I] sound, and not the long [i] sound.

Glory is pronounced with a single *r* that begins on the second syllable (*glo-ry*), and not as if it had a double *r* (*glor-ry*). The *o* vowel is a diphthong [ou] and should not be sung as the vowel *aw* [ɔ].

Get is pronounced with the short [ɛ] vowel, and not as [I], which only works in "Git along little doggies, git along!"

"We wish you a Merry Christmas" most often sounds like it has a *shoe* in the phrase. Do not connect the *sh* of *wish* to the word *you*. Leave a slight space between these words to omit the shoe! This same directive applies to the common phrase "The Lord bless () you and keep you."

When the consonant *t* precedes the consonant *y*, the two are often sound together as *ch. Put your* becomes *puchour*, and *what you* becomes *whachu*. These consonants must be separated if the integrity of both words is to be maintained.

Our should not be pronounced as the word *are*. Think of the word *our* as being *hour*. Madeleine Marshall calls the vowel combination in this word a "triphthong" and notates it as [ɑʊə]. Another triphthong combination is [aiə], as in the word *ire* (1953, p. 174).

Diction Training

The following outline contains three major divisions: Vocal-Tract Freedom, Pronunciation Exercises, and Consonant Group Drill. Each division comprises six sequential exercises, for a total of eighteen exercises in diction training. This outline is given for teacher-training purposes only and is not intended as the total sequence for group instruction. Diction training builds upon the foundations of training in respiration, phonation, and resonant tone production.

PART IV. DICTION-TRAINING OUTLINE

Vocal-Tract Freedom

1. Jaw Flex
2. Jaw Prop
3. Pharyngeal Openers
4. Forward Tongue
5. Chin-facial Massage
6. Tongue Flex

Word Pronunciation

1. Tongue Twisters
2. Final Consonants
3. Hissing Sibilants
4. The Three Rs
5. Song Études
6. IPA Studies

Consonant Articulation

1. Voiceless Plosives
2. Voiced Plosives
3. Voiceless Sibilants
4. Tuned Continuants
5. Voiced Continuants
6. Aspirates

VOCAL-TRACT FREEDOM

Goal: The student will develop the technique of singing with an open throat, through vocal-tract conditioning exercises involving the relaxation and flexibility of the vocal articulators.

Vocal authorities have long considered singing with an open throat conducive to good singing. The characteristics of an open throat are a relaxed jaw, a relaxed larynx, a feeling of openness in the pharynx, and a tongue that is relaxed and forward in the mouth (not grooved). These conditions are basic to proper sound production if optimal voice quality and projection are to be achieved.

Maintaining an open throat is not an easy task for a singer. Muscle tension in the oral and pharyngeal areas is quite common and is often the result of the body trying to compensate for poor breath management. The muscles of the swallowing action may exert some influence on the vocal tract in order to help the vocal process when foundational technique is inadequate. A tight jaw, elevated larynx, constricted pharynx, and rigid and retracted tongue are all characteristics that prove harmful to resonant tone production when the muscles of the swallowing action are used for singing. Overt action must be taken to check for, and guard against, the presence of swallowing action in the vocal process. The following vocal-tract conditioning exercises are given as a means of developing the open-throat condition for good singing and flexibility of the articulators.

Level 1: Jaw Flex (Exercise 10)

Drop Jaw.   Stretching the muscles of the jaw periodically is good for increased jaw flexibility. Direct the students to drop the jaw in the following manner: Place the tips of the index fingers on either side of the head just in front of the ears at the base of the "pinna," the spot where the jaw hinges to the synovial cavity. Place the thumbs under the rear of the jaw. Drop the jaw from the hinge, and feel the indentations that appear when the jaw opens. Have the students maintain a light pressure on the indentations while vocalizing on pure vowel sounds. Direct the students to check their jaw-drop positions periodically with this exercise.

Chewing Exercise.   Direct students to chew with a loose jaw while saying *yah-yah-yah-yah-yah*. Repeat the chewing action while singing up and down a five tone scale (1–2–3–4–5–4–3–2–1).

Level 2: Jaw Prop (Exercise 25)

Students will have difficulty maintaining the vertical and flared position of the vowels when they are introduced. Direct them to prop their jaws open using one of the techniques below.

Two-Finger Jaw Prop. Drop the jaw and push the flesh of each cheek between the teeth with the first two fingers; keep the thumbs under the chin (Figure 10–2).

Fist Jaw Prop. Drop the jaw and press the fists of the hands into the cheeks with the knuckles resting under the cheekbones and the fingers resting on the jaw (Figure 10–3). Keep the arms and elbows elevated, which will help to keep the sternum high.

Hand Jaw Prop. Drop the jaw, resting it in the cradle of one hand, with the lower lip protruding between the thumb and index finger. With the thumb on one side of the face, press the flesh of the cheek between the teeth; press the index finger on the other side flat under the cheekbone (Figure 10–4). This prop is best used with adolescents.

Each of the three jaw-prop positions requires that students do not cover their mouths with their hands or contort their mouths into irregular shapes. At all times the lips are to be uncovered and flared. Use the jaw prop as a means of establishing resonance on all vocalises that use vowels only. Obviously, this position is not conducive to the singing of words with consonants. Alternate the singing of vocalises with and without the jaw prop. The jaw prop helps to counter the trigger of the swallowing action, which is in the pursed lips. By keeping the jaw down and the cheeks hollow, one keeps the larynx in the at-rest position.

Level 3: Pharyngeal Openers (Exercise 40)

The following pharyngeal openers help to relax the major muscles of the pharynx that interfere with resonant tone production.

Sigh. Direct students to speak a high laryngeal *uh* in the lower adjustment (shallow jaw opening). Notice the elevation of the larynx. Direct students to speak a low laryngeal *ah*, as in a sigh (deep-jaw opening) in the lower adjustment. Note the relaxation of the larynx and the open-throat feeling. Sing vocalises while maintaining this feeling of a sigh. Maintain the low-laryngeal, open-pharyngeal feeling.

Cool Spot. Direct students to inhale through an open mouth, forming a "cool spot" at the rear of the soft palate. Note that the cool spot is a feeling conducive to the open throat. Sing vocalises while maintaining this feeling of the cool spot.

Inner Smile. Direct students to smile inside the mouth with lips lightly closed and teeth parted (like a stifled yawn). Nostrils should flare slightly. Note how the inner smile opens the oropharynx. Sing vocalises while maintaining this feeling of an inner smile.

Level 4: Forward Tongue (Exercise 55)

A rigid, swallowed tongue is often noted among young singers. The tongue should be carried forward in the mouth, with the tip resting at

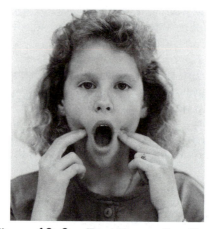

Figure 10–2.   Two-Finger Jaw Prop.

Figure 10–3.   Two-Fist Jaw Prop.

Figure 10–4.   One-Hand Jaw Prop.

the base of the lower front teeth. It never should be grooved, or drawn down, for any vowel.

Direct students to rest the tip of the tongue at the base of the lower front teeth. Speak the vowel sequence *oo-oh-ah-ay-ee* without moving the tip of the tongue from its frontal resting position. Rest a finger on the chin, but be certain that the jaw moves only a little. Note that it is possible to form all five vowels without moving the front of the tongue. It is the back of the tongue that forms the vowels in the pharynx and oral cavity. Direct students to sing the vowel sequence *oo-oh-ah-ay-ee* on a sustained pitch, keeping the tongue in its forward resting position.

Level 5: Chin–Facial Masssage (Exercise 70)

Direct students to massage the facial muscles of the cheeks with rotating motions of the fingertips. Note the need for relaxation in these muscles. Now massage the muscles under the chin with rotating motions of the thumbs. Note the need for relaxation in these muscles.

Tension in the muscles under the chin (geniohyoid and mylohyoid muscles) may be determined by placing the index finger up into the soft area under the chin. Direct students to swallow and note the "kick" of the contracting muscles as they work to elevate the larynx for swallowing. Any such tension works against resonant tone production.

Direct students to try to detect tension in the muscles under the chin while singing sustained pitches. Note that any rigidity or bulging of muscles under the chin is wrong and will harm singing by elevating the larynx. Direct students to relax the muscles under the chin consciously by massaging away any tension in this area.

Level 6: Tongue Flex (Exercise 85)

The tongue should be free and relaxed for singing. Often it is not because it is employed in a semiswallowing state that is tense and retracted. This is a result of "throat singing" and lack of support.

To detect tongue rigidity, direct students to place the tip of the tongue at the base of the lower front teeth and arch the tongue forward from the back. (Note that the tip of the tongue does not extend beyond the lower front teeth.) Retract the tongue and flex it forward and back repeatedly without moving the jaw up and down. The motion should be easy and without any jaw interference. If the student cannot move the tongue easily in this flexing motion, it is a sure sign that the tongue is tense and being drawn back into the pharynx for singing. Remediate this condition by slow flexing of the tongue.

Repeat the tongue-flex exercise while droning a pitch in the lower adjustment. Some students will not be able to do this immediately and will need to return to flexing without phonation. Gradually work into the drone and then into a sustained pitch in the lower and upper adjustments. The sound should be free and full, and the tongue should flex easily if it is not being retracted into the pharyngeal area. A tense tongue is an indication that the tongue is being engaged in a partial swallowing position for singing. If this is the case, slow repetition of the tongue flex is necessary to correct this condition.

WORD PRONUNCIATION

Goal: The student will develop the technique of singing with accurate and intelligible word pronunciation through exercises involving both enunciation of vowels and articulation of consonants.

The following pronunciation exercises make the student aware of the difference between speaking diction and singing diction. The singer's diction must be distinct, uniform, and intelligible when combined with the singing voice. This type of production requires that the vocal articulators be relaxed and flexible, yet capable of rapid and exaggerated articulation. Uniform vowel-color enunciation and distinct consonant articulation are fundamental to intelligible singing.

Level 1: Tongue Twisters (Exercise 11)

Nursery Rhymes. Gaining articulator flexibility can be accomplished through the recitation of tongue twisters. Direct students to speak with exacting articulation the following:

> From Wibbleton to Wobbleton is sixteen miles,
> From Wobbleton to Wibbleton is sixteen miles,
> From Wibbleton to Wobbleton, from Wobbleton to Wibbleton,
> From Wibbleton to Wobbleton is sixteen miles.

Use other nursery rhymes and tongue twisters that are appropriate for the age levels. Those in Dr. Seuss's *ABC Book* are especially good. Use good British diction in the articulation of these exercises.

Advanced Tongue Twisters. More advanced tongue twisters can be used with older students, such as the following:

1. Momma made me mash my M&Ms. (sing on sustained pitches)
2. Aluminum, linoleum, aluminum, tin.
3. Toy boat, . . . (repeat five times in rapid succession).

Level 2: Final Consonants (Exercise 26)

Emphasized. Final consonants must be greatly exaggerated in order to be heard. Sing words ending in final consonants, giving more emphasis to the consonants than the vowels. Sing the following words to various counts (4, 3, 6, etc.), indicating the place for the final consonant with a slight karate chop of one hand against the other (visual signal):

1. not, kick, church, cat, pop, etc.
2. budge, dog, load, bribe, job, etc.

Interpolated **uh.** Singing with orchestral or band accompaniment may necessitate an increase in the amount of emphasis on the final consonants by the interpolation of a vocal *uh* after each final consonant. Direct students to sing words ending in final consonants, giving a vocal *uh* after each consonant. Sing these words on one pitch to various counts and indicate the place for the final consonant with the visual karate chop:

1. *not(uh), kick(uh), pop(uh),* etc.
2. *budge(uh), dog(uh), load(uh),* etc.

Level 3: Hissing Sibilants (Exercise 41)

Troublesome Final **s, sh, and c.** The troublesome elongation of these sounds can be remedied by deemphasizing the sounds or by directing the students to drop the jaw immediately upon execution of these consonants. A hissing sibilant cannot be sustained when the teeth are parted! Rehearse students in singing words ending with the hissing sibilants by deemphasizing the final consonants or by dropping the jaw immediately after execution.

Visual Cue. A visual cue may be given for the quick release of hissing sibilants. Extend the hand forward for sustaining a word such as *peace.* Release (cutoff) the word by lightly touching the index finger to the thumb and then springing them open. The spring-open action should remind the students to part the teeth immediately after the soft *c* has been sounded. Be certain not to interpolate a vocal *uh* after the sounding of a final sibilant.

Level 4: The Three Rs (Exercise 56)

The American **r (as in run).** The American *r* (tongue pulled back) is sung when preceded by a consonant or when it begins a word, but it is never sung when it appears before a consonant. Sing the words *try. run,* and *burn* on sustained pitches. In the first two words, the *r* is sung in the America style, but it must be softened (tongue forward) in the word *burn* because the *r* precedes a consonant.

The American *r* should not be overly emphasized or used in the wrong place. It is not sung before a pause, but it is always sung before a vowel as quickly as possible. It is a tuned continuant, but should not be prolonged. Sing the tune "Row, Row, Row Your Boat," moving quickly through the American *r* to the vowel sound.

The Flipped r. The "flipped" *r* is sung between two vowels within a word or between a word ending in an *r* and a word beginning with a vowel. It requires only one flip of the tongue and should not be treated as the double *r* in Italian, which is rolled. Sing the words *spirit, very,* and *redeemer of* on sustained pitches, flipping the tongue once for the *r* between vowels. Students who cannot flip an *r*, should speak *veddy, veddy, veddy, veddy* as quickly as possible. This will eventually become *very* with the flipped *r*.

The Soft r. Soften the *r* when followed by a consonant, pause, or rest. This is done by keeping the tip of the tongue forward instead of retracted as it is for the American *r*. Sing the words *arm, father like,* and *for me* on sustained pitches, softening the *r* for each word.

Sing the beginning of the "Lord's Prayer" ("Our Father"), sustaining the *er* of *Father* with the tongue retracted in the American-*r* position. Note the irritating *rrrr* sound and lack of vowel quality. Now omit the *er* altogether and sing *Fathuh*. Note the rather affected quality without any *r*. Lastly, sing *Father* with a soft *r* (i.e., tongue forward). Note that more vowel quality is present when the soft *r* is used. Direct students to put a slash mark (\) over every *r* in words in which the *r* should be softened (or omitted).

Madeleine Marshall (1953) recommends that the *r* before a consonant not be sung at all. This is an optional approach to dealing with this troublesome *r* problem. However, when a word ending in *r* is followed by a word beginning with *r*, only the second *r* is sounded (e.g., *her riches*). In this case, the first *r* is omitted. The omitted *r* is more useful in choral singing than in solo singing.

Level 5: Song Études (Exercise 71)

Short songs études that emphasize articulation problems are useful for diction study. All song texts, however, should be studied for pronunciation problems.

"The Alphabet Song" (Example 10.1). This song can be sung in unison or in parts. Keep the diction light and crisp. The melismatic section is especially good for developing vocal agility.

EXAMPLE 10.1. THE ALPHABET - attributed to Mozart

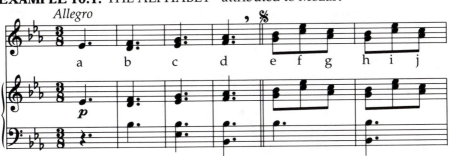

"The Pop Song" (Example 10.2). Use the best British diction (even a little affectation). Sing as a round, and watch the following pronunciation problems:

1. *bot-tle*   not   *bod-dle*
2. *po-puh*   not   *pop*
3. *don't*   not   *don't*
4. *put-your*   not   *putchore*
5. *dust-pan*   not   *dusspan*
6. *vinegar*   *not*   *vinegarrr*
7. *anduh*   not   *and (except in fish 'n' chips)*
8. *pepper*   *not*   *pepperrr*
9. *lo-t*   not   *lot*

Level 6: IPA Studies (Exercise 86)

The following six IPA studies were prepared by Renee Ferrell (a middle school choral director in Athens, Texas) for her middle school choirs.[1] The material has been adapted for inclusion in this text.

There are five steps in presenting each short lesson: (1) review of previous lessons, (2) preparation in which the students echo the director, who speaks the word containing the vowel sound to be taught, (3) presentation of the IPA symbol with proper execution, (4) spoken practice, and (5) written practice. One lesson can take several sessions, and for elementary students, each lesson should be separated into two parts, presenting only one vowel each time.

Lesson 1: [ɑ] and [ɔ]

[ɑ] as in father *(ah)*
1. Review: the importance of developing singing diction.
2. Prepare: *father, John, God, not, was.*
3. Present: [ɑ]. Description: This is an open, front vowel. Place the tongue low (not grooved), letting it slightly touch the front teeth. Drop the jaw by lowering the bottom back teeth. Flare the lips.
4. Practice: *father, heart, star, far, part, dark, calm* (silent *l*).

[ɔ] as in awful *(aw)*
1. Review: [ɑ] as in *father.*
2. Prepare: *awful, all, law, talk, fall, ought, Mark.*

[1] R. Ferrell, "English Diction and the International Phonetic Alphabet," *Choristers Guild Letters,* Feb. 1987, pp. 147–153. Used by permission.

EXAMPLE 10.2. "The Pop Song"(Traditional).

3. Present: [ɔ]. Description: drop the jaw. The lips protrude slightly to create a vertical oval. The tongue remains forward, arched in the back. A singer who consistently pronounces *aw* as *ah* is probably not opening his or her mouth wide enough.

4. Practice: *cause, taught, Paul, bought, yawn, call, song.*

5. Game for practice and review of Lesson 1: the teacher will say the sentence and the students will orally guess the missing word in the blank using correct diction, and then write the symbol for the words using [ɑ] or [ɔ]. (The IPA symbol is always printed.)

 1. Matthew, _____, Luke, and _____. (*Mark* [ɔ], *John* [ɑ])
 2. He has a _____ of gold. (*heart* [ɑ])
 3. It is not near, it is _____ away. (*far* [ɑz])ʔ
 4. And _____ created the heavens and the earth. (*God* [ɑ])
 5. A thunder _____ is loud. (*storm* [ɔ])
 6. Noah built an _____. (*ark* [ɔ])

Lesson 2: [æ] [ɛ]

[æ] as in *cat* (*a*)

1. Review: [ɑ] as in *father* and [ɔ] as in *all*.
2. Prepare: *cat, happy, lamb, Sam.*
3. Present: [æ]. Description: For this open front vowel, slightly arch the tongue and let it touch the lower front teeth. Drop the jaw more than normal for this vowel sound.
4. Practice: *stand, man, sand, that, sat, band, cat, happy, lamb.*

[ɛ] as in *let* (*eh*)

1. Review all previous vowels.
2. Prepare: *let, fed, dead, said, wed.*
3. Present [ɛ]. Description: Relax the lower lip. Drop the jaw more than usual for this vowel. Slightly raise the front of the tongue. Do not spread the lips into a smile.
4. Practice: *wed, fed, let, met, head, bread, shepherd, send, pen, ten.*
5. Game for practice and review of Lesson 1–2 (directions as before):
 1. I won't _____ you go! (*let* [ɛ])
 2. The shepherd's job is to _____ the sheep. (*tend* [ɛ])
 3. Mother and _____ are at work. (*father* [ɑ])

4. I want _____ of it. (*all* [ɔ])
5. The black _____ meowed loudly. (*cat* [æ])
6. This is the _____ of the quiz. (*end* [ɛ]).

Lesson 3: [I] and [i]

[I] is in *sit* (*ih*)

1. Review: *father* [ɑ], *saw* [ɔ], *man* [æ], *let* [ɛ].
2. Prepare: *sit, is, sin, big, pit.*
3. Present: [I]. Description: Drop the jaw more than normal for this vowel, and raise the upper lip. Place the front of the tongue forward, touching the lower teeth. Note: When a word ends in an unstressed *y*, the *y* is pronounced [I]. The word *silly* is pronounced sIlI.
4. Practice: *lip, big, is, him, winter, sick, divine, beautiful, holy.*

[i] as in *he* (*ee*)

1. Review all previous vowels.
2. Prepare: *he, me, sleep, meet, heat.*
3. Present: [i]. Description: The tongue is arched and raised, touching the lower front teeth. The jaw is relaxed more than normal for speech.
4. Practice: *me, sleep, weep, feet, he, three, each, sheep.*
5. Game for practice and review of Lessons 1–3.
    1. Please let me _____ in the morning. (*sleep* [i]).
    2. If you don't _____ up, your singing will be poor. (*sit* [I]).
    3. How still and _____ the wind is today. (*calm* [ɑ]).
    4. My _____ flew off my head! (*hat* [æ]).
    5. He _____ and broke his arm. (*fell* [ɛ]).
    6. The leaves fall in _____ (*autumn* [ɔ]).

Lesson 4: [u] and [U]

[u] as in *too* (*oo*)

1. Review all previous vowels.
2. Prepare: *too, do, soon, lose, shoe.*
3. Present: [u]. Description: Round the lips, but keep the jaw relaxed. Arch the back of the tongue, and let the tip touch the lower front teeth.

4. Practice: *room, moon, roof, soon, too, do, shoe, lose, June, through.*

[U] as in *book* (*u̇*)

1. Review all previous vowels.
2. Prepare: *book, could, stood, full, put.*
3. Present: [U]. Description: Slightly protrude and round the lips while keeping the jaw relaxed. The tongue is slightly raised in the middle; the tip is forward.
4. Practice: *look, good, took, book, put, full, beautiful, would, could.*
5. Game for practice and review of Lessons 1–4:
    1. The sky is _____. (*blue* [u])
    2. In choir, we learn to _____ a _____. (*sing* [I], *song* [ɔ])
    3. The pail is _____ _____ water. (*full* [U], *of* [ɔ])
    4. Be sure you _____ eight hours of _____ each night. (*get* [ɛ], *sleep* [i])
    5. The sea is very still and _____. (*calm* [ɑ])
    6. How do you _____. (*do* [u]).

Lesson 5: [o] and [ɜ]

[o] as in *obey* (unstressed)

1. Review all previous vowels.
2. Prepare: *obey, omit, police, polite, memory, desolate, omnipotent.*
3. Present: [o]. Description: Say *aw,* then slightly arch the back of the tongue from the *aw* position. Flare the lips forward and relax the jaw.
4. Practice: *obey, omit, police, polite, memory, desolate, omnipotent.*

[ɜ] as in *bird*

1. Review all previous vowels.
2. Prepare: *bird, burn, river, her, sir.*
3. Present: [ɜ]. Description: Place the jaw in the *eh* position, and then raise the back of the tongue. The sides of the tongue slightly touch the upper teeth, and the lips flare.
4. Practice: *bird, burn, river, her, sir, wonderful, ever, turn, learn.*
5. Game for practice and review of Lessons 1–5.

1. The robin is a red _____. (*bird* [ɜ])
2. It is not _____ to talk with your mouth full. (*polite* [o])
3. I _____ the ball through the window! (*hit* [I])
4. Oh say can you _____. (*see* [i])
5. Don't give me _____ story! (*that* [æ])
6. I am _____ and can't eat anything else. (*full* [U])
7. You _____ too much on the telephone. (*talk* [ɔ])
8. _____ there be peace on earth. (*let* [ɛ])
9. I ate _____ much. (*too* [u])
10. It was _____ the right thing to do. (*not* [ɑ])

Lesson 6: [ʌ] (stressed) and [ə] (unstressed)

[ʌ] as in *up* (*uh*)

1. Review all previous vowels.
2. Prepare: *up, none, unto, cup, us.*
3. Present: [ʌ]. Description: The lips are relaxed. The tongue moves back and down; the tip touches the lower gums.
4. Practice: *us, trumpet, suffer, trust, cup, sun, up, funny, bun, done.*

[ə] as in *quiet*

1. Review all previous vowels.
2. Prepare: *endeth, presence, quiet, tablet, symbol.*
3. Present: [ə]. Description: This symbol represents the vowel sound occurring in an unstressed syllable. It can be spelled many different ways, and the sound produced can take on the coloring of other vowels, depending on the spelling of the word in which it is used. It is the "neutral" sound of the voice and is not a good vowel for singing. The jaw should have more depth in the direction of the *ah* vowel to add more color to this sound. However, do not replace [ɑ] for [ə].
4. Practice: *endeth, purpose, sadness, angel, sudden, present, Christmas.*
5. Game for practice and review of Lessons 1–6.
    1. The _____ rises in the _____ and sets in the west. (*sun* [ʌ], *east* [i])
    2. December 25th is _____. (*Christmas* [I], [ə])
    3. I will _____ my mother and _____.
       (*obey* [o], *father* [ɑ])

4. Don't _____ down just _____. (*sit* [I], *yet* [ɛ])

5. Who _____ the cat in the _____? (*put* [U], *hat* [æ])

6. In choir we _____ to sing correctly. (*learn* [ɜ])

7. Don't let the ladder _____ down. (*fall* [ɔ])

8. I don't know what to _____ with you. (*do* [u])

CONSONANT ARTICULATION

Goal: The student will develop the technique of singing with distinct articulation of consonants, through exercises involving flexible, rapid, and often exaggerated use of the vocal articulators.

The following consonant group drills are to be used for exercising the articulators with each sound classification of consonants. One-measure rhythm patterns using the various consonant groups should be spoken by the instructor and echoed by the students. (This is an alternative approach to using other rhythm syllables). The instructor should use much exaggeration of articulation when appropriate to the class of consonants. Note also the phrases given for practicing clean and crisp articulation.

Level 1: Voiceless Plosives: *p, t, k, ch* (Exercise 12)

Echo Rhythm Drill. Say the consonants in this class while improvising various rhythm patterns (one measure in common time). Employ much exaggeration in the explosion of these consonants. Direct students to echo the patterns. Students also may lead the exercise.

Phrase. Speak and sing the following phrase: "Put that cat out of that chair."

Level 2: Voiced Plosives: *b, d, g, j* (Exercise 27)

Echo Rhythm Drill. Say the consonants in this class while improvising various rhythm patterns (one measure in common time). Employ much exaggeration in the explosion of these consonants. Direct students to echo the patterns. Students also may lead the exercise. These subvocal consonants are preceded by a vocal buzz, which is not tuned.

Phrase. Speak and sing the following phrase: "Big dogs jump and dig the ground."

Level 3: Voiceless Sibilants: *f, s, th, sh* (Exercise 42)

Echo Rhythm Drill. Say the consonants in this class while improvising various rhythm patterns (one measure in common time). Alternate heavy and light stresses, heavy on *f* and *th* and light on *s* and *sh*. Direct students to echo the patterns. Students also may lead the exercise.

Phrase. Speak and sing the following phrase: "Thanks for friends with food to share."

Level 4: Tuned Continuants: *m, n* (Exercise 57)

Sustained m *and* n. Direct students to say the following, elongating the *m* and *n*: *moo-moh-mah-meh-mee* and *noo-noh-nah-neh-nee.* Sing the exercise on a sustained pitch. Tuned continuants should begin ahead of the beat so that the vowel begins on the beat.

Phrases. Sing the first line of "My country 'tis of thee," beginning the *m* of *My* before the first beat. Sing the word *Amen* with emphasis on the *m* and *n*. The instructor may indicate where the *m* and *n* close by touching the index finger to the thumb.

Level 5: Voiced Continuants: *v, z, th, zh* (Exercise 72)

Echo Rhythm Drill. Say the consonants in this class while improvising various rhythm patterns (one measure in common time). Employ much exaggeration in the explosion of these consonants. Direct students to echo the patterns. Students also may lead the exercise. Be sure to sing each of these consonants on pitch.

Phrase. Speak and sing the following phrase: "The pleasure of thy company is requested."

Level 6: Aspirates: Voiceless *h*, Voiced *wh* (Exercise 87)

Echo Rhythm Drill. Say the consonants in this class while improvising various rhythm patterns (one measure in common time). Employ much exaggeration in the aspirate of these consonants. Direct students to echo the patterns. Students also may lead the exercise. Note that for *wh*, the aspirate precedes the *w* (i.e., *hw*).

Phrase. Speak and sing the following phrase: "How and when and where, he wails."

STUDY AND DISCUSSION QUESTIONS

1. Define the terms *diction, pronunciation, enunciation,* and *articulation.*
2. Discuss how vowels serve as the basis of tone quality and color.
3. What are the three goals of uniform vowel enunciation and the three goals of distinct consonant articulation?
4. Give the five primary vowel colors for singing and the IPA symbol for each.
5. Discuss the main problem in singing short-vowel colors and a technique for dealing with this problem.
6. What is a diphthong and how should most diphthongs be sung? Which diphthong is the exception in its execution?
7. Give the anatomical origin for each of the following articulators: labial; velar; lingual; glottal; dental; alveolar ridge.
8. Give the consonants for each of the following classifications: voiceless plosives, voiced plosives, voiceless sibilants, tuned continuants, voiced continuants, and aspirates.
9. What are the four characteristics of an open throat? Suggest some ways to encourage an open pharyngeal area.
10. When stretching the jaw, care must be taken to lower the jaw from what point? What will this prevent?
11. What are the names of the muscles of the jaw (chin) that often constrict while singing and need to be consciously relaxed?
12. A tense tongue in singing is often caused by what?
13. How should consonants be executed in relation to vowels?
14. How can hissing sibilants be remedied?
15. State the "three *r*s" and how each is to be sung.
16. Discuss the differences between sung-speech and rhythmic diction. In general, why should sung-speech diction not be used in music of an ethnic origin?
17. How is the consonant *w* to be sung?
18. What two tuned continuants should not be prolonged or started ahead of the beat? What two tuned continuants should be prolonged and started ahead of the beat?
19. What does it mean to "implode" a consonant?
20. What is the rule for the singing of *the* before a vowel and before a consonant?

References

CHRISTY, VAN A. (1970). *Foundations in singing*. Dubuque, IA: Wm. C. Brown.

FERRELL, R. (1987). English diction and the international phonetic alphabet: Six lessons teaching the twelve basic vowels. *Choristers Guild Letters, 38*(7), 147–153.

FISHER, R. E. (1986). Choral diction with a phonological foundation. *The Choral Journal, 27*(5), 13–18.

HERMAN, S. (1988). *Building a pyramid of musicianship*. San Diego: Curtis Music Press.

MARSHALL, M. (1953). *The singer's manual of English diction*. New York: Schirmer Books.

MAY, W. V., & TOLIN, C. (1987). *Pronunciation guide for choral literature*. Reston, VA: Music Educators National Conference.

URIS, D. (1971). *To sing in English: A guide to improved diction*. New York: Boosey & Hawkes.

WARING, F. (1951). *Tone syllables*. Delaware Water Gap, PA: Shawnee Press.

WILSON, H. R. (1954). *Artistic choral singing*. New York: G. Schirmer.

11

EXPRESSION 〜

Goal: The student will develop the ability to sing expressively, through exercises related to variation of phrasing, dynamics, tempo, range, and agility.

Good singing is more than a well-supported, resonant tone. Good singing is expressive; it conveys the meaning and life of the text. Students need to be taught the expressive elements of singing in order to be made more conscious of how those elements contribute to the whole of the singer's art.

While much of the ability to express music is the responsibility of the conductor and teacher (i.e., interpretation), there are a number of technical aspects of expressive singing that can, and should, be learned by the students. Too often these techniques of expression are learned in a haphazard way; learning in this manner often fails to establish the broad concepts necessary for transfer from one selection of music to the next.

Students should know what constitutes a musical phrase and how it moves and breathes. They should know the differences among dynamic levels and the various musical tempi. Agility and a wide range are important characteristics by which good singing is recognized. All of these elements of expression are isolated and studied in this method as a means of refining and polishing the singing process. It then becomes the job of the instructor to integrate these expressive elements into the song repertoire of the students.

Expressive singing seems to come more naturally to some people than to others. However, this does not mean that students cannot be taught to be expressive in singing. It only means that some are endowed with a greater capacity to express themselves than others. The affective nature is present in everyone, and all can learn, to some degree, to use it expressively. Just as the basic mechanics of singing can be learned, so can the ability to express in song be learned.

Developing Musical Sensitivity

One of the ways in which an expressive language can be developed in students is to involve them in the evaluation process. How often are singers asked to provide input as to the vocal sound of a singer or group of singers? Questions of blend, tone color and quality, tempo, dynamic level, diction, and the like are most often left to the discretion of the conductor. If, however, students are asked periodically to separate from the group and evaluate the singing for musical concepts, a critical ear can be developed that rarely is developed within the group. Ask a student during a rehearsal to separate and listen for contrasts in dynamic levels; he or she must now deal with this problem as a listener rather than a performer. The importance of dynamics is heightened in the student's mind. Make students a part of the evaluation process, and they will develop a keener sense for the expressive whole of the art of singing.

When possible, have your students listen to other groups of singers through live performances or recordings. Students need the opportunity to hear and experience voices or choirs other than their own. Opportunities to hear other singers can develop a positive ability to discern the strengths and weaknesses evident in the singing process.

The Affective Nature

Students listen to pop music because of the way it makes them feel. Yet, it almost has become unfashionable among some music teachers to discuss the feeling or mood of a song or choral composition. "Let the music speak for itself," they say. There seems to be an attitude that teachers should not force their feelings or interpretations on students, as a musical selection can mean many different things to many different people.

It is true that one musical composition can convey a multitude of feelings and that teachers should not unduly influence students as to personal interpretation. However, a group discussion concerning the mood of a composition can cause students to think about the music they are singing in ways previously unexplored. While no one interpretation may be agreed upon, the process of getting into the mind of the poet or author and composer will help the students to associate more closely with the expressive content of the music. If feeling provides such strong motivation for active listening to music, how can the affective nature of singing be omitted from any vocal-music program?

The beauty of group singing in a classroom or choir lies in its corporate nature. There are few places in life or the school curriculum where people actively join together in a group effort to share their feelings and thoughts about life. Whatever its benefits, expressive group singing is a tradition of humankind that has as its basis this need to share and express what makes people human. These affective elements are a natural extension of this innate need to share and are powerful in a group effort, especially among adolescents. The expressive elements of vocal music should not be ignored.

The Text

Much of the expressive nature of singing has its origin in the text. This unique characteristic of vocal music—words—makes it especially appealing to youth. Textual considerations, however, create problems for the vocal instructor with which the instrumental instructor does not have to contend. The whole problem of singing diction adds another layer to vocal teaching and can impede greatly the process of expressive music making and learning.

Vocal instructors most often teach music and text simultaneously. Students, especially those who do not read music well, seem to bond music and word, thus facilitating the learning process. The danger in this mode of teaching is that little attention is paid by the instructor to the pronunciation of the text while the notes are being learned. After the notes are learned, the instructor then tries to correct pronunciation problems that have become ingrained and bonded to the notes. Correction at this stage is ineffectual and wastes time.

Music learning for singers should begin with the words first, separate from the notes, or the notes first on a neutral syllable. In either case, the text should be taught separately from the notes. The instructor should analyze the text for proper enunciation and articulation in preparation for teaching and mark the score with helpful reminders of the correct pronunciations. (IPA symbols are helpful in this process.) Thus, when the composition is introduced to the students and the textual considerations have been planned, the instructor can model the correct pronunciation from the beginning. Older students should be encouraged to have a pencil at each class and to mark the score as directed. Once the pronunciation of the words is established, the meaning of the text may be discussed and/or note learning commence.

Regarding the effective and expressive communication of text, Don Neuen writes:

> The paramount rule of communication is that no two consecutive notes, syllables, or words should receive equal emphasis. Singers must constantly make use of crescendo, stress, and diminuendo, whether it be in groupings of a few notes or a sixteen-measure phrase. A chorus can do this

within a given dynamic level. There should be no static plateaus of sameness [1988, p. 45].

Word-meaning emphasis, or "tone painting," also must be recognized:

> Each word has a special meaning or texture: "Fire" should not sound like "ice," "love" not like "hate," nor "sing" like "talk." By the same token, highly charged words such as "power," "peace," and "beauty" should not receive the same emphasis as "it," "the," and "of" [p. 45].

Neuen concludes his discussion of the importance of textual considerations by stating:

> The sound of a great chorus is dependent upon energy—energy in the mental and physical attitude of the singer, the buoyancy and lifting of the tone, and the effective dramatic communication of both text and melody. All of these must be a consistent part of the learning and rehearsal process from the beginning. Every director needs to develop a positive and energetic concept of a great choral sound and teach it effectively and consistently [p. 45].

The Musical Phrase

The life of music is in the "line," or phrase. The instructor should consistently shape phrases to reflect the intentions of the composer. Plenty of forethought must be given to this matter, and students can also be involved in this process, as reflected in Level 6 (phrase sculpting) of this method.

Every phrase has a forward momentum that reaches a peak and then subsides. This may be thought of as a wave that builds and builds and then breaks before rushing to shore. A lack of drive in this forward momentum process results in dull and lifeless singing. Jean Ashworth Bartle states:

> No musical phrase ever "sits there." It must have energy and vitality. Even the softest and slowest phrase must have momentum and direction. To achieve this, I often tell the children to sing with soft vowels and loud consonants. The children must be told to send the phrase forward and not to sing the phrase note by note, mechanically [1988, pp. 26–27].

The fine singing of the Toronto Children's Choir under Jean Ashworth Bartle is evidence that her children practice what she preaches!

Sally Herman's "pyramid of musicianship" places "artistic expression" at the top, where students experience what it means to be a musician. Herman has devised the following "rules of articulation" that have worked well with her adolescent singers:

- If a voice part moves differently from most of the others, emphasize that part.
- When singing a dotted note followed by a shorter note, either crescendo on the dotted note, accent the short note, or put a slight "click" or space between the two notes. Never breathe after a dotted note unless it is the last note of a phrase or followed by a rest.
- Always crescendo on long notes unless you are at the end of a phrase where a resolution calls for a diminuendo.
- If an octave leap occurs in only one voice part (usually the bass), separate the two notes and accent the second note.
- Renew sequential patterns on the offbeat rather than on the beat by putting a slight separation at the point of renewal.
- Accent offbeats when the syllabic stress of the text allows.
- Continue stressing a strong syllable with a crescendo following the attack [1988, p. 41].

Expressive Singing

Teaching students to sing expressively is a rewarding task. Linda Swears writes:

> Expressive choral singing is disciplined singing. The expressiveness of any given piece is dependent upon the attention and input of individual chorus members and the conducting of the choral teacher. No matter how disciplined a group may be, if the conductor beats out time and does little more, the music will be lifeless. Expressive singing is constantly being created through the mutual communication of the choral teacher and the chorus [1985, p. 112].

Expression Training

The following outline contains three major divisions: phrasing, dynamic and tempo variation, and range and agility. Each division comprises six sequential exercises, for a total of eighteen exercises in expression training. This outline is given for teacher-training purposes only and is not intended as the total sequence for group instruction.

PART V. EXPRESSION-TRAINING OUTLINE

Phrasing

1. Down 5–Up 5
2. Phrase Extension
3. Breath Techniques

4. Meaning and Mood
5. Physical Movement
6. Phrase Sculpting

Dynamic and Tempo Variation

1. Six Dynamic Levels
2. Seven Tempo Markings
3. Accelerando and Ritardando
4. Crescendo and Decrescendo
5. Sudden Dynamic Changes
6. Messa di vòce

Agility and Range Extension

1. The Light Portamento
2. Increasing Agility
3. The Arpeggio
4. Agility and Range 1
5. Agility and Range 2
6. Melismatic Singing

PHRASING

Goal: The student will develop the technique of expressive phrasing through exercises involving the development of musical line as it relates to musical structure and overall musical performance.

Word phrases and melodic phrases together form the bases of musical meaning. Not only must students be able to sing phrases musically, they must also be able to recognize and understand what constitutes a phrase of music. Comparisons of musical phrases to similar structures in written language can be a helpful technique to foster better understanding of the importance of phrasing in music. If a phrase in prose or song is broken in the wrong place, its meaning can be obscured or changed. Students need to be taught what constitutes a musical phrase.

Level 1: Down 5–Up 5 (Exercise 13)

Down 5. Sing the vocalise in Example 11.1 easily on *oo* with one breath, at a moderate tempo. Students should be told that "one breath length" of music is known as a musical "phrase."

EXAMPLE 11.1.   Vocalise: Down 5.

Keep the interval fa-mi very high. As students are introduced to the remainder of the pure vowels, vary the vowels on succeeding repetitions. Changed male voices may sing one octave lower. Transpose downward by half steps at least a minor third. Play "How low can you go?" Keep the lips forward and jaw relaxed. Advise students to keep the tone light. Do not push in the lower adjustment, but do exercise it. All pitches below middle C can be sung safely in the pure lower adjustment.

Students should be led to recognize a musical phrase (a breath length) in every song they sing. Speak often of phrases so that the term becomes a common part of the students' vocabulary.

Down 5–Up 5.   Sing both of the vocalises in Example 11.2 at slow tempi. Emphasize the extended nature of the phrases. Sing each phrase to one breath, varying the vowels on each succeeding repetition. Changed male voices may sing one octave lower. Transpose downward and upward a minor third by half steps. Caution students singing in the treble clef to keep the tone light and unforced.

EXAMPLE 11.2.   Vocalise: Down 5–Up 5.

Level 2: Phrase Extension (Exercise 28)

"America."   This well-known song (Example 11.3) is typically chopped into short segments when sung. The musical line, however, calls for only three phrases in the song. Direct the students to sing the phrases as marked in the example given here, breathing only at the breath marks (comma) above the staff. Note that in the first musical phrase are three word phrases marked off by commas. The second and third musical phrases have two word phrases each. Direct students to sing the musical phrases.

EXAMPLE 11.3.   Vocalise: "America" (H. Carey).

Other Familiar Songs. Direct students to sing correctly other familiar songs in which musical phrases are typically broken. The carol "Silent Night, Holy Night" is a good example. Encourage the students to sing two-measure phrases in the first four measures, rather than four one-measure phrases. ("Silent night __ holy night,' all is calm __ all is bright.")

Level 3: Breath Techniques (Exercise 43)

Catch Breath. The "catch breath" is a partial breath taken between phrases when there is a need to continue the vocal line without seriously interrupting its flow. Caution should be taken that the catch breath not be used between syllables of a word or after a very short note, a preposition, or an article. Students also should be warned against any sudden dynamic change following a catch breath. If anything, the entrance after a catch breath should be somewhat softer so as not to interfere with the legato line.

Direct students to count aloud two measures in common time using "1 and 2 and 3 and 4 and . . . ," with a catch breath where the "and" after "4" would be in the second measure. Once the technique is understood, making sure that 1 is never late on the downbeat, increase the counting to a rapid tempo, which forces a quick breath on the "and" after "4." Do not permit a gasping of air for the catch breath. Inhalation should be as quiet as possible. A catch breath properly taken is a low breath. Monitor for abdominal movement outward on the catch breath.

A visual cue may be given by the instructor to reinforce the movement of the students' abdominal walls upon inhalation. Place the palms of the hands together in front of the abdominal area and spring the hands outward on the catch breath.

Staggered Breathing. The technique of staggered breathing is one in which the various members of a singing group breathe at different times in order to carry over a long phrase. To do this correctly, the singer must soften the pitch before and after the breath so that breaks in the tonal line will not be audible. If possible, the breath should be taken within a long note (half or whole), and not when passing from one pitch to another. In this way, the same vowel color is maintained.

Direct students to sustain a pitch on the *ah* sound. Fade the pitch, breathe quietly, and return softly to the same pitch. Repeat the sequence over two measures in common time, assigning half the students to breathe in the first measure and half to breathe in the second measure. Repeat with three and four measures, dividing the group into thirds and quarters for staggered breathing.

Direct students to sing the "Octave Alleluia" (Example 11.4) very slowly on one breath. Do not breathe between the two *alleluias.* Stagger the breathing within each syllable of the second *alleluia.* Do not breathe

EXAMPLE 11.4.   Vocalise: "Octave Alleluia."

between syllables. Maintain a very legato line and guard against flatting with good breath support and high half steps.

Level 4: Meaning and Mood (Exercise 58)

Meaning.   Read the words of the text aloud as a poem, not just as metered lines. Ask children about the meaning of specific phrases, and determine if there are phrases or words they do not understand. Give appropriate historical or social background to texts when appropriate.

Mood.   Lead a discussion about words of emotion, such as *love, hate, happiness,* and *pride.* How can these words be reflected in the singing, facial, and postural responses? Find such words in song texts and discuss how these would best be sung.

Direct the students to make a list of the songs in their repertoire by mood. What should be the desired response from the audience, and how can the mood of each song best be communicated?

Level 5: Physical Movement (Exercise 73)

Physical movement can aid the development of phrasing in group singing. The Dalcroze approach to music learning is based upon this concept. The following exercises are offered as a means of developing a sense of phrasing through physical movement.

Conducting.   Direct students to conduct phrases as they sing, using free-flowing diagonal curves (left to right, and vice versa) of the arms and hands to equate arm movement with the phrasing and flow of the music.

Physical-Response Exercises

1. Direct students to lean forward (not side to side!) with the weight on the forward foot as the phrase peaks.

2. Direct students to move in a circle while singing. Change directions at the ends of phrases.

3. To help students become more aware of the way their entrance grows out of the introduction, have them begin a movement that characterizes the style of composition as soon as the introduction begins and continue the movement throughout their entrance. Slow, sweeping gestures of the arm across the space in front of the body or circular motions of the hands can be used for a fluid, lyrical line. For a martial composition, marching could be used.

4. Direct singers to maintain the energy of the phrase through long notes by silently clapping the underlying beats. The claps should move away from the body if a crescendo is desired and toward the body for a diminuendo.

Level 6: Phrase Sculpting (Exercise 88)

Word Phrases. Direct the students' attention to the text, having them read it aloud. Decide where the phrases are, and read in unison from phrase to phrase. Draw line diagrams (long curved lines over the words) on the chalkboard to indicate the length of the phrases. Decide where the breaths (pauses) should be placed. Define words that may not be understood. Discuss the meaning of the text with the class.

Note the important words of the text. Circle these on the board. Strike out unimportant words, such as articles. Then decide if any of the important words have syllables that should be stressed more than others, and underline those that should receive more stress, or "inflection." Read the text again with greater emphasis on the circled or underlined words and syllables than on the words struck out.

Musical Phrases. Teach students to breathe at the ends of musical phrases. If musical phrases become unusually long, the catch breath or staggered breathing may need to be used.

Students need to understand that the musical phrase must be sung to the very end. The dropping or fading of musical lines is as common as dropping the voice at the ends of sentences when speaking. However, breathing between phrases without a notated rest demands that the time for breathing be taken from the last note of the first phrase. The second phrase must never be late in starting.

Matching the character of the word phrase to the musical phrase is another important aspect of musical expression. A good composer will match the two very carefully. When this does not occur, the musical phrase usually takes precedence.

The most important aspect of technique for musical phrasing is that of forward motion, without which singing becomes dull. Every phrase has a musical shape that can be sculpted as well on the chalkboard. Moving toward and away from the peak of each phrase can be drawn using waveforms that build and subside over the musical line (Figure 11–1).

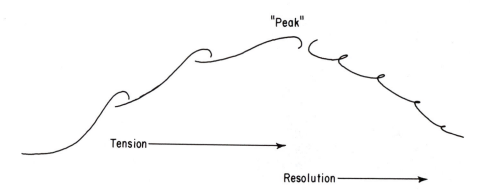

FIGURE 11–1.   Waveforms for Phrase Shaping.

Musical phrases may peak near the beginning (first phrase of "Joy to the World") or near the end ("o'er the land of the free" from "The National Anthem"). Most, however, peak near the middle, creating an arch-shaped melody. Direct students to sculpt the shape of musical phrases using waveforms, as in the following example from "Simple Gifts," a Shaker tune (Figure 11–2).

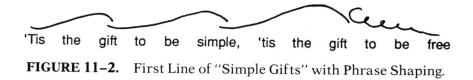

'Tis   the   gift   to   be   simple,   'tis   the   gift   to   be   free

FIGURE 11–2.   First Line of "Simple Gifts" with Phrase Shaping.

DYNAMIC AND TEMPO VARIATION

Goal: The student will develop the techniques of both dynamic and tempo variation through exercises involving degrees of loudness-softness and fastness-slowness.

Variation of dynamics and tempo are extremely important to expression in singing. A dull and lifeless performance is likely to result when the subtleties of these concepts are ignored.

Level 1: Dynamic Levels (Exercise 14)

Terms and Meanings.   Students need to be taught the fundamental levels of dynamic variation so as to establish a relative criterion by which to establish any indicated intensity level. A dynamic-levels chart is given here as one way in which to build a fundamental knowledge of dynamic levels. Six basic dynamic levels are given. It is important to establish levels for mezzo forte and mezzo piano with elementary students, as these are the middle dynamic levels at which most elementary students should sing. Singing too softly usually results in an unsupported sound, and singing too loudly forces the voice. The dynamic ranges of adolescents should be expanded as vocal development progresses.

Students should learn to interpret the Italian dynamic terms and symbols, as well as to place them in order from softest to loudest. Dynamic levels are relative and call for the instructor to make personal judgments concerning appropriate intensities for each age group. Drill students on the fundamentals of the chart. After much study, give them a blank chart to fill in, to test their knowledge.

DYNAMIC LEVELS

Level	Symbol	Italian Term	English Meaning
6	ff	*fortissimo*	very loud
5	f	*forte*	loud
4	mf	*mezzo forte*	moderately loud
3	mp	*mezzo piano*	moderately soft
2	p	*piano*	soft
1	pp	*pianissimo*	very soft

Dynamics Drill. To secure an understanding of the six dynamic levels, direct the students to count "1 an' 2 an' 3 an' 4 an' . . . " at the various levels given. The instructor should point to the levels in succession, and then jump from one level to another. This exercise is fun and requires the students to respond quickly to visual cues.

Level 2: Tempo Markings (Exercise 29)

Terms and Meanings. Students need to be taught the fundamental levels of tempo variation so as to establish a relative criterion by which to establish any indicated tempo. The tempo-markings chart is given here as one way in which to build this fundamental knowledge. A mobile made of the different terms is another means by which to visualize these tempo markings in the classroom.

Seven basic tempo markings are given. These seven markings are the basic tempi about which students should be knowledgeable. Students should learn to interpret the Italian tempo terms and symbols, as well as to place them in order from slowest to fastest. Tempo markings are relative in music prior to Beethoven. However, the use of a standard metronome is recommended for class use when establishing the approximate tempi in the chart. Drill students on the fundamentals of the chart. After much study, give them a blank chart to fill in, to test their knowledge.

TEMPO MARKINGS

Level	Italian Term	English Meaning
7	presto	very fast
6	allegro	fast
5	allegretto	moderately fast
4	moderato	moderately
3	andante	moderately slow
2	adagio	slow
1	largo	very slow

Tempo Drills

1. To secure an understanding of the seven tempo markings, direct students to count "1 an' 2 an' 3 an' 4 an' . . . " at the various tempos given. The instructor should point to the levels in succession, and then jump from one level to another. This is a fun exercise and requires the students to respond quickly to visual cues.

2. The instructor also may set a tempo by counting "1, 2, 3, 4, . . . " while the students continue the count silently until the twelfth beat, which they mark together with a clap. The slower the tempo, the more difficult this exercise!

3. The metronome can be used in tempo discrimination. Set the metronome to the various speeds of the tempo chart and ask students to determine the tempo aurally. If the metronome also has a light, elementary students love to have the room lights turned out while the tempo is being flashed.

Level 3: Accelerando and Ritardando (Exercise 44)

Terms and Meaning. Add the terms *accelerando* (gradually faster) and *ritardando* (gradually slower) to the tempo chart (Level 2). Again, students should be expected to know the Italian tempo terms and their meaning in English.

Tempo Drill. To secure the students' understanding of accelerando and ritardando, direct them to sit forward in their chairs and lightly tap the heel of one foot on the floor (keeping the ball of the foot on the floor!) to your vertical pulse directing. Students should tap once for every downstroke of the hand or baton. Gradually increase and decrease the tempo, directing the students to maintain the pulse of the direction. The faster the tempo, the smaller the pulse; the slower the tempo, the larger the pulse. Monitor any rushing or lagging of tempi. Students will tend to rush the accelerando and lag on the ritardando. Insist that the students maintain the tempo given them.

Some fun can be had with the heel-tapping exercise by directing the students to freeze the tapping when the instructor's directing motion stops. Invariably, a number of students will get caught when they fail to stop soon enough. This exercise has the added benefit of forcing students to pay close attention to conducting gestures.

Level 4: Crescendo and Decrescendo (Exercise 59)

Terms and Meaning. Add the terms *crescendo* (gradually louder) and *decrescendo* (gradually softer) to the dynamics chart (Level 1). Again, the students should be expected to know the Italian dynamic terms and the English meaning.

Dynamic Drills

1. To secure the students' understanding of crescendo and decrescendo, direct them to crescendo by counting aloud "1 an' 2 an' 3 an' 4 an' ...," followed by decrescendo counting backward "4 an' 3 an' 2 an' 1 an'...." Students will tend to decrease the volume of the decrescendo too quickly. Do not permit the support to sag on the decrescendo.

Vary the above routine with a crescendo and decrescendo of eight counts each, and sing various sustained pitches by counting, using *doo-doo,* or pure vowels; work for an even crescendo and decrescendo.

2. To counter the tendency to increase volume on ascending vocal lines and decrease volume on descending lines, direct students to sing an ascending arpeggio (1–3–5–1) while executing a decrescendo. Sing a descending arpeggio (1–5–3–1) while executing a crescendo.

3. Direct students in the vocalise shown in Example 11.5, monitoring for breath support throughout the vocal line. Sing this vocalise at a

EXAMPLE 11.5. Vocalise: Crescendo and Decrescendo.

slow tempo, gradually building to the first note of the second measure before beginning the decrescendo. Direct students to relax the throat and drop the jaw as they increase the breath pressure into the crescendo.

Level 5: Sudden Dynamic Changes (Exercise 74)

Terms and Meaning. Add the terms *subito forte* (suddenly louder) and *subito piano* (suddenly softer) to the dynamics chart (Level 1). Again, students should be expected to know the Italian dynamic terms and the meanings in English.

Dynamic Drills

1. For reinforcing sudden (subito) dynamic changes, have singers sit for soft passages and stand for loud passages. Alternate counting loudly from 1 to 4 for standing with counting softly from 1 to 4 for sitting. Alternate thumbs up (loud) with thumbs down (soft).

2. The "sforzando" (sfz) is a forceful accent built upon the marcato thrust of the abdominal musculature. Repeat the marcato-thrust exercises in preparation for the following sforzando exercise. Speak and then sing the word *Help!* on a unison pitch or chord, using an abdominal thrust. The explosive nature of the sforzando must come from the abdominal musculature, not the throat. An intentional pulling-in of the abdominal support must be consciously present. Monitor this exercise closely for vocal abuse, and do not prolong its practice with young voices.

Level 6: Messa Di Voce (Exercise 89)

Term and Meaning. The messa di voce (swell, < >) differs from the crescendo-decrescendo in that the latter usually occurs over a series of notes, whereas the messa di voce occurs over just one note, usually a longer one. It is a technique used in legato singing to give life and vitality to the individually sustained tones. Add this term to the dynamics chart (Level 1).

Dynamic Drills

1. Direct students to sing whole notes with a slight swelling and softening of dynamic level, as in Example 11.6. Monitor so that the tone is not softened too quickly.

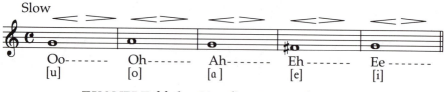

EXAMPLE 11.6.   Vocalise: Messa di voce 1.

2. The vocalise given in Example 11.7 is enhanced if the accompanist plays the second beat of each quarter-note pattern a little louder than beats 1 and 3. Maintain support throughout the swell of each tone. Beat 1 begins piano and immediately swells into a mezzo forte on beat 2, which fades immediately to piano on beat 3. For maximum effect, sing the vocalise very slowly as indicated.

EXAMPLE 11.7. Vocalise: Messa di voce 2.

AGILITY AND RANGE EXTENSION

Goal: The student will develop the techniques of both agility and range extension through exercises involving increasing articulation demands (syllabic, neumatic, melismatic) over a gradually increasing vocal range.

Students must first learn to sing syllabically—that is, with one note per syllable. Most songs, however, contain examples of two notes per syllable (neumatic) or three or more notes per syllable (melismatic). These latter two types of singing are more difficult to master and should be practiced until fluency is achieved.

Singing with an adequate range is basic to expressive singing. While range should increase with maturity (grades 1–12), it often does not for many students. By the sixth grade, students should have achieved a vocal range of two octaves (g to g^2). Vocal ranges of high school students will vary, depending upon the voice classification.

Level 1: The Light Portamento (Exercise 15)

Young students often have trouble learning to sing two different successive pitches on one syllable. The following vocalises concentrate on developing the ability to sing in a neumatic style (two pitches per sylla-ble). Caution students not to slur between pitches, but rather to use a light "portamento," a light, quick, scarcely audible glide between the pitches involved.

"How Are You?" (Example 11.8).   This vocalise is for students in the primary grades. The instructor sings the first two measures, and the student answers accordingly in the second two measures. Other questions such as "What are you doing?" also may be substituted.

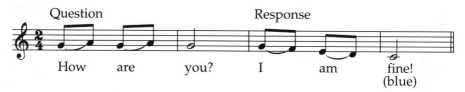

EXAMPLE 11.8.   Vocalise: "How Are You?"

Chant.   The "Alleluia" (Example 11.9) is for students beyond the first grade. Each measure is sung by a soloist (instructor or a student) and echoed by all the class. The first measure is syllabic, and the second and third measures include both syllabic and neumatic articulation. Be sure that the soloist is able to provide a good vocal model for the echo.

EXAMPLE 11.9.   Vocalise: "Alleluia 1" (Chant).

"La-Be-Da-Me" (Example 11.10).   Use this vocalise only as stu-dents advance in vocal development and are working through the mid-dle adjustment. Sing it with a light, rapid gliding so as to obtain a smooth carryover between pitches. Caution students not to slur be-tween pitches. The vowel sounds are those of the IPA system.

EXAMPLE 11.10.   Vocalise: "La-Be-Da-Me."

Level 2: Increasing Agility (Exercise 30)

The following vocalises expand the students' ability to sing with more agility (i.e., more notes per syllable). Keep the singing light and moving from the breath impulse.

Chant. This "Alleluia" (Example 11.11) requires that students sing one-, two-, and three-note groupings. Singing the chant slowly will encourage good breath support and control.

EXAMPLE 11.11. Vocalise: "Alleluia 2" (Chant).

"One and a Six" (Example 11.12). The following vocalise is fun, catchy, and good for agility building as well as chordal feeling. Four notes are sung per syllable. Use the abdominal-pulse exercise to encourage the pulsing of each note of the phrase.

EXAMPLE 11.12. Vocalise: "One and a Six."

For elementary students, the bass-clef part should be sung an octave higher, the whole exercise being sung in the key of D. For changing voices, the bass-clef part can be sung an octave higher. Exchange parts between voices on the repetitions, and transpose upward by half steps.

Level 3: The Arpeggio (Exercise 45)

The basic arpeggio (Example 11.13) is one of the best exercises to promote agility and extend range. Parts 1 and 2 are to be sung staccato, and part 3 legato, a more advanced technique that requires better breath support and should not be introduced too soon in the vocal sequence. Direct students to sing lightly and not to carry the lower adjustment sound in its pure form up into the middle or upper adjustment.

EXAMPLE 11.13. Vocalise: Arpeggios.

Level 4: Agility and Range 1 (Exercise 60)

Sir John Stainer is the composer of the vocalise in Example 11.14. It is a classic vocalise for the development of the young voice. Begin by singing each note on *loo* before attempting to sing each measure on one syllable. This vocalise may be sung by changed and unchanged voices at the pitch and octave written or by changed male voices an octave lower. It is excellent for developing the upper adjustment of male and female voices. Monitor the shift to the upper adjustment as the vocal line ascends. Keep the vocalise light and flowing.

EXAMPLE 11.14. Vocalise: Range, Agility 1 (from C. E. Johnson, *The Training of Boys' Voices,* Oliver Ditson Co., 1906).

Level 5: Agility and Range 2 (Exercise 75)

The vocalise in Example 11.15 is to develop legato-staccato agility and range extension. Remind the students not to slur the first two notes, but rather to lift over to the second pitch of each four-note grouping. Direct the students to keep the *foo-foo* very crisp and bright. Begin slowly and increase the tempo as agility increases. It may be sung by all voices as written or by changed male voices an octave lower.

EXAMPLE 11.15.   Vocalise: Range, Agility 2 (from C. E. Johnson, *The Training of Boys' Voices,* Oliver Ditson Co., 1906).

Level 6: Melismatic Singing (Exercise 90)

The ability to sing many notes per syllable is an advanced technique based on abdominal pulsing. Most young students have trouble singing one vowel to many notes (melisma).

"Gloria."   Direct this familiar chorus of the carol "Angels We Have Heard on High" (Example 11.16) as a simple means of introducing students to the melisma. Sing the eighth-note melismas on *doh-doh-doh-doh* until students have progressed so far in vocal development that they can articulate the separate *o* vowel cleanly from the breathing

EXAMPLE 11.16. Vocalise: "Gloria" (Traditional).

musculature. Direct students to think the *o* of each melisma for each eighth note. Review of the rolling-pulse exercise is helpful to accomplish this feeling of bouncing the *o* from below! Any melismatic passage must be sung lightly if it is to be clean and agile.

Pulsing Sixteenths (Example 11.17). Begin this sixteenth-note vocalise slowly and gradually increase the tempo. Direct students to sing each sixteenth note on *doo*. As vocal development progresses, remove the *d* and sing only the vowel *oo*, which must be pulsed from the breathing musculature. Do not interpolate an *h* for each note, as this only slows down the execution and develops a bad singing habit for melismatic runs. Transpose upward a minor third by half steps.

EXAMPLE 11.17. Pulsing Sixteenths.

STUDY AND DISCUSSION QUESTIONS

1. What are the five expressive elements that students should learn for expressive singing?
2. How can students be involved in the evaluation process for singing?
3. Why do students listen to pop music? What implications does this have for the teaching of expressive singing?
4. Suggest some ways for teachers to help students to think about the mood or feeling of music they are singing.

6. What is the problem in teaching words and music simultaneously? How can this problem be remedied?
7. What are some aids in writing pronunciations into the text?
8. What is the paramount rule of communication?
9. The sound of a great chorus is dependent on what factor?
10. Suggest some ways in which students can be involved in determining phrase shape.
11. Describe the parts of a phrase that can be shaped.
12. What should be done with a voice part that moves differently from most of the other parts?
13. What is a catch breath? When is it used? Students should be warned against doing what after a catch breath?
14. What is staggered breathing? How can it be taught?
15. In what direction should students be taught to lean into phrases?
16. Breathing between phrases without a notated rest demands that the time for breathing be taken from where?
17. When the word phrase does not match the musical phrase, which usually takes precedence?
18. What is the most important technique for musical phrasing?
19. When an arpeggio is to be sung, what two directions should be given?
20. What three directions should be given for singing a melisma?

References

BARTLE, J. A. (1988). *Lifeline for children's choir directors*. Toronto: Gordon V. Thompson Music.

HERMAN, S. (1988). Unlocking the potential of junior high choirs. *Music Educators Journal, 75*(4), 33–36, 41.

NEUEN, D. (1988). The sound of a great chorus. *Music Educators Journal, 75*(4), 43–45.

SWEARS, L. (1985). *Teaching the elementary school chorus*. West Nyack, NY: Parker.

12

VOCAL-TECHNIQUE SUMMARIES

The following five outlines represent an overview of each of the main areas of vocal development in the method: respiration, phonation, resonant tone production, diction, and expression. By reviewing each of the outlines sequentially, the reader will gain greater insight into the scope and sequence of the curriculum. Note that each main part is divided into three subdivisions, each of which is divided into six levels of exercises. The numbering of each exercise corresponds to the particular level (1–6) for which each exercise is assigned. There are a total of ninety graded exercises in the method, many of which have multiple parts.

Following the five main outlines are the three learning sequences in which the various exercises are arranged, in the order in which they are to be taught. It is intended that the teacher will use these learning-sequence outlines as a handy reference for lesson planning. Beside each exercise is given the page number for that specific technique in the main body of the text.

There are three learning-sequence outlines. Outline 1 contains six levels and is to be used when the method is begun in grades 1–3. Outline 2 combines the six original levels into three groupings: I–II, III–IV, and V–VI. This outline is to be used when the method is begun in grade 4 or 7, and enables more coverage of exercises in a shorter amount of time. Outline 3 combines the exercises into two groupings: I–III and IV–VI, and is to be used when beginning the method in grades 9/10–12.

PART I. RESPIRATION-TRAINING OUTLINE

Posture Development

1. Muscle Movers
2. Body Alignment
3. Posture Practice
4. Face Lift
5. Active Posturing
6. Mental Posturing

Breathing Motion

1. Natural Breathing
2. Deep Breathing
3. Breath Suspension
4. Breath Rhythm
5. Tired Dog Pant
6. Hot Dog Pant

Breath Management

1. Abdominal Lift
2. Breath Stream
3. Breath Articulation
4. Breath Pulse
5. Breath Extension
6. Costal Control

PART II. PHONATION-TRAINING OUTLINE

Lower Adjustment

1. Animal Farm
2. Voice Placement
3. Energized Voice
4. Upper Wheelie

5. Accented Pulse

6. Choric Speech

Upper Adjustment

1. Animal Farm

2. Marcato Thrust

3. Staccato Bump

4. Upper Wheelie

5. Sustained Howl

6. Soundscape

Adjustment Coordination

1. Animal Farm

2. Woofers and Tweeters

3. Voice Inflectors

4. Spiral Wheelie

5. Sustained Bleat

6. Vocal Glissando

PART III. RESONANT TONE PRODUCTION OUTLINE

Vocal Resonance

1. Sustained Humming

2. Staccato Koo-koo

3. The Attack

4. Rolling Pulse

5. Intonation

6. Warm-up Tunes

Uniform Vowel Colors

1. The Model Vowel

2. Solfège Patterns

3. Vertical Vowels

4. Legato Movement

5. Short Vowels
6. Diphthongs

Vocal Coordination

1. Pitch Exploration
2. Upper to Lower
3. Octave Lift
4. Lighten Up
5. Midvoice Balancing
6. Ho-ho Choruses

PART IV. DICTION-TRAINING OUTLINE

Vocal-tract Freedom

1. Jaw Flex
2. Jaw Prop
3. Pharyngeal Openers
4. Forward Tongue
5. Chin–Facial Massage
6. Tongue Flex

Word Pronunciation

1. Tongue Twisters
2. Final Consonants
3. Hissing Sibilants
4. The Three Rs
5. Song Études
6. IPA Studies

Consonant Articulation

1. Voiceless Plosives
2. Voiced Plosives
3. Voiceless Sibilants
4. Tuned Continuants

    5. Voiced Continuants

    6. Aspirates

PART V. EXPRESSION-TRAINING OUTLINE

Phrasing

    1. Down 5–Up 5

    2. Phrase Extension

    3. Breath Techniques

    4. Meaning and Mood

    5. Physical Movement

    6. Phrase Sculpting

Dynamic and Tempo Variation

    1. Six Dynamic Levels

    2. Seven Tempo Markings

    3. Accelerando and Ritardando

    4. Crescendo and Decrescendo

    5. Sudden Dynamic Changes

    6. Messa di voce

Agility and Range Extension

    1. Light Portamento

    2. Increasing Agility

    3. The Arpeggio

    4. Agility and Range 1

    5. Agility and Range 2

    6. Melismatic Singing

LEARNING-SEQUENCE OUTLINE 1, GRADES 1–6

(when begun in grades 1–3)

Level 1

Level 2

Level 6

Part I: Respiration   **Page**

Part II: Phonation

Part III: Resonant Tone Production

Part IV: Diction

Part V: Expression

LEARNING-SEQUENCE OUTLINE 2, GRADES 4–6 or 7–9

(when begun in grade 4 or 7)

Levels 1–2 (grade 4 or 7)

Part I: Respiration

Levels 3–4 (grade 5 or 8)

Part I: Respiration

Part II: Phonation

Part III: Resonant Tone Production

Part IV: Diction

Levels 5–6 (grade 6 or 9)

Part I: Respiration

Part II: Phonation

Part III: Resonant Tone Production

LEARNING-SEQUENCE OUTLINE 3, GRADES 9/10–12

(when begun in grade 9 or 10)

Levels 2–3 (grade 9 or 10)

Part I: Respiration

Levels 4–6 (grades 11–12)

Part I: Respiration

Part II: Phonation

Page

RECORD KEEPING

The following exercise record will be helpful to the instructor for keeping a record of which exercises have been done on what days. The exercises are grouped according to the five main areas and the three subdivisions of each. It is suggested that the teacher photocopy these pages so that multiple copies exist (permission given).

Keep track of which exercises are used and when by writing the date of each day in the blanks following the names of each exercise used on that particular day. For example, if exercises 1, 2, and 3 were done on September 10, the instructor would write "9/10" in the next open blank after each of those three exercises. Some exercises, such as the muscle movers, will be used repeatedly; others build in importance and will be returned to infrequently for review purposes only. By keeping track of the exercises, the instructor will have a visual overview of what exercises have been used in each particular subdivision and area. This will help in the pacing and planning process. It also will aid in the vocal-technique evaluation process when trying to recall exactly which exercises have been covered in each grading period.

Vocal Technique for Young Singers

EXERCISE RECORD   Class: _____

RESPIRATION

POSTURE DEVELOPMENT_____
- 1 Muscle Movers _____
- 16 Body Alignment _____
- 31 Posture Practice _____
- 46 Face Lift _____
- 61 Active Posturing _____
- 76 Mental Posturing _____

BREATHING MOTION_____
- 2 Natural Breathing _____
- 17 Deep Breathing _____
- 32 Breath Suspension _____
- 47 Breath Rhythm _____
- 62 Tired Dog Pant _____
- 77 Hot Dog Pant _____

BREATH MANAGEMENT_____
- 3 Abdominal Lift _____
- 18 Breath Stream _____
- 33 Breath Articulation _____
- 48 Breath Pulse _____
- 62 Breath Extension _____
- 78 Costal Control _____

PHONATION

LOWER ADJUSTMENT_____

    4 Animal Farm_____

    19 Voice Placement_____

    34 Energized Speech_____

    49 Lower Wheelie_____

    64 Accented Pulse_____

    79 Choric Speech_____

UPPER ADJUSTMENT_____

    5 Animal Farm_____

    20 Marcato Thrust_____

    35 Staccato Bump_____

    50 Upper Wheelie_____

    65 Sustained Howl_____

    80 Soundscape_____

ADJUSTMENT COORDINATION_____

    6 Animal Farm_____

    21 Woofers and Tweeters_____

    36 Voice Inflectors_____

    51 Spiral Wheelie_____

    66 Sustained Bleat_____

    81 Vocal Glissando_____

RESONANT TONE

VOCAL RESONANCE_____

    7 Sustained Humming_____

    22 Staccato Koo-koo_____

37 The Attack_____

52 Rolling Pulse_____

67 Intonation_____

82 Warm-up Tunes_____

UNIFORM VOWEL COLORS___

 8 The Model Vowel_____

23 Solfège Patterns_____

38 Vertical Vowels_____

53 Legato Movement_____

68 Short Vowels_____

83 Diphthongs_____

VOCAL COORDINATION___

 9 Pitch Exploration_____

24 Upper to Lower_____

39 Octave Lift_____

54 Lighten Up_____

69 Midvoice Balance_____

84 Ho-ho Choruses_____

DICTION

VOCAL-TRACT FREEDOM___

10 Jaw Flex_____

25 Jaw Prop_____

40 Pharyngeal Openers_____

55 Forward Tongue_____

70 Chin–Facial Massage_____

85 Tongue Flex_____

WORD PRONUNCIATION

11 Tongue Twisters

26 Final Consonants

41 Hissing Sibilants

56 The Three Rs

71 Song Études

86 IPA Studies

CONSONANT ARTICULATION

12 Voiceless Plosives

27 Voiced Plosives

42 Voiceless Sibilants

57 Tuned Continuants

72 Voiced Continuants

87 Aspirates

EXPRESSION

PHRASING

13 Down 5–Up 5

28 Phrase Extension

43 Breath Techniques

58 Meaning and Mood

73 Physical Movement

88 Phrase Sculpting

DYNAMIC/TEMPO VARIATION

14 Dynamic Levels

29 Tempo Markings

44 Accelerando/Ritardando

59 Crescendo/Decrescendo

74 Sudden Dynamic Change																
89 Messa di voce																
AGILITY, RANGE EXTENSION																
15 Light Portamento																
30 Increasing Agility																
45 Arpeggio																
60 Agility, Range 1																
75 Agility, Range 2																
90 Melismatic Singing																

POSTSCRIPT

The amount of material covered in this method may appear to be overwhelming to the teacher who has never been involved in a regular program of voice instruction. Indeed, there is much here, but the multiplicity of the exercises is meant to provide a great variety of ways in which to improve the singing voices of children and adolescents. Not all of the exercises will work with every student.

Perhaps the best advice is to begin with exercise 1, and if that is successful, proceed to 2, 3, and so on. Take one exercise at a time, master it yourself before trying to teach it, and begin. Do not look at the big picture too soon or you may become fearful of not accomplishing anything. Just take one exercise at a time and proceed slowly. If your students learn only to stand and breathe properly, they will have accomplished much!

At a recent conference a music teacher who has used this method for several years approached the author to relay how helpful he had found the techniques in teaching his students to sing. He said, "If people will only do what you say repeatedly in your workshops—take it one exercise at a time, follow the sequence, go slowly—the results will be there."

This method, of course, need not be followed as a "method" at all, but rather as an "approach" to better singing. Those teachers who feel comfortable in teaching students to sing may wish to pick and choose from among the exercises to supplement their own program of voice development.

The author believes that most people want to learn to sing. Many students, however, are embarrassed by their voices and thus display an unwillingness to sing. You may find disgruntled students when you begin a program of voice development, but stay with it—the results will come. Students must know that singing is not a gift for only a few but a skill for all to enjoy. Stress that singing has to be learned, just as writing has to be learned, or mathematics, or anything else worth knowing. Very few students sing "naturally" without help, but most people can be taught to sing with help. Go to it!

INDEX